D1188507

CONFEDERATE MILITARY HISTORY

Volume
II

CONFEDERATE
MILITARY HISTORY

A LIBRARY OF CONFEDERATE
STATES HISTORY, IN THIRTEEN
VOLUMES, WRITTEN BY DISTIN-
GUISHED MEN OF THE SOUTH,
AND EDITED BY GEN. CLEMENT
A. EVANS OF GEORGIA....

VOL. II.

The
Blue & Grey
Press

973.73013
C748
v.2

Printed in the United States of America

191479

CONTENTS—MARYLAND.

ILLUSTRATIONS—MARYLAND.

CONTENTS—WEST VIRGINIA.

MARYLAND

BY

BRIG.-GEN. BRADLEY T. JOHNSON.

BRADLEY T. JOHNSON

CHAPTER I.

WHEN the New World was disclosed to the Old, the
belief of all civilized people was that the heathen
had no rights which Christians ought to respect
—that he and his country belonged of right to the
strongest taker; and it became a curious article of a
more curious faith that murder and robbery were efficient
means for propagating the faith of Christ and magnify-
ing the glory of God.

The Pope made short work of the whole matter, for he
divided the new world east and west by a degree of longi-
tude and made a present of one-half to the Spaniard
and the other half to the Portuguese—"Ad majoram glori-
am Dei"—to the greater glory of God. This process of
simple division was not satisfactory to the fair-haired,
blue-eyed race that dominated the island in the North Sea.

Love of enterprise, commercial daring, politics, religious conditions—all contributed to stimulate exploration
and investigation. One Englishman spent his life search-
ing for El Dorado—the land where gold abounded; a
Spaniard spent his hunting the "Fons Vitæ"—the fountain of perpetual youth, the waters of which renew forever the waning forces of vitality. But while the Spaniard ransacked two continents for silver and gold, found
them and ruined his posterity, the French, actuated by no
nobler ideals, made settlements in North America, the
main inspiration of which was the desire to possess the
great fisheries on the north-eastern coast. The English,
in the main, had higher aims, and wider, larger aspira-
tions. Political conditions at home exasperated religious

differences, and the only hope of liberty seemed to be to transplant the old institutions of Britain—liberty of person, security of property, freedom of thought—to the wilderness, and there secure them forever by the ancient safeguards devised by the experience, the wisdom and the courage of their ancestors—habeas corpus, trial by jury, representative self government. So, at the beginning of the seventeenth century, many gentlemen in England emigrated with their property and their servants to the forests of New England, then including the north continent from the lakes to the gulf. With them they carried the opinions of their time and generation. The possession of the heathen was lawful and laudable sport for Christian men, and they straightway put them to the sword, seized their lands, their wives and their children, and divided them and all prisoners taken in war as slaves of the conquerors. This was the universal rule among all the English except in Pennsylvania and in Maryland. In the first the influence of Penn, in the last that of the Jesuits, saved them from such crimes against humanity. But the necessities of the new society, the constant struggle with nature, the forest, the flood, the fire, all made involuntary and controlled labor exceedingly valuable, convenient, comfortable and necessary. And when to the captive Indians were added cargoes of savage, cannibal Africans, no man could deny that it was a Christian duty to civilize them and teach them to work. Therefore, involuntary servitude existed in all the English colonies from the very first, and it was not until the American revolution stirred up generalizings and theories about the rights of man, that the idea got abroad that slavery was wrong. In the New England States it had long ceased to be necessary, for population had increased and roads been constructed, so that society was able to protect itself. It was troublesome, annoying, unprofitable. Slaves of different races—Indian, white and negro—confused the social order, and it was best to get rid of them. But it was not as a moral question, but as an economical one, that it was dealt with.

So when the Constitution of the United States and the Union by, through and under it were framed, formed and organized, it was silent on the subject of slavery by name, but provided for its protection by requiring that persons held to service, escaping from one State to another, should be delivered and returned to their masters on demand. Without this provision no constitution could have been adopted and no union formed

But the cotton-gin was invented, by which the cultivation of cotton became extremely profitable and slaves became valuable property. There was a great movement of capital and population to the cotton country, and the new States rapidly grew up and demanded admission into the Union. By the gradual abolition of slavery north of the Chesapeake the free States had been approaching control of the Senate of the United States, until the cotton-gin reversed the order, and it seemed as if the slave States would secure permanent control of the Union.

Then began an agitation in the North, superficially moral and religious, but really and substantially political; professedly to do away with the great crime of slavery, in fact to check and destroy the aggrandizement of the Southern power. The first clear issue between the forces was on the application of Missouri to be admitted as a State of the Union. Missouri was a slave State and her admission would destroy the equilibrium between the two systems in the Senate of the United States. So Missouri was kept out until a free State could be hitched to her and thus the balance of power preserved. This was in 1821. In divers ways the struggle between the powers exhibited itself. Congress for years had levied duties on imports, whereby Northern manufacturers were encouraged and protected. Northern manufacturers were enriched and the rest of the country taxed for their benefit. In 1831 a tariff law was passed which was resisted by

South Carolina, and the issue of arms was only averted by the retreat of the Federal government, by concession and by compromise.

The king of England at the beginning of the seventeenth century claimed the proprietorship of the North American continent, which claim was disputed by the Spaniard in the South and the French in the North. New England was hemmed and bounded by New Spain, New France, and the ambition and the courage and enterprise of England were roused to the conquest of the new world. The spirit that had shattered the Grand Armada and won for commerce the freedom of the seas, was directed to new countries and new States to be founded in North America, where the institutions, the habits, the sentiment and the society of their ancestors were to be transplanted, cultivated and developed, as they had been a thousand years before from the forests of Germany to the shores of Britain. The leading nobility and gentry, sailors, soldiers, and merchants of England were aroused to this great enterprise. They formed the Virginia company and received a grant from the king of that part of North America unoccupied by French or Spaniards. The enterprise of settlement, transportation and support of colonies proved too much for the company, and its grant was taken away with its charter, and the crown resumed its rights. Then grants were made to individual proprietors. Noblemen and gentlemen about the court secured these great favors, which they hoped would be the foundation of fortune to their posterity, just as the grants of the Norman conqueror had founded great houses and families which had controlled England for six centuries. Among them was Sir George Calvert, a Yorkshire knight of moderate fortune, but of an old family, whose ancestors had filled important offices in the Low Countries under the kings of Spain, and high positions at the court of France. He, in association with Sir Francis Arundel of Wardvin (whose daughter, Lady Anne Arundel, his son Cœcilius married, applied for grants of land in the new country.   Both died before the grant was prepared, and Cœcilius Calvert then procured to be framed a charter or grant, which was the wisest and most liberal in its terms of any issued up to that time to an English subject.   The charter granted to him and his heirs forever the territory on the north of the Potomac, and extending from the Atlantic ocean to the first springs of the Potomac, and along the 40th degree of north latitude from the Delaware river to the meridian of the first fountain of the Potomac river.   Together with this great grant of land and water, about 13,000 square miles, the proprietary was vested with all the powers of the Bishop of Durham, who from the earliest times had exercised absolute dominion over the palatinate of Durham and such power of martial law as was necessary in tempestuous times to preserve society and protect the border.   The charter provided for self-government by the freemen; it secured them all the rights of Englishmen, and laid the solid foundation of a happy, friendly, contented society. The proprietary, in his capacity of palatine, regulated social laws and behavior.   The motto of the Calverts is "Fatti Maschii, Parole Foemine"—Deeds are manly, words are womanly, or as it has always been rendered, "Courage and Chivalry."   The standard of the proprietary was borne in battle by a grand standard-bearer, who was an officer of great dignity and authority.   One was killed at the battle of the Severn, between the Cavaliers and Roundheads, in 1654, and his widow received a grant of land and was treated with great distinction by the proprietary.

But the controlling force of the colony was the spirit of Baltimore, who in his instructions to his governors insisted that there should be no broils about religion or politics. Every man should be secured in the right to his opinion. Free thought was guaranteed to every Marylander, and free speech as well, except so far as free speech infringed on the rights of his neighbors, when it was strictly suppressed.   Therefore, in the very foundation of Maryland was deeply laid the idea of toleration of different opinions among neighbors, of consideration for their feelings, and, as a logical consequence, of readiness at all times to help them, to protect them, and to assist them in all the struggles of life. There never was a more homogeneous, sentimental society than that planted on the Chesapeake. "One for all and all for one" was the animating spirit for generations.

While the northern settlements were torn and blood-drenched and fire-blasted by intolerance, when the flames of burning witches lighted New England, and the air echoed with the lash of whipped Baptists, no man was ever molested for his opinions in Maryland—while Marylanders controlled the palatinate. Several times during that stormy epoch, which cost a king his crown in England and the people their liberties, there had been struggles between the Cavalier and Roundhead parties in Maryland, in which the latter were successful as their friends and relatives in England had been. But in all that tension of feeling there was never but one issue of arms in which blood was spilled. Therefore Maryland grew and prospered without those bitter memories which in New England and in Virginia separated class from class and divided neighbor from neighbor. And whenever their neighbors on the south side of the Potomac were harassed by the savages on their borders, the Marylanders were prompt and generous in spending life, blood, and treasure in their defense. There never was an Indian war in Maryland. The policy of the palatine, so broad and generous and just, prevented quarrels with the natives, and they were always friendly with the Marylanders. There were bloody invasions from south of the great river, from the west and from the north, but no rising ever occurred of Maryland Indians. Generosity with justice was the fundamental rule of dealing with them, and this rule of right acts upon all who practice it, as well as upon those on whom it is practiced. Respect for the weak, regard for the truth, a willingness and a desire to help those who need help, become controlling principles of life, and selfishness is eradicated as much as it is possible for human nature to be changed.

Thus developed the Maryland character. Love of country and of friends, regard for truth and justice, toleration of differences of opinion, for five generations had been the directing influence of their lives. So when in 1774 news came that the people of Boston had been shot down in their streets by men in red coats, the people rose as one man. From Mills' Creek, whence Braddock had marched twenty years before to disaster and death, to St. Mary's, where free thought had been proclaimed first in all the world, the men of Maryland mustered in companies and battalions, and in two weeks the province was organized for defense. It raised money and provisions which it sent to Boston, and, inasmuch as the port of Boston was closed to trade, formed an association pledging the people of Maryland, men, women and children, never to use any imported goods until justice was done to Boston, just as ten years before it had refused to recognize the Stamp Act. When the farmers of New England met and drove the British regulars at Breed's Hill, the prompt response of Maryland was a battalion of riflemen which marched from Frederick to Boston, 550 miles, to reinforce their brethren. Maryland had no interest in this fight. She enjoyed a just and liberal government. Her people made their own laws, levied their own taxes and expended them for their own benefit, and there was no friction between them and the government. Their governor, Sir Robert Eden, was one of the most popular gentlemen in the province. But when the word went out that Boston needed assistance, every country committee, every court, every provincial assembly proclaimed with one voice, "The cause of Boston is the cause of all," and from that hour to the signature of the definite treaty of peace, Maryland never faltered in her support of the cause of her

Md 2

friends and neighbors. She lavished her last man and her last dollar to sustain that cause. No British soldier ever trod the soil of Maryland except during the short march from the head of Elk to Brandywine. She was never invaded, she was never molested; but she was true to her friends. There were no Tories in Maryland. A loyalist regiment was formed on the eastern shore, but its elements were so inefficient and incongruous that it was at once removed to Nova Scotia, where it perished from the memory of man and left hardly a trace behind.

Such were the men who moulded, formed and developed the society which was to face the crisis and do the duty of the times of 1859-65. It is our duty to tell how they did it.

In all discussions Maryland was on the side of the Union. She had given Colonel Washington, of Virginia, to the continental army as its commander-in chief, by and through her deputy in Congress in 1775, Thomas Johnson. She had made the first move for the Union in 1785. She had supported Washington all through the war and in the subsequent struggles and differences about the articles of Confederation, the Constitution and the Union. When, therefore, a party arose in the North which inculcated hatred toward the South, Maryland abhorred the apostles of malice and ill-will and sympathized more closely with the minority and weaker party. "Fatti Maschii, Parole Foemine" was the controlling sentiment of the men whose ancestors had stood with Stirling at Long Island until they were destroyed and the American army saved; whose charge at Eutaw had saved Greene's army; whose dash at Cowpens had driven the British line; whose bayonets at Guilford had broken the solid front of the Grenadier Guards—these men all believed in standing by their friends, reckless of risk, regardless of consequences. "With my friend—right or wrong—with my friend" is the complement of the State motto, "Courage and Chivalry."

So, as it became clearer in 1858-59-60 that the aggressions and attacks of the North on Southern society were not to be confined to discussion and vituperation, but were to be directed by physical force, Maryland, though utterly and entirely opposed to secession, or disunion, as a remedy or relief, still began to prepare herself for an uncertain future. Her legislature in 1860 appropriated seventy thousand dollars to arm the militia of the State and entrusted the distribution of them to Thomas Holliday Hicks, governor, and his adjutant-general.

In 1859, the Democratic party, then struggling to rescue the State from the Know Nothings, whose governor Hicks was, selected Bradley T. Johnson as chairman of the State committee and the direction of the struggle was entrusted to his hands. In 1860 he was a delegate from Maryland to the Democratic national convention at Charleston and represented Maryland in the committee on resolutions. In that committee Maryland always voted with the Southern States. When that convention held its adjourned meeting in Baltimore, the majority of the Maryland delegation, with the chairman of its State committee, withdrew with the Southern States and united in nominating Breckinridge and Lane, and Maryland voted for Breckinridge and Lane when Virginia was divided and other Southern States failed to support the movement. After November, 1860, it became clear to the younger men that war was imminent. In high excitement and peril young men see more clearly than old men. They have more energy, more clearness of vision, more promptness, more decision. They were all ardent sympathizers with the South. The old men—the ex-governors, ex-United States senators, ex-judges—all brought the weight of their characters to bear against connecting Maryland with the secession movement. And there was a profound disapprobation all through the State, with all classes, against any attempt to dismember the Union. But two per cent of her people were in favor of disunion. Some few of the young men, ardent, impetuous, devoted to ideas, believed that disunion was the only possible relief from the constant insults and aggressions of the North, its oppression and its selfish power.   They were convinced that with the political power in the hands of a section and a party, the cardinal dogma of whose faith was, " He shall take who hath the power, and he shall keep who can!" all the power of government would be directed toward the aggrandizement, the pecuniary aggrandizement, of those who wielded it, and that the minority in numbers and in wealth would become the serfs of the strongest, just as had been the case in all history.   They thought that wealth would flow from the many to the few; that capital would accumulate in sections and in classes, as it had done in the dead hands of religious corporations in England before Henry VIII, and then dispersed and distributed by his revolutionary measures, and just as the feudal system all over Western Europe had built up in the middle ages concentrated power of the barons, who owned all the land, reduced the people to vassalage and produced the French Revolution and its horrors of blood and fire. They believed that Northern society, directed by the same principles, without conscience, without sense of right or justice, would evolve the same conditions with the same consequences, and that the only salvation for Southern society was absolute and entire separation under a different government; that slavery furnished the only solution of self-government based on universal suffrage, and the only organization of labor and capital which had survived, or could survive the change of social conditions in ages of development and progress.   They were disunionists *per se;* but they were few and scattered and exerted no influence on the public opinion.   Their enthusiasm, their earnest conviction, did impress themselves on the mass, and when the time came the fire of their ardor kindled the State from mountain to ocean.

So the time went on.   State after State of the South seceded from the Union.   State after State of the North organized, armed and drilled her militia.   In February, 1861, the Southern party of Maryland, led by the young men, called a conference convention to meet in Baltimore to confer together and decide what the honor and the interests of Maryland required her to do in the crisis. Honor first—interest last!   That conference met and was such a demonstration of physical strength, of resolute purpose and of intelligent design, that it alarmed the conservative sentiment.   But in February no action could be taken.   Virginia had not moved, and it was uncertain how or when she would move, for the South or against it.

The governor of Maryland, Thomas Holliday Hicks, professed to be an ardent Southern man.   The young men did not believe him, put no confidence in him.   The old men, Union to the core, old Whigs, conservative by education and by nature, did trust him and insisted that Maryland should do nothing without the action of her constituted authorities, her governor and her legislature. The party of action urged a call of the general assembly. The governor protested that he was then in correspondence with the governors of the border States and that they would devise and execute means to save the Union and to preserve the peace.   The conference adjourned until the middle of March, by which time Lincoln would be inaugurated and the Federal government pass from the hands of the State rights Democracy to the successors of the Federal party that Jefferson and the Democracy had expelled in John Adams' time.

In Lincoln's inaugural he avowed the determination of the party in power " to retake, reoccupy and repossess the forts, arsenals, dock-yards and other property of the United States which had been seized in the Southern States by State authority."   This meant *war!*   But still the conservatives of Maryland could not understand it. They clung to their idea that talk, palaver, negotiation would weather the storm, and that the tornado could be stilled by resolving and asserting that the wind was not blowing.   As soon as the conference convention reassembled on the 12th of March in Baltimore, the party of action asserted itself.   Judge Chambers, ex-United States senator and ex-judge of the court of appeals, was made president, and a committee on resolutions appointed. The majority of the committee reported a set of resolutions of generalities—devotion to the Union, and opposition to disorder and disturbance of the public peace. The minority, through the chairman of the State committee, who was a member of the conference and of the committee, reported that any "attempt by the Federal government to retake, reoccupy or repossess the forts, arsenals and dock-yards now controlled by the Southern States, would be an act of war by the Federal government on the States, would operate *ipso facto* as a dissolution of the Union, and would remit to each State its original sovereign right to provide for its own safety and welfare, in any manner it decided to pursue." These resolutions would have been passed, but they met such violent opposition from the old men (Judge Chambers declared he would leave the chair and the convention if they were passed) that their author left the conference in disgust and returned home, where he promptly organized a military company for home defense and to resist invasion by foreign troops moving from the North to attack the South. The conference sent commissioners to Richmond to learn from the convention there in session what was the prospect of Virginia's taking position.   They could learn nothing, for Virginia herself did not know.

CHAPTER II.

ON April 12, 1861, South Carolina fired on Fort Sumter, and on April 15th President Lincoln issued his proclamation, calling on the States for 75,000 militia "to maintain the Union and to redress wrongs already too long endured." He did not specify the wrongs nor the period of endurance. With the proclamation went out from the secretary of war a requisition on the governors of each of the States for the State's quota of the 75,000 troops. Virginia promptly responded by passing her ordinance of secession on the 17th, not, however, to take effect until it had been ratified by a vote of the people, to be cast on the 24th of May; and the governor of Virginia, John Letcher, moved Virginia troops to Harper's Ferry and "retook, reoccupied and repossessed" that property of Virginia which she had ceded to the Union for the common welfare and mutual benefit of all the States, East and West, North and South. Now that it was being diverted to the injury of part and the exclusive use of one section, Virginia resumed the control of her ancient territory. Had she had the power, she would have had the right "to resume possession, control and sovereignty" of all the six States she had ceded to the Union, northwest of the Ohio river. But, alas, her own children, born of her blood and bred of her loins, were foremost in striking at the heart and life of their mother. The Northwest was the most ardent in "suppressing the rebellion,"the forerunner of which had been independence from the British nation and the right of self-government for the English in America, and had breathed into their nostrils the breath of Statehood.

15

With the defiance of old Virginia, went that of North Carolina, Tennessee, Kentucky and Missouri, who spurned the demand of the government back of it for men and arms to make war on brethren, kinsmen and fellow citizens. Kentucky tried the impracticable rôle of neutrality, but she was soon overrun by Federal troops. Governor Hicks assured the people that no troops should be sent from Maryland, unless it was to defend the national capital. The mayor of Baltimore, George William Brown, also issued his proclamation, expressing his satisfaction that no troops would be sent from Maryland to the soil of any other State. "If the counsels of the governor," he said, "shall be heeded, we may rest secure in the confidence that the storm of civil war which now threatens the country will at least pass over our beloved State and leave it unharmed, but if they shall be disregarded a fearful and fratricidal strife may at once burst out in our midst." So the governor and the mayor. The first knew well that in the strife of the elements, which was about to burst, in which the foundations of the mountains would be broken up and the winds of the tempest would sweep the land, the cry of "Peace! Peace!" was but the whining of babes—for Governor Hicks was no fool. He was a shrewd, sharp, positive man. He knew what he wanted and he took efficient means to procure it. He wanted to save Maryland to the Northern States. He believed the Union was gone. In the Southern Confederacy, Maryland must, in his opinion, play a subordinate part and he, himself, fall back into the political obscurity from which he had been recently raised. With the North, Maryland in possession of the national capital, protected by the Northern navy through her bay and great rivers, would be a conspicuous power, and he, as her governor, would fill a distinguished rôle. He knew that Maryland was as ardently Southern as Virginia. The Marylanders are the more excitable race. They are ardent, sympathetic and enthusiastic.

And they were afirè at the threat of invasion of Virginia. Had the governor hinted at his ulterior hopes and designs—at his purpose to keep Maryland quiet until she could be occupied by Northern troops and delivered, tied and manacled, to the Union authorities—had he given open ground for suspicion of treachery, the State would have risen, he would have been expelled, his government eradicated, and a revolutionary government of action instituted.

Mayor Brown was a high-minded, just and honorable gentleman. But he was a lawyer and an old man. He was devoted to his State and to his city, and no purer patriot ever lived than George William Brown. But he believed in *law*; he could conceive of nothing higher than law. Force to him meant riot, and in a great city riot always means arson, robbery, murder and license. The mayor believed that with the police and the fire departments he could control revolution and subdue the fires of insurrection. He faithfully did his duty as he saw it. He and his police commissioners tried to keep the peace, and in three months all were landed in Federal prisons, where they were incarcerated for fourteen months, beyond the reach of habeas corpus, without charge or indictment. Maryland thus suffered "the crucifixion of the soul," for her heart was with the Confederacy and her body bound and manacled to the Union.

On April 18th a battery of United States artillery under Major Pemberton, accompanied by six companies of unarmed Pennsylvania militia, arrived by the Northern Central railroad from Harrisburg at Baltimore and marched via Howard street to the Baltimore & Ohio railroad station at Camden street, whence they were promptly dispatched to Washington. They were escorted through the city by a howling mob, who displayed secession flags (the Palmetto flag of South Carolina being conspicuous), and who emphasized their feelings by cheers for "Jeff Davis and the Southern Confederacy." They were un-

Md 3

armed and as weak looking as a drove of cattle as the regulars escorted them through the streets. But the telegraph flamed out the news of the secession of Virginia, and at night the story of the capture of Harper's Ferry by the Virginia troops, with whom were Marylanders led by Bradley Johnson. The town was afire the night of the 18th. From all quarters came tidings of troops from the North and West, concentrating on Baltimore. The efficient militia of Massachusetts, under Maj.-Gen. Benjamin F. Butler, a man of ability, vigor and executive capacity, were on the march to protect the capital and to save the nation.

The New York Seventh, the ideal soldiers of peace parades, but in reality a gallant and game set, was filling its ranks, its cartridge boxes and its haversacks, and standing at attention, waiting word of command and tap of drum. Pennsylvania was rallying to the call of her great governor. The Democracy of the West, roused by Douglas, was rising as one man to defend the flag, and one serried, unbroken line of steel stretched from the northeast corner of Maine to the Mississippi river, ready to march forward to invade, to crush and to conquer the South. There could be no misunderstanding as to the meaning of all this. It meant *war*—nothing but *war*. War by one section on another. War urged on by hatred, by malice, by greed, by desire for conquest, to overthrow institutions existing before the republic, to destroy a social order which had given the world soldiers, statesmen and philosophers, the peers of any who had ever lived. The common people of Maryland understood it. The plain people think with their hearts, and *hearts* on questions of right and wrong are more unerring than heads. They were all for the South, and they were all for arming and fighting—fighting there on the spot—the first man or men who should presume to attempt to cross Maryland to get at Virginia. But the upper class is always conservative. The ex-governors, the ex-senators, the ex-judges everywhere are always afraid. The " have beens " ever recur to the peaceful times when they directed affairs, and always will be abhorrent of noise, of tumult, of violence, of force and of change. They cannot be leaders in revolution. Maryland at this crisis of her history was cursed by just such "conservatism." It was caused by her geographical position. She could only follow. She can never lead in such a crisis. She lacked young leaders. Kentucky was in a worse situation, for her leaders led her into the quagmire of neutrality. Missouri was better off, for Jackson and Price on the one side and Frank Blair on the other were positive men, and promptly ranged the people of the State in arms, for their respective sides. Maryland had sons who were educated soldiers. Robert Milligan McLane came of soldier blood. His grandfather, Allan McLane, had been the comrade of Light Horse Harry in the campaign of Valley Forge and had led the Delaware Legion, as Lee had the Virginians. McLane graduated at West Point, served with distinction in the Florida campaign, but after that left the army and entered politics in Maryland. He had served in the State legislature, as representative in Congress from Maryland, and occupied a conspicuous place in the confidence of the State rights Southern people of Maryland. George W. Hughes had served with distinction for many years in the army of the United States and had won the grade of colonel in Mexico. He was now living in affluence and retirement on his plantation in Anne Arundel county. The party of action, the young men, looked to these old soldiers for advice and leadership. But they were too old soldiers to plunge into a fight without troops, arms, ammunition or a commissary department. Bradley Johnson and other young men were ready, but they had neither the experience nor the knowledge to qualify them for immediate leadership.

So on the night of April 18, 1861, Maryland was standing alert, braced up, ready to charge at the word. Vir-

ginia had seceded, the North was marching.   Maryland
was the outpost to receive the first attack.   At that hour
there was no division of opinion.   The State rights clubs
had been flying the secession flag, the stars and bars of
the Confederacy, and the palmetto of South Carolina.
The Union clubs had over their halls the stars and
stripes; but during the afternoon of April 18th the Union
flags were hauled down and the State flag of Maryland
everywhere substituted.   And the black and gold was
everywhere saluted with cheers, with shouts, with
tears.   The telegraph gave hourly notice of the approach
of the enemy.   General Butler had left Boston; he had
passed New York; he had gone through Philadelphia;
he was on the Susquehanna.   What next?   Maryland
held her breath.   Through New England their route had
been an ovation.   Down Broadway in New York the people went wild, as they did through New Jersey and Philadelphia.   There were eleven companies of Massachusetts
troops attached to the Sixth Massachusetts under command of Colonel Jones.   At Philadelphia an unarmed
and ununiformed mob of Pennsylvanians, called a regiment, under Colonel Small, was added to Colonel Jones'
command.   They came in a train of thirty-five cars and arrived at the President street station at 11 'a. m.   Thence
it was the custom of the railroad company to haul each
car across the city, over a track laid in the street, to Camden station of the Baltimore & Ohio railroad, a distance of a little over a mile.   Nine cars with seven companies got through to Camden station.   But that was as
much as human nature could bear.   The mob of infuriated men increased every minute and the excitement
grew.   The stones out of the street flew up and staved
in the car windows.   The drivers unhitched their teams,
hitched to the rear of their cars and made all haste back
to President Street station, where had been left the unarmed Pennsylvanians and the rest of the Massachusetts
regiment.   These men were marched out of the station,

formed in front of it, and then moved in a column of fours toward Camden station. In the meantime the railroad track had been torn up, the bridge on the south dismantled and obstructed, and the march of the troops was necessarily laborious and very slow. The streets were packed with a dense mass of infuriated and excited men, encouraged by the apparent retreat of the troops and the success of the opposition to them. The foremost files had to force their way through this pack of humanity. George William Brown, mayor of the town, with a gallantry and chivalry beyond imagination, for he was a Southern man and certified his fidelity by fourteen months' imprisonment in Union dungeons, placed himself by the side of the captain of the leading company and forced their way through the crowd. No man in Baltimore was more loved, respected and admired than Brown, and his escort of the "invader" was submitted to while he was present. But as soon as he had passed stones began to hail on the column. The officers became rattled. Instead of halting and confronting their enemy, they accelerated the step until the march became a half run. Then a pistol went off; then a musket; then two muskets, three muskets cracked, and citizens fell and died in their tracks. Then reason fled. The mob tore the muskets out of the hands of the soldiers and shot them down. One man jerked the sword out of the hand of an officer and ran him through with it. Frank Ward, a young lawyer, snatched the flag out of the hands of the color bearer and tore it from the lance, and while making off with it was shot through both thighs. He survived though, to serve gallantly as adjutant of the First Maryland regiment, and is alive to-day. Marshal Kane had gone to the Camden station to protect the troops there, when news came of this mêlée on Pratt street. He swung fifty policemen down the street in a double-quick, formed them across the street in the rear of the soldiers and ordered their pursuers to "halt." They halted, and then with the mayor of Baltimore in front, the chief of police in rear, the baited, harried, breathless preservers of the Union reached Camden station, where they were loaded on trains and dispatched, panic-stricken, to Washington.

Outside the city limits, however, after the danger had passed, some heroic soul signalized his devotion to the flag by shooting in cold blood Robert W. Davis, a reputable and well-known citizen and merchant, whose crime was alleged to have been a cheer for Jeff Davis and the South. That evening, April 19th, Marshal Kane telegraphed to Bradley T. Johnson at Frederick: " Streets red with Maryland blood. Send expresses over the mountains of Maryland and Virginia for the riflemen to come, without delay. Fresh hordes will be down on us to-morrow. We will fight them and whip them or die."

Johnson, since the failure of the conference convention of March to act, had been engaged in organizing companies of minute men to resist invasion, by bushwhacking or any other practicable method. He had corresponded with the captains of many volunteer companies in the State, and all were moving toward concert of action. The receipt of Kane's telegram was the match to the magazine. By seven o'clock on the 20th the Frederick company was assembled, took possession of the moving train on the Baltimore & Ohio railroad to Baltimore, and by eleven o'clock marched down Baltimore street to Monument Square. Monument Square was the forum of Baltimore, where the citizens always assembled in times of peril to consult and determine that the commonweal should receive no harm. They were the first reinforcements to Baltimore. Next came two troops of cavalry from Baltimore county, and next the Patapsco Dragoons from Anne Arundel rode straight to the city hall and presented themselves to Mayor Brown to assist in the defense of the city. The afternoon papers of the 19th spread all over the State during the next day, and the State rose. Early on the morning of the 20th the city council appropriated $500,000 for the defense of the city, to be used at the discretion of the mayor. The banks furnished the money in two hours. Capt. Wilson Carey Nicholas, with the Garrison Forest Rangers—afterward Company G., First Maryland regiment, seized the United States arsenal at Pikesville, where there was a deposit of antiquated arms and a considerable supply of gunpowder. All the city companies of militia were under arms in their armories. Col. Benjamin Huger, of South Carolina, who had been in command at Pikesville for some years, but who had just resigned from the army of the United States, was made colonel of the Fifty-third regiment, Maryland militia, composed of the Independent Grays and the six companies of the Maryland Guard. The command was admirably instructed, drilled and officered, and a majority of its officers and men afterward served in the army of the Confederate States. The mayor issued a notice calling on all citizens who had arms to deposit them with the commissioner of police, to be used in the defense of the city, and upon all who were willing to enroll themselves for military service. Under this call over fifteen thousand volunteers were enrolled and partly organized on Saturday, the 20th, and Col. Isaac R. Trimble was assigned to command them. The railroad stations and State tobacco warehouses were used for drill rooms. On Saturday night the bridges on the railroads leaving north from Baltimore were burnt or disabled by a detachment of police and of the Maryland Guard, acting under the orders of Governor Hicks. The governor was in Baltimore during the attack on the troops and was carried off his feet and out of his head by the furor of the hour. He gave the order to burn the bridges. He afterward strenuously denied giving it, but he gave it.

On Sunday morning, April 21st, the Howard County Dragoons, Capt. George R. Earltree, came in, and by the boat two companies from Easton, and news came that the companies from Harford, Cecil, Carroll and Prince

George's were on the march. Three batteries of light artillery were out on the streets, and the city was braced up in tense excitement.

Just after the people had gone to church on that day, about half-past ten, two men rode down Charles Street, in a sweeping gallop, from beyond the boundary to Lexington and down Lexington to the city hall. They shouted as they flashed by, '' The Yankees are coming, the Yankees are coming!'' Twenty-four hundred of Pennsylvania troops, only half of them armed, had got as far as Cockeysville, twenty miles from Baltimore, where they had been stopped by the burnt bridges, and had gone into camp. These couriers of disaster brought the news of this fresh invasion and it flashed through the city like an electric shock. The churches dismissed their congregations, their bells rang, and in the twinkling of an eye the streets were packed with people—men and women in the hysterics of excitement pressing guns, pistols, fowling pieces, swords, daggers, bowie knives, every variety of weapon, upon the men and beseeching them to drive back the hated invader. In an hour Monument Square was packed, crammed with such a mass of quivering humanity as has rarely been seen in human history.

Early that morning the mayor had gone to Washington on a special train to see the President and General Scott at the invitation of the former to the governor and mayor to visit him for conference as to the best way to preserve the peace. They arrived at an understanding that no more troops were to be marched through Baltimore. They were to be brought from Harrisburg down to the Relay House on the Northern Central railroad, seven miles north-west of the city, and thence by rail to Washington. General Scott proposed this plan to the President, *if the people of Maryland would permit it and would not molest the troops*. But if they were attacked, the general of the army said, he would bring troops from Perryville by

boat to Annapolis and thence by rail to Washington. The President and General Scott both seemed to take it for granted that the Potomac would be blockaded.   Mayor Brown returned from Washington with the assurance that the detachment at Cockeysville would be ordered back, and that no troops should attempt to pass through Baltimore.   The wires were all cut north of the city and all communication by rail or telegraph between the capital and the Northern States was absolutely closed for several days.   The Eighth Massachusetts, with Brig.-Gen. B. F. Butler, arrived at Perryville on the 20th, took the steamboat Maryland, and arrived at Annapolis on the 21st.   On the 22d, the governor called an extra session of the general assembly to meet at Annapolis on the 26th. On the 24th the governor, "in consequence of the extraordinary state of affairs," changed the place of meeting to Frederick.   On its meeting there the Hon. James Murray Mason appeared before it, as a commissioner from the State of Virginia authorized to conclude a treaty of alliance, offensive and defensive, between the two States. The legislature had been elected in 1859 and was charged with no mandate for revolutionary times.   Ten members from Baltimore were elected at a special election held in that city on the 24th, in the place of the delegation returned as elected in 1859, but unseated on account of fraud and violence at the election.   The new members were the leading men of the town—merchants, lawyers, representatives of the great business of commerce and trade of a great city.   They were John C. Brune, Ross Winans, Henry M. Warfield, J. Hanson Thomas, T. Parkin Scott, H. Mason Morfit, S. Teakle Wallis, Charles H. Pitts, William G. Harrison, and Lawrence Langston. It was evident in twenty-four hours that "conservatism" would rule the councils of the general assembly, as it had done those of the governor, and that all the influence of that body would be exerted against any action by the
Md 4

State looking toward taking part in the revolution, which it was clear, was upon the whole country.

Captain Johnson had brought back his company from Baltimore, armed with Hall's carbines, an antiquated and rejected breechloader, and had got his men into some sort of shape. He remained in Frederick at the request of the State rights members of the legislature to guard and protect them from the Unionists of the town, who were loquacious and loud in their threats against " the Secesh." And the legislature was prompt to range itself on the side of peace and Union. It met on the 26th of April. On the 27th it issued an address disclaiming all idea, intention or authority to pass any ordinance of secession. It appointed Otho Scott, Robert M. McLane and William J. Ross commissioners to confer with the President of the United States and see what arrangements could be made to preserve the peace of the State. On May 6th these commissioners reported that they had had an interview with the President, and that he had assured them that the State of Maryland, so long as she did not array herself against the Federal government, would not be molested or interfered with, *except so far as it was necessary for the preservation of the Union.* But neither governor, general assembly nor commissioners to the President had the faintest conception of the real state of things in Maryland. She was devoted to the Union. She was hostile to secession. She abhorred the men who precipitated the Gulf States into revolution. She had no sympathy with slavery, for she had emancipated more than half her slaves and had established a negro State of Maryland in Africa, where she was training her emancipated servants to take control of their own destiny as free men, and this colony she supported by annual appropriations out of her public taxes. There was no involuntary servitude in Maryland, for as soon as a servant became discontented he or she just walked over the line into Pennsylvania, where they were safely harbored and concealed.

Therefore there was no sympathy in Maryland for the proceedings convulsing the Southern States. But the proclamation of the President, calling for 75,000 men "to redress wrongs already too long endured," changed the whole situation in the twinkling of an eye. It was no longer union or disunion, secession or State rights. It was a question of invasion and self-defense. The President had declared war on her sister State. Was Maryland to support that war, or was she to stand by with hands folded and see her friends and kindred beyond the Potomac put to the sword and the torch? War on a State was against the common right. The cause of each was the cause of all; and precisely as Maryland had responded in 1775 to the cry of Massachusetts for assistance, so now did the people of Maryland, over governor, over general assembly, over peace commissioners, respond to the call of Virginia. The peace commissioners reported on May 6th. On the 8th Captain Johnson, having secured from Mason an engagement that all troops that would go from Maryland should be promptly received into the army of the Confederate States, and from Colonel Jackson, in command at Harper's Ferry, permission to rendezvous on the Virginia side, opposite Point of Rocks, marched out of Frederick to that place, crossed the Potomac and reported to Capt. Turner Ashby, then posted there with his troops of horse. Ashby was to feed the Marylanders until further orders. This pioneer company showed the way, and in a few days detachments of companies began to straggle in—the débris of Trimble's fifteen thousand enrolled volunteers in Baltimore. Some marched with a semblance of order from Baltimore to the Point of Rocks. Some straggled in by twos and threes. Some came in squads on the railroad. But the State was aflame and a steady stream of gallant youth poured into the rendezvous at Point of Rocks and Harper's Ferry. By May 21st there were the skeletons of eight companies collected at Point of Rocks.

Co. A.   Capt. Bradley T. Johnson.
Co. B.   Capt. C. C. Edelin, at Harper's Ferry.
Co. C.   Capt. Frank S. Price.
Co. D.   Capt. James R. Herbert.
Co. E.   Capt. Harry McCoy.
Co. F.   Capt. Thomas G. Holbrook.
Co. G.   Capt. Wilson Carey Nicholas.
Co. H.   Capt. Harry Welmore.

They were mustered into the service of the Confederate States on May 21st and 22d by Lieut.-Col. George Deas, inspector-general on the staff of Gen. Jos. E. Johnston, who in the meantime had superseded Colonel Jackson in command at Harper's Ferry. Captain Johnson, as senior captain, refused to recognize the Virginia authorities. Relying on the promise of Mr. Mason, he insisted that the Marylanders should be received into the army of the Confederate States, and not into the army of Virginia. On May 21, 1861, Virginia was not one of the Confederate States. He believed that Maryland ought to be represented in the army by men bearing arms and her flag. It was impossible for her to be represented in the political department of the government; therefore it was of vital importance that the flag of Maryland should always be upheld in the armies of the Confederate States. In these eight companies there were about five hundred men. They effected a temporary organization among themselves under their senior captain, and sent up through the regular channels to President Davis their application to have their battalion organized into the army of the Confederate States, with Charles S. Winder, late captain Ninth infantry, U. S. A., as colonel, and Bradley T. Johnson as lieutenant-colonel.

CHAPTER III.

MARYLAND'S OVERTHROW.

WHILE the city of Baltimore was in a frenzy of excitement, on Sunday, the 21st of May, at the approach of the Pennsylvanians from Cockeyville, Brig.-Gen. Benjamin F. Butler, with a Massachusetts regiment, landed at Annapolis, whither he had proceeded by a steamer from Perryville on the Susquehanna. The next day, the 22nd, he was reinforced by the New York Eighth and pushed up the Annapolis & Elkridge railroad to its junction with the Washington branch of the Baltimore & Ohio Railroad. On May 5th he took possession of the Relay House, nine miles from Baltimore, where the main branch of the Baltimore & Ohio railroad leading to Harper's Ferry and the West unites with the Washington branch, which leads to Washington, thirty miles distant. His troops were the Eighth New York, the Sixth Massachusetts and Major Cook's battery of Boston light artillery. He promptly fortified the position with earthworks and artillery. All trains going west and south were searched, and scouts scoured the surrounding country. On the 8th of May communication between Washington and the North was further strengthened by a new route by water from Perryville to Locust Point, and thence by rail to Washington. On the night of May 13th General Butler, with the major part of his command, entered Baltimore, seized Federal Hill, which commands the city, fortified it with fifty heavy guns, and Baltimore was in his control. He acted with intelligence and promptness, and to him the Union side was greatly indebted for restoring communications between the capital city and the United States. The United States having control of the bay and the great rivers emptying into it—the Patapsco, the Patuxent and the Potomac, all parts of the State were dominated by Federal guns. The Northern frontier was open, with the Baltimore & Ohio railroad from Wheeling and the West, the Northern Central railroad from Harrisburg and the central North, and the Baltimore, Wilmington & Philadelphia railroad from New York and New England, and the North, West and East in arms to pour down over these great avenues of travel to subjugate Maryland and to protect the capital. It was too late for Maryland to act with the Confederacy. There never had been an hour when she could have struck a blow for independence. It was impossible to move before Virginia. Virginia did not move until May 24th, when Maryland was bound hand and foot to the Union by the overwhelming force of the army of occupation.

The general assembly of the State acted with the dignity and courage of a Roman senate. On the 10th of May, the State in the grip of the Federal army, the committee on Federal relations of the house of delegates, Severn Teakle Wallis, Esq., chairman, made a report that for exact statement, for force and for logic was excelled by no paper of that epoch. They said:

"Whereas, in the judgment of the General Assembly of Maryland, the war now waged by the government of the United States upon the people of the Confederate States is unconstitutional in its origin, purposes and conduct; repugnant to civilization and sound policy; subversive of the free principles upon which the Federal Union was founded, and certain to result in the hopeless and bloody overthrow of our existing institutions; and,

"Whereas, the people of Maryland, while recognizing the obligations of their State, as a member of the Union, to submit in good faith to the exercise of all the legal and constitutional powers of the general government, and to join as one man in fighting its authorized battles, do reverence, nevertheless, the great American principle of self-government, and sympathize deeply with their Southern brethren in their noble and manly determination to uphold and defend the same; and,

"Whereas, not merely on their own account, and to turn from their own soil the calamities of civil war, but for the blessed sake of humanity and to arrest the wanton shedding of fraternal blood in a miserable contest which can bring nothing with it but sorrow, shame and desolation, the people of Maryland are enlisted with their whole hearts on the side of reconciliation and peace;

"Now, therefore, it is hereby resolved by the General Assembly of Maryland, that the State of Maryland owes it to her own self-respect and her respect for the Constitution, not less than her deepest and most honorable sympathies, to register this, her solemn protest, against the war which the Federal government has declared against the Confederate States of the South and our sister and neighbor, Virginia, and to announce her resolute determination to have no part or lot, directly or indirectly, in its prosecution.

"Resolved, That the State of Maryland earnestly and anxiously desires the restoration of peace between the belligerent sections of the country; and the President, authorities and people of the Confederate States having over and over, officially and unofficially, declared that they seek only peace and self-defense, and to be let alone, and that they are willing to throw down the sword the instant the sword now drawn against them shall be sheathed—

"The senators and delegates of Maryland do beseech and implore the President of the United States to accept the olive branch which is thus held out to him, and in the name of God and humanity to cease this unholy and most wretched and unprofitable strife, at least until the assembling of the Congress at Washington shall have given time for the prevalence of cool and better counsels.

" Resolved, That the State of Maryland desires the peaceful and immediate recognition of the independence of the Confederate States, and hereby gives her cordial consent thereto, as a member of the Union, entertaining the profound conviction that the willing return of the Southern people to their former Federal relations is a thing beyond hope, and that the attempt to coerce them will only add slaughter and hate to impossibility.

" Resolved, That the present military occupation of Maryland being for purpose which in the opinion of the legislature are in flagrant violation of the Constitution, the General Assembly of the State in the name of her people does hereby protest against the same and against the arbitrary restrictions and illegalities with which it is attended, calling upon all good citizens at the same time, in the most earnest and authoritative manner, to abstain from all violent and unlawful interference of every sort with the troops in transit through our territory, or quartered among us, and patiently and peacefully leave to time and reason the ultimate and certain re-establishment and vindication of the right.

" Resolved: That under existing circumstances it is inexpedient to call a Sovereign Convention of the State at this time, or to take any measures for the immediate organization or arming of the militia."

These resolutions passed the Senate, ayes 11, nays 3; House, ayes 43, nays 12. General Butler replied to this defiance by seizing Baltimore the very night these resolutions passed. He *acted*, they *resolved!* An equally significant incident had occurred in Baltimore just the week before. Judge William F. Giles, judge of the district court of the United States for the district of Maryland, issued the writ of habeas corpus on May 4th to Major Morris, commanding at Fort McHenry, commanding him to produce before the court without delay the body of John George Mullen, an enlisted soldier, one of the garrison of the fort who sought his discharge on the ground of minority. Under the law of the United States it was unlawful to enlist a minor under eighteen years of age in the military or naval service without the consent of his parent or guardian. Mullen alleged in his petition that he was under the lawful age and had been enlisted illegally. Major Morris neither produced the man nor made any response to the mandate of the writ; but on May 7th he addressed a letter to Judge Giles, in which he peremptorily refused to obey the writ. In this first trial of strength between law and arms, law became silent, as usual. On May 25th John Merryman, one of the first citizens of Baltimore county, was arrested at his home by a squad of soldiers and locked up in Fort

McHenry. The next day Roger Brooke Taney, chief
justice of the Supreme court of the United States,
assigned to the fourth circuit, of which Maryland formed
a part, issued the writ of habeas corpus to General Cadwallader, commanding at Fort McHenry, requiring him
to produce the body of Merryman before the circuit court
of the United States for the district of Maryland, at
Baltimore, on Monday, May 27th. The chief justice
issued the writ on Sunday! On Monday Colonel Lee, aide-
de-camp to General Cadwallader, appeared in the court
and said that General Cadwallader's other engagements
prevented his appearing in person, but had sent him to
express the general's regrets and read the chief justice a
letter, which the aide proceeded to do. The general said
that Merryman had been arrested for open and avowed
hostility to the United States, and that he had been
authorized by the President of the United States to suspend the
writ of habeas corpus in such cases, which he had done.
The chief justice ordered an attachment to issue against
General Cadwallader and sent the marshal of the court
to arrest the general and bring him before the Court.
Upon the marshal's proceeding to Fort McHenry with a
few deputy marshals he sent in his card and official designation through the sentry at the gate to the commanding officer. After a reasonable time the messenger came
back with the message that there was no answer to the
marshal's card and that he would not be permitted to
enter the fort. The marshal made return of these facts
to the court, and the chief justice directed the clerk to
make an entry on the record of the court that the writ of
habeas corpus having been disobeyed by General Cadwallader, an attachment for contempt had issued against
him, which he had resisted, having a superior force at
his command to any which the court or its marshal could
control, and he subsequently filed his opinion in the case,
in which he demonstrated beyond a cavil that the President of the United States has and can have no authority at

Md 5

any time, under any circumstances, to suspend the writ of habeas corpus, and directed the entire record to be certified to the President of the United States for his information and action.

On the 14th of May the legislature adjourned, and Ross Winans, a member of the house of delegates from Baltimore City—the head of the firm of Ross Winans & Co., the greatest manufacturers of locomotive engines and railroad cars in the world—was arrested by General Butler at the Relay House on his way home. Ross Winans was not only a man of great wealth, one of the millionaires of the day, but he was a man whose moral character, whose genius, whose breadth of mind and greatness of heart, whose culture and whose courage would have made him distinguished in any country in the world. His arrest was intended to terrorize the State. It had the effect of rousing it like the long roll. The legislature, at its adjourned session of June 22d, declared that "The unconstitutional and arbitrary proceedings of the Federal executive have not been confined to the violation of the personal rights and liberties of the citizens of Maryland, but have been extended into every department of oppressive illegality, so that the property of no man is safe, the sanctity of no dwelling is respected, and the sacredness of private correspondence no longer exists; and,—

"Whereas, the Senate and House of Delegates of Maryland, recognizing the obligations of the State, as far as in her lies, to protect and defend her people against usurped and arbitrary power, however difficult the fulfillment of that high obligation may be rendered by disastrous circumstances, feel it due to her dignity and independence that history should not record the overthrow of public freedom, for an instant, within her borders, without recording likewise the indignant expression of her resentment and remonstrance;

"Now, therefore, be it resolved, That the senate and house of delegates of Maryland, in the name and on behalf of the good people of the State, do accordingly register this their earnest and unqualified protest against the oppressive and tyrannical assertion and exercise of military jurisdiction within the limits of Maryland, over the persons and property of her citizens, by the government of the United States, and do solemnly declare the same to be subversive of the most sacred guarantees of the Constitution and in flagrant violation of the fundamental and most cherished principles of American free government.''

The legislature of Maryland was composed of brave, high-minded and patriotic men, but it was dominated by the spirit of conservatism, which cannot understand how anything can be right which is unlawful, nor any process expedient or necessary which is illegal. The conservatives never could, never did understand that they were in the midst of a revolution. They stood by constitutional rights. They held on to the claim of constitutional guarantees—to habeas corpus—to trial by jury—to free speech—to law—until they and their constitutional guarantees were landed in Fort Lafayette or the military prisons in New York and Boston. They stood by their faith then and never ceased to protest that they could not be imprisoned without warrant, nor held without bail. They were right in doctrine, but they were imprisoned and held.

The minority party in the State, the party of action in the legislature, never hoped for the secession of the State after the delay of Virginia. After the 24th of May Maryland was a Federal garrison. But they did hope for action—a league offensive and defensive with Virginia, with all that that implied. They introduced into the legislature a bill to provide for a committee of safety to be elected by the legislature, to which should be committed the duty of defending the State and her people and to exercise all the powers of government. The bill appropriated $5,000,000 to be applied by the committee of safety for the defense of the State. The banks in Baltimore had raised $500,000 for the defense of the city in three hours, and the banks of the State would have supplied $5,000,000 for the defense of the State in a week. The plan of the projectors of the committee of safety was to arm the militia. They expected to equip forty thousand men as promptly as the Northern States had armed and equipped their volunteers, and they knew that Maryland volunteers would take arms as quickly as those of Massachusetts and Ohio. They did not propose to carry the State out of the Union, but they intended to arm their young men and command the peace in the State. When that failed, as fail they knew it would, the State would be represented by forty thousand armed and equipped volunteers who would carry her flag in the front line and would make her one of the Confederate States in fact, if not in name.

These were the intentions of Captain Johnson and men of his age in the legislature and in the State, and they were constant and ardent in pressing them in the general assembly. The Conservatives, however, preferred the processes of the law, and could not understand how force could decide questions of right. It would be better to bring trespass *quare clausum* against Butler at the Relay for digging trenches and piling up earthworks, to sue out injunctions against illegal arrests and a mandamus to make Cadwallader respect Taney's writ of habeas corpus!

The committee on Federal relations agreed on their report May 7th that it was inexpedient to take any steps toward the organization and arming of the militia, though it was not made until the 10th. But on the 8th Johnson and his company marched to Virginia. At the Point of Rocks he arranged with Capt. James Ashby to ride into Frederick, seize the governor and carry him off to Virginia and thus break up the State government and throw it into the hands of the legislature, who would be obliged to take charge during the interregnum. A notice to this effect was sent to the leaders in the legislature and they promptly dispatched T. Parkin Scott, member from Baltimore City, to Johnson, then on the Maryland Heights with the Maryland battalion, demanding that he cease his enterprises and let them alone. He obeyed them and they went to prison; while he went into the field.

The battalion at Harper's Ferry was helpless. Company A was the only company that pretended to be armed, and it carried Hall's carbines, which had been procured in Baltimore by its captain. This arm was the original breechloader manufactured at Harper's Ferry for the United States army, and was so inefficient that it was promptly condemned and discarded. Hence it was sold cheap to innocent militiamen. But the others didn't have even these worthless carbines. They had rushed off from home, fired by the enthusiasm of those days in Baltimore, had stolen rides on the cars or had walked to Point of Rocks and to Harper's Ferry where they were fed. Provisions were plenty, but they had no clothes, blankets, tents, cooking utensils—nothing that soldiers need and must have to be of any service. They had no government to appeal to for arms. In fact, they were outlaws from their own State government. They were too proud to go back home; stay and fight they would and must. All around them were warm-hearted comrades who shared their blankets with them at night and their rations by day. Unless something could be done to keep them together, unless they could be armed, equipped and legally organized, they must inevitably dissolve, be absorbed in surrounding commands, and thus Maryland lose her main hope and best chance to be represented by her own sons, bearing her flag in the army of the Confederate States.

At this crisis Mrs. Bradley T. Johnson came forward and offered to go to North Carolina and apply there for arms and equipment. She was the daughter of the Hon. Romulus M. Saunders, for a generation a leading and distinguished member of Congress from North Carolina, and by appointment of Polk, minister plenipotentiary and envoy extraordinary to Spain, with a special mandate to purchase Cuba and pay one hundred millions for it. His young daughters were with him and were introduced to court and presented to the queen. There they became intimate with Eugenie de Montijo, countess de Teba, who afterward became empress of the French. Mrs. Johnson was then in the prime of her youth, handsome, graceful, accomplished. She had left her comfortable home in Frederick with her little boy, a lad five years old, to follow her husband. She now volunteered to serve him. She was the only hope of Maryland. Captain Johnson applied to Colonel Jackson for advice in this emergency. Jackson ordered that Mrs. Johnson be furnished with escort and transportation and that she start at once. On May 24, 1861, she left the camp of Companies A and B at the Point of Rocks, escorted by Capt. Wilson Carey Nicholas, Company G, and Second-Lieut. G. M. E. Shearen, Company A, to go to Raleigh via Richmond. At Leesburg they found that Alexandria had that day been occupied by the Federals and thus communication southward cut. Returning, she and her staff went up to Harper's Ferry and thence by Winchester and Strasburg and Manassas Junction to Richmond and Raleigh, where she arrived on the night of the 27th. The next morning, accompanied by her father and her escort, she applied to Gov. Thomas H. Ellis and the council of state for arms for her husband and his men. There were on that council some plain countrymen, in their home spun, but they bore hearts of gold. It was a picturesque incident. Here this elegant, graceful, refined young lady, whose family was known to every man of them, and to some of whom she was personally known—there the circle of grave, plain old men taking in every word she uttered, watching every movement. Her father, Judge Saunders, one of the most illustrious citizens of the State, as simple, direct, frank a gentleman as ever lived, had put his daughter forward to tell her plain story in the fewest and simplest words possible. She said: " Governor and gentlemen, I left my husband and his comrades in Virginia. They have left their homes in Maryland to fight for the South, but they have no arms, and I have come to my native State to beg my own people to help us. Give arms to my husband and his comrades, so that he can help you!"

" Madam," said one of the council, old, venerable and gray-haired, slapping his thigh with a resounding blow, —" Madam, you shall have everything that this State can give." And the order was made then and there, on the spot, at the instant, that she should be supplied with five hundred Mississippi rifles and ten thousand cartridges, with necessary equipments. This at the time when, in the language of the day, every cartridge was worth a dollar.

But her visit and her errand lighted the greatest enthusiasm among her fellow countrymen. The constitutional convention of North Carolina was then in session. It was the most illustrious body of Carolinians that ever assembled. The members of it called a meeting at night in the capitol, under the leadership of Hon. Weldon H. Edwards, president of the convention, Chief Justice Thomas Ruffin of the supreme court of the State, her father, Judge Saunders, and others. The meeting was held in the hall of the house of commons, was presided over by ex-Gov. Thomas S. Reid and was attended with great enthusiasm. The cause of the Marylanders was espoused with ardor, the meeting making a liberal contribution of money on the spot. Hon. Kenneth Raynor, ex-member of Congress, addressing the meeting, said:

" If great events produce great men—so in the scene before us we have proof that great events produce great women.   It was one that partook more of the romance than of the realities of life.   One of our own daughters, raised in the lap of luxury, blessed with the enjoyment of all the elements of elegance and ease, had quit her peaceful home, followed her husband to the camp, and leaving him in that camp, has come to the home of her childhood to seek aid for him and his comrades, not because he is her husband, but because he is fighting the battles of his country, against a tyrant.''

He paid a high tribute to the patriotism and love of liberty which eminently characterized the people of Maryland.   '' They were fighting our battles, '' he said, '' with halters round their necks.''

On the 29th Mrs. Johnson left Raleigh with her escort and her arms, and her route was a continued ovation. At every town, at every station, the people had gathered to see the woman who was arming her husband's regiment, and they overwhelmed her with enthusiasm and hearty sympathy.   At Petersburg a substantial sum of money was handed to her, and stopping at Richmond she procured from John Letcher, governor of Virginia, a supply of camp-kettles, hatchets, axes, etc., and with the money in her hands, ordered forty-one wall tents made at once.   On the 31st of May she left Richmond with her arms, ammunition and supplies.   At Manassas Beauregard gave her an order to take any train she might find necessary for transportation and to hold all trains subject to her orders.   She rode in the freight car on her boxes of rifles.   Companies A and B had during her absence been moved up to Harper's Ferry to unite with the rest of the command, and on June 3, 1861, after an absence of ten days from camp, she returned and delivered to her husband the results of her energy, devotion and enthusiasm.   The following receipt from the chief of ordnance of Stonewall Jackson's command has probably no parallel in the history of war:

" Received, Ordnance Department, Harper's Ferry, Va., June 3, 1861, of Mrs. Bradley T. Johnson, Five Hundred Mississippi rifles (cal. 54) Ten Thousand cartridges and Thirty-five Hundred caps.

G. N. COCHRANE, Master of Ordnance.''

Such an incident of courage, of heroism, of devotion and of enthusiasm thrilled that army through every rank and fiber. Colonel Jackson, then in command at Harper's Ferry, afterwards the world-famous " Stonewall," called on her, with his staff, and thanked her. The officers of the battalion in meeting:

"Resolved—That the thanks of the Maryland Line be tendered to Mrs. Captain Bradley T. Johnson for her earnest, patriotic and successful efforts in arming and equipping the Maryland Line.

"Resolved—That we, the officers, pledge ourselves and for our men that the arms she has obtained shall at the close of the war be returned to the State of North Carolina, without stain or dishonor.

"Resolved—That these resolutions be signed by the officers of the meeting and presented to Mrs. Johnson.

JAMES R. HERBERT, President.
I. G. W. HARRIOTT, Secretary.''

She forthwith returned to Richmond for clothes and the tents. She secured cloth for uniforms, by permission of Governor Letcher, by purchasing it from the mills where it was manufactured for the State of Virginia, and she paid for making it up into uniforms. Shoes, blankets and underclothes were supplied by Col. Larkin Smith, quartermaster-general; and the tents had been ordered on her way back from North Carolina. On June 29th she started back for camp with forty-one tents, and uniforms, underclothes and shoes for five hundred men. She had paid out ten thousand dollars, the contribution of enthusiastic North Carolinians and Virginians.

CHAPTER IV.

MARYLANDERS ENLIST, AND ORGANIZE TO DEFEND VIRGINIA AND THE CONFEDERACY.

WHILE these events were occurring at Harper's Ferry, considerable numbers of Marylanders were rendezvousing at Richmond. The enrolled men commanded by Colonel Trimble, called out by the board of police commissioners, were drilled in a more or less efficient way in Baltimore, until the meeting of the legislature at Frederick, when they were disbanded. Johnson's company, at the same time, having left Frederick and gone to the Point of Rocks, furnished the nucleus around which gathered the men thus dismissed by the police authorities. They formed the eight companies mustered into the service of the Confederate States by Lieutenant-Colonel George Deas. But the volunteer companies, the Baltimore City Guard, the Maryland Guard, the Independent Grays, were as well instructed, as well officered as any American volunteers ever are, and some of them had historical reputations to maintain, for their companies had fought at North Point. They, therefore, regarded themselves as superior to the undrilled crowd that Captain Johnson was "licking into shape at Harper's Ferry," as they put it, and proceeded to Richmond, where they at once put themselves in accord with the Virginia authorities. Marylanders were to be embodied into three regiments, armed and mustered into the service of Virginia, who was to adopt them. In carrying out this plan Governor Letcher issued commissions to Francis Q. Thomas, ex-captain United States army, as colonel of the First; to Bradley T. Johnson as lieutenant-colonel of the Second, and to Alden

Weston, major of the Third. It was in the plan to consolidate these three into one if they failed to fill up into full regiments. Captain Johnson promptly declined the commission sent him by Governor Letcher, refusing to enter the military service of Virginia on the distinct ground that Maryland must be represented by Maryland regiments, and for Marylanders to accept service under Virginia would be to sacrifice the rights of the State to the services of her own sons. It was their duty, he believed, to give their own State the benefit of their service and of such reputation as they might be fortunate enough to win. Following this line of duty, he had caused the eight Harper's Ferry companies to be mustered into the army of the Confederate States, and he urged by every means in his power the consolidation of all Marylanders into the Maryland Line. This proved to be utterly impracticable. They were all volunteers; away from home there was no State sentiment, no home opinion to direct or control their conduct, and they selected their associates and comrades from contiguity, from friendship and from relationship. Men of Maryland descent were scattered all over the Confederacy, and thousands of young men who got through the lines sought out their relations and kinsmen in nearly every regiment of the army. The Maryland Line was the ideal of Lieut.-Col. George H. Steuart and of Maj. Bradley T. Johnson, and for two years they labored to collect the Marylanders. All influences from home were directed to the same end. The flag, made in Baltimore and brought over by Hetty Carey, was inscribed "First Regiment Maryland Line." But not until 1863 was any considerable force embodied under that name.

In the early summer of 1861 the way to Virginia was open and thousands of ardent youth left home and friends to fight for the South. In a few months, however, Maryland was hermetically sealed. Her bays were patrolled by gun boats, her rivers were picketed, and a barrier of bayonets sought to keep back the current of sympathy that day and night flowed to the South. All over the State, the women, irrepressible as ever in times of excitement, flaunted the Confederate red and white in the faces of the army of occupation. The babies wore red and white socks, the girls red and white ribbons—with red and white bouquets at their girdles and on their hearts, the young lads red and white cravats. The larger boys were sent South by their mothers, sisters and sweethearts. Regular lines of communication were established, with stations and pass words and signs for the "underground," as it was called. They made their way by steamer down to the Patuxent—on to the eastern shore. They bought, "borrowed" or "captured" small boats, sail or with oars, and they put out in the darkness over the waters to find the way to Dixie. The gun boats searched bay and inlet with their strong lights and their small boats. Sometimes they caught the emigrés and more frequently they did not. When they did the Old Capitol and Point Lookout military prisons were the swift doom of the unfortunates, where they languished for months, half clad and nearly starved. This blockade running went on over the Potomac from the Chesapeake to the District of Columbia, right under the surveillance of the Federal authorities. When the watch became too vigilant and the pickets too close along the rivers, the Marylanders made their way up through the western part of the State, where the sentiment was generally Union, and forded the river from Hancock up to the mountains. Working through the mountains of West Virginia, through the perils of the bushwhackers and Union men, ten thousand times worse than from Union pickets, they made their way, ragged, barefoot, starving, down to some camp in the valley of Virginia, where they were welcomed with warm hearts and open hands. During all that time the condition of the Southern people of Maryland was like that of the Cavaliers during the Puritan domination in

England. They were tied to home by a thousand imperative duties, but their hearts were "over the water with Charlie." Every Southern family had a son over there. Every Southern woman, young or old, had her heart there with lover or brother or son. There were few husbands, for the enlisted Marylanders were generally youths unmarried. The field officers, Elzey, Steuart and Johnson, were the only married officers of the First Maryland regiment.

Social life in Baltimore was almost obliterated. Spies, male and female, of all social ranks, permeated everything. You could not tell whether the servant behind your chair at dinner, or the lady by your side, whom you had taken to the table, were not in the employ of the Federal provost-marshal. But force never compels ideas, and hearts are beyond the power of bayonets. During all that period, when nurses were arrested because the babies in their arms wore red and white socks, when young ladies were marched to the guard-house because they crossed the street rather than pass under the Union flag suspended over it as sign and proof of domination — during all that red time communication with Richmond was incessant and reliable. Word would be passed by a nod on the street, by a motion of the hand, and time and place given in a breath. And in one of the parlors of one of the greatest houses of the town, blazing with every luxury that wealth and culture could buy, one or two score beautiful women would meet, doors and windows sealed, to see the messenger and to hear the news "from Dixie." Every story of a Maryland boy who had died in battle for the right, every exploit of a Marylander that had thrilled the army, every achievement of the First Regiment of the Line, was recited and repeated and gone over, until human nature could stand no more, and "In Dixie's land I'll take my stand, and live and die for Dixie" would burst from the throng and make indistinct vibrations on the outer air. At one of these mystic meetings of the faithful at the Winns house, on Monument street, the messenger produced James R. Randall's grand war song—"My Maryland." It was read aloud and reread until sobs and inarticulate moans choked utterance. Hetty Carey was then in the prime of her first youth, with a perfect figure, exquisite complexion, the hair that Titian loved to paint, a brilliant intellect, grace personified, and a disposition the most charming—she was the most beautiful woman of the day and perhaps the most beautiful that Maryland has ever produced. Her sister, Jenny Carey, was next to her in everything, but Hetty Carey had no peer. While this little coterie of beautiful women were throbbing over Randall's heroic lines, Hetty Carey said: "That must be sung. Jenny, get an air for it!" and Jenny at the piano struck the chorus of the college song, "Gaudeamus igitur," and the great war anthem, "Maryland, My Maryland," was born into the world. It went through the city like fire in the dry grass. The boys beat it on their toy drums, the children shrilled it at their play, and for a week all the power of the provost-marshal and the garrison and the detectives could not still the refrain—

"The despot's heel is on thy shore,
            Maryland!
His torch is at thy temple door,
            Maryland!"

for it was in the hearts of the people and it was true!

The rendezvous of the drilled volunteers produced three crack companies under Capt. E. R. Dorsey, Baltimore City Guards; Capt. Wm. H. Murray, Maryland Guards, and Capt. J. Lyle Clarke, Independent Grays. And soon after was organized another company under Capt. Michael Stone Robertson, of Charles county, whose company came from the counties of St. Mary's, Calvert and Charles. These Richmond companies were mustered into the service of Virginia, May 17th and 18th and June 17th. Captain Clarke elected to take his company into the Twenty-first Virginia regiment. It served its year with great eclat and was the crack company of that part of the army. The other three were united to the battalion at Harper's Ferry. Virginia troops had by that time been taken *en masse* into the army of the Confederacy. That battalion was reorganized into six companies, so as to equalize them above the minimum required by the law of the Confederacy, and thus the First Maryland regiment was formed, with Capt. Arnold Elzey, late United States artillery, as colonel; Capt. George H. Steuart, late United States cavalry, as lieutenant-colonel, and Bradley T. Johnson as major. It consisted of 500 men armed with Mrs. Johnson's rifles, calibre 54, and 220 men (the three Richmond companies) with Springfield muskets and bayonets. The drill and style of the Richmond companies set the standard for the rest, and during their whole service there never was anything but the most devoted comradeship and the most generous feeling. The only rivalry was "Who shall get there first!"

Soon afterward Capt. R. Snowden Andrews mustered into Confederate service his battery, which during the next four years won undying fame on a hundred fields as the First Maryland artillery. Next came the Baltimore light artillery, known later as the Second Maryland, Capt. John B. Brockenbrough. The Latrobe artillery, Third Maryland, Capt. Henry B. Latrobe; and the Chesapeake, Fourth Maryland, Capt. William Brown, were organized and mustered into the service early in 1862 and served with distinction, the Third Maryland in the army of the Southwest with Johnston and Kirby Smith, and the Fourth Maryland in the army of Northern Virginia. Capt. George R. Gaither brought to Virginia a part of the Howard Dragoons, a troop of which he had been captain in Howard county, with horses, arms and accoutrements, and mustered them into the First Virginia cavalry, Col. J. E. B. Stuart, as

Company K of that élite corps.   A troop of cavalry composed of Marylanders was mustered into the Sixth Virginia under Capt. J. Sturgis Davis.   Subsequently five troops of Marylanders were collected under Davis and were known as the Davis Battalion, of which he was commissioned major.   Capt. Elijah V. White, of Montgomery county, organized a dashing troop of Marylanders as escort and headquarters guard for General Ewell, which was afterwards enlarged into the Thirty-fifth Virginia battalion, commanded by Lieut.-Col. "Lije" White.   It was a Maryland command.   Harry Gilmor in the valley of Virginia in 1863-64 collected a number of Marylanders into troops and formed a battalion known as the Second Maryland, or Gilmor's battalion, of which he was commissioned lieutenant-colonel.   He and they operated in the valley of Virginia and rivaled Mosby by their daring exploits behind the enemy's lines and against his supply trains; and in the lower valley, operating against and breaking the Baltimore & Ohio railroad, occupied and kept employed a large body of the enemy's infantry and cavalry from Harper's Ferry to the Ohio river.   In December, 1860, South Carolina had sent a recruiting officer to Baltimore, and he enlisted there and sent to Charleston five hundred men who were placed in the Lucas battalion of artillery and Rhett's First South Carolina artillery. They served with fidelity, gallantry and distinction in the defense of Fort Sumter, for a large part of the garrison of that fortress during its bombardment were Marylanders.

During the autumn of 1862 seven troops of Marylanders were collected under Lieut.-Col. Ridgely Brown, from Montgomery county, as the First Maryland cavalry.   When the First regiment was mustered out of service August 12, 1862, on account of its depleted ranks, which had been worn threadbare by Jackson's Valley campaign and the Seven Days battles, the men who were mustered out were largely collected by Captains Herbert, Murray and Goldsborough, who formed three new companies, which with others formed the Second Maryland infantry battalion, of which Herbert became lieutenant-colonel commanding, and Goldsborough major. The Second Maryland was officered by trained and experienced soldiers. Almost every one of its captains had seen more than one year's service in the army of northern Virginia, and its field officers had been among the brightest captains in the "Old First," as the First regiment was always designated in the hearts and words of its old members. The Second Maryland infantry and the First Maryland cavalry were in the valley of Virginia about Harrisonburg in the winter of 1862 and 1863. Co. F of the cavalry was recruited by three rich young Baltimoreans—Augustus F. Schwartz, captain; C. Irving Ditty, first lieutenant, and Fielder C. Slinghoff, second lieutenant. They furnished uniforms, horses, accoutrements and arms for their company at an immense expense, for everything except horses had to be smuggled through the blockade from Baltimore.

In January, 1862, Elzey and the field officers of the First having been promoted at First Manassas, July 21, 1861, Colonel Steuart, while on leave at Richmond, procured an order to be issued by the adjutant-general of the Confederate States, that all Marylanders on application to the adjutant-general would be transferred to the Maryland Line, then consisting of the First regiment, in the army of the Potomac under Joe Johnston at Manassas. This measure resulted in no practical, good result. The Marylanders were generally quick, bright, valuable young fellows, and commanding officers were not willing to part with them. Many were taken on the staff, commissioned and non-commissioned, at division, brigade and regimental headquarters, and when one did apply in writing for a transfer, his paper was pigeon-holed and lost on its way up to the adjutant-general. The order added very few men to the Maryland Line.

Md 7

CHAPTER V.

WHEN Virginia became one of the Confederate States by the vote of her people, May 24, 1861, the Confederate government, Mr. Jefferson Davis being President, removed to Richmond from Montgomery, Ala., and assumed the charge of military operations all over the Confederacy. The fixed idea of President Davis was that the first necessity was to save the Confederate States from invasion; for invasion, he argued, would demoralize the negro population and make inefficient the labor of the South behind the armies, which must rely on slave labor for food and clothes. Therefore the Confederate government undertook to cover the entire front, from the Chesapeake bay to the western frontier. In carrying out this strategy, armies were collected in Virginia at Norfolk; at Aquia Creek on the Potomac; at Manassas Junction, thirty miles from Alexandria; at Harper's Ferry, the junction of the Shenandoah and Potomac and the mouth or entrance of the valley of Virginia; and at Grafton, west of the mountains on the Baltimore & Ohio railroad. At Harper's Ferry the Potomac and Shenandoah break through the Blue Ridge and form a gorge of surpassing grandeur and picturesqueness. Mr. Jefferson once said in his notes of Virginia that the view from Loudoun heights on the Virginia side was worth a voyage across the Atlantic to see. The Virginians never got over it. Harper's Ferry was Thermopylæ and Mont Blanc combined. It was an impregnable fortress of nature. John Brown agreed with them—about the only thing he did agree with them about—and seized Harper's Ferry as the base of his proposed negro insurrection in 1859. So the very first step taken in Virginia, after secession was agreed to, was the seizure of Harper's Ferry. Governor Letcher ordered the volunteers of the valley there within five hours after the convention passed the ordinance of secession on April 17th, and about dusk on the 18th, the Second Virginia regiment, Colonel Allen, with several detached companies and with James Ashby's and Welby Carter's troops of cavalry from Fauquier and Loudoun, took possession of the place, with its workshops and machinery. The Union officer that was posted there as the regular guard with a detachment of half a hundred infantry, retired after having set fire to the armory, where a large number of muskets were stored, and to the storehouses and machine shops. The Virginians got in in time to save most of the buildings and the machinery, and a large lot of gunstocks was afterwards shipped to Fayetteville, N. C., for the Confederate armory at that place.

Col. Thomas J. Jackson, a professor of the Virginia military institute, was assigned to command the post, which the Virginia authorities considered the one of greatest importance, responsibility and danger; for it was to protect the valley of Virginia from the Potomac to the North Carolina and Tennessee line. Virginia troops were poured into the place. Captain Johnson, as we have seen, procured from Colonel Jackson permission to rendezvous the Marylanders there and at the Point of Rocks, and by June 1st had collected about five hundred men. As soon as Virginia had joined the Confederacy, President Davis, equally impressed with the value and importance of this Thermopylæ, assigned to command it Gen. Joseph Eggleston Johnston, the second in rank of the generals of the Confederate army. Johnston ranked next to Lee, but was his equal in experience in war. He was a Virginian by birth and blood, and knew all about the Virginia fetish about Harper's Ferry

While the President was pouring troops from Arkansas, from Mississippi, from Alabama, from South Carolina, into Harper's Ferry, Johnston knew that it was a trap, a deadfall, for the soldier who attempted to hold it. It was commanded on the east by the Maryland heights beyond the Potomac, and on the south by heights on the other side of the Shenandoah.

The Confederate States government was then offering every inducement for Maryland to join it. It exempted Maryland from its declaration of war against the United States, and it was tender of her territory and her feelings. When, therefore, Johnston saw the absolute necessity of holding Maryland heights, he saved the invasion of Maryland by sending Marylanders to occupy the position. He ordered Captain Johnson with his eight companies, and Col. Blanton Duncan with his First Kentucky regiment, to take the Maryland heights, fortify and hold them. They did so while Johnston strained every nerve to strip Harper's Ferry of everything that could be made of use to the Confederacy. By June 15th he had cleared out the place, brought the Marylanders and the Kentuckians from the mountains and evacuated Harper's Ferry. A large Federal army had been collected at Chambersburg, Pa., thirty miles to the north of Johnston, under command of Major-General Patterson. For several days Patterson had given signs of restlessness unmistakable to an old soldier of Johnston's caliber, and the very day Johnston moved out of Harper's Ferry, Patterson marched south from Chambersburg. The former moved to Charlestown, Va., the latter to Hagerstown, Md. On June 17th, Patterson crossed the Potomac at Williamsport and Johnston went into line of battle at Bunker Hill, a place halfway between Martinsburg and Winchester. The Confederates were delighted at the prospects of another battle of Bunker Hill on the 17th of June. But a large portion of Patterson's army were sixty-day men, and when their time expired they marched home, General Patterson and the remnant of his troops following in such temper as they might to the Maryland side. Patterson having recrossed the Potomac, Johnston fell back to Winchester, where he proceeded to organize his incongruous troops into brigades and divisions. One brigade, the Fourth, was formed of the First Maryland, the Tenth and the Thirteenth Virginia and the Third Tennessee, and Col. Arnold Elzey of the First Maryland was assigned to command it. The Fourth and Third brigades constituted a division under the command of Brig.-Gen. E. Kirby Smith. The field officers of the First Maryland were commissioned to date from June 17, 1861. The first duty the regiment was set to perform under its new field officers was on the day after the arrival at Winchester. On June 19th, Lieutenant-Colonel Steuart was directed to return to Harper's Ferry by railroad train and complete the destruction of the shops and Federal property left on the evacuation of the 15th. This duty Colonel Steuart executed with great intelligence. Instead of burning up a great magazine of seasoned and shaped gunstocks, which he found abandoned, he loaded the whole outfit on a train of cars and hauled them back with his command to Winchester. The service was so valuable and so exceedingly sensible that the commanding general rewarded it with a special order of approbation. Steuart and the Marylanders enjoyed the unique distinction of being probably the only command that was ever decorated by a special order for *disobedience of orders*. General Johnston had sent them on this detail with distinct and positive orders to burn everything burnable. They brought off a trainload of most valuable plunder, and the commanding general honored them thus:

"Headquarters, Winchester, June 22, 1861.
Special Order.
The commanding general thanks Lieutenant-Colonel Steuart and the Maryland regiment for the faithful and

exact manner in which they carried out his orders of
the 19th instant at Harper's Ferry.

He is glad to learn that owing to their discipline, no
private property was injured, and no unoffending citizen
disturbed. The soldierly qualities of the Maryland regiment will not be forgotten in the day of action.

By order of Gen. JOSEPH E. JOHNSTON.''

The Confederate strategy in the early part of 1861 was
to hold armies, or army corps, within supporting distance
of each other along the exposed frontier of Virginia.
If one army was attacked the corps to the right and left
of it was to move promptly to its assistance. Patterson,
after retiring beyond the Potomac, was heavily reinforced
and recrossed the river, threatening Johnston at Winchester. Johnston, on the other hand, covered his front
so thoroughly with cavalry patrols and pickets as to in-
terpose an impenetrable veil between Patterson and
himself.

On July 18, 1861, General McDowell moved out of Alexandria on Beauregard at Fairfax Court House. Beauregard retired behind Bull Run. McDowell on the 19th
made a heavy reconnoissance in force and found Beauregard's position. The latter called on Johnston for help.
He left Winchester in the morning of the 18th and
marched to Piedmont, on the Manassas Gap railroad,
whence his troops were hurried by rail to Manassas
Junction. In the meantime McDowell had thrown his
right around Beauregard's left, turned his position, and
at daylight of the 21st attacked him, driving everything
before him as he marched down the right bank of Bull
Run. By midday the Confederates were in retreat,
their line broken and their position forced. About
noon, the Fourth brigade, Colonel Elzey, arrived at the
junction of the Manassas Gap and Orange & Alexandria
railroads. The command was at once disembarked.
McDowell's heavy guns were pounding away toward the
east, the first hostile fire the men had ever heard. They
were formed: First Maryland on the right, Third Ten-

nessee, Tenth Virginia, Thirteenth Virginia. By the time they were ready to move, Kirby Smith rode up in a strain of tense excitement. He assumed charge of the brigade. The other part of his division was not up—"The watchword is Sumter, the signal is this," throwing his right hand to his forehead, palm outwards. " Go where the fire is hottest; forward march!"

The excitement of the first fight, the growing fire, the spreading volleys, braced up the men. At the order "double-quick" they struck out in a trot, down by the junction, past the cluster of huts and houses, thence straight as the crow flies toward "where the fire was hottest." After a run of a few miles the column was halted to breathe and load. Then on again. Wounded men coming back cried, " Go back. We are all cut to pieces. Go back. You'll all get killed!" But the Fourth brigade kept steadily on. As it passed a clump of pines on the right, a sharp volley from a squad of the Brooklyn Zouaves knocked General Smith over the neck of his horse and Elzey resumed command. By that time the day had advanced to three or four o'clock. The field was dotted with retreating men, hurrying ambulances, flying wagons. Just to the right was a squad of cavalry. A shell burst over them and the cavalry scattered. Running over two lines lying in ranks on the ground, still Elzey pressed on to the left. Entering a wood, beyond which was heavy musketry firing, he formed line of battle. Smith at Manassas had detached A. P. Hill with the Thirteenth Virginia to hold one of the fords of Bull Run. With three regiments remaining Elzey pressed straight to the front. Getting nearly through the wood, he halted inside the edge of it. In front were a branch and a worm fence; beyond it an open field gently rising for four hundred yards into a considerable elevation. On the ridge stood a line of battle. Uniforms were no designation, as the line showed no colors. Cried Elzey to his aide-de-camp, Charles Couter, of Prince George's,

Maryland: "Couter, give me a glass—give me a glass, quick." Just at that instant the breeze blew out the flag on the hill. It was the stars and stripes. "Fire!" cried Elzey, and the whole line delivered its volley. "Charge!" he shouted. The Marylanders had six companies of Mississippi rifles and three companies of bayonets. But over the fence the whole line went with a yell—up the hill—through the Yankee line, or rather where it had been. It had gone, dissolved into mist. Elzey pressed right on. He was behind McDowell's right and he never stopped to draw breath. The whole Union line crumpled up, and First Manassas was won. As the Maryland colonel rode proudly down on the right of his line, Beauregard dashed up, filled with enthusiasm— "Hail! Elzey, Blucher of the day!" and in a moment President Davis came up with General Johnston. "*General Elzey*, I congratulate you," said the man who made generals. Elzey was promoted brigadier-general, Steuart colonel, Johnson lieutenant-colonel, and E. R. Dorsey, captain Company C, major—all to date from July 21st, the day of the great victory.

The First Maryland was pushed on in pursuit of the rout over the Stone bridge and along the turnpike until dark, and then hastily recalled to Blackburn's ford to meet an apprehended attack. Next, moving at daylight, it went out with the First Virginia cavalry under Col. J. E. B. Stuart to Fairfax Court House, when, for the first time, the extent of the disaster to the Union army was understood and appreciated. During the night of the 21st no one had any idea of the ruin and rout that overwhelmed the enemy. On the march of the 22nd, J. E. B. Stuart, an Indian fighter, could not believe his eyes, nor the reports his scouts brought him. The roads, the woods, the fields were filled with inconceivable débris— overturned carriages, ambulances, artillery limbers, lunch baskets, champagne, even gold pieces were found, and Stuart suspected it was a ruse to lure him into an ambush. As the morning wore on, however, the thing became too plain to doubt, and Fairfax Court House settled it. The court house and yard were packed full of new tents, new overcoats, new uniforms. The infantry went into camp, and cavalry scouts pursued their way down to the suburbs of Alexandria, and by night Stuart reported to Johnston and Beauregard that there was no organized force south of the Potomac.

This is no place to discuss the reasons why the Confederates did not take Washington on the 23rd of July, 1861. Two days' march would have brought them to the Long Bridge, J. E. B. Stuart could have occupied it by noon of the 22nd, and the army could have marched comfortably over it. It is easy to see all this now. It was not so apparent on the 22nd of July. The Fourth brigade, Colonel Elzey, reached the Court House the afternoon of the 22nd, where the First Maryland had preceded them, and the command went into camp at Fairfax Station, a few miles distant.

The whole army passed the rest of the summer in drills, in marches, in sudden alarms, in being instructed in the duties of a soldier—first and most important of which is to know how to make bread. Bad cooking that summer killed more than Yankee bullets. But the Marylanders were full of spirit. They sang, they yelled, they shouted, they romped like a pack of schoolboys, and they were pets in the army. If a quick march was to be made, the Marylanders were sent on it. If a surprise was planned by J. E. B. Stuart and the cavalry, the Maryland regiment was ordered to support him, and to this day the survivors remember an eighteen-mile march through the rain and mud to catch a regiment of Yankee cavalry at Pohick Church, which had strayed that far into the woods and which Stuart proposed "to lose" with the help of the First Maryland. They mustered seven hundred and twenty rifles and muskets. Their uniform was a French kepi (a little gray cap), a natty gray round-

Md 8

about, collar and sleeves bound with black braid, and a similar stripe down the gray trousers. They were all boys The age of the First Maryland rank and file would not have averaged nineteen, nor their height over five feet eight, nor their weight above one hundred and thirty-five pounds. They were generally beardless boys, with the spirits, the enthusiasm, the devotion of boys. A large per cent were gentlemen by birth and culture. All were gentlemen at heart and principle. Exiles from home, volunteers to help a friend, staking life for love, they must of necessity have been impressed with an ardent sentimentality and a devotion beyond the ordinary standard of humanity. Around the camp-fires, on the lonely picket, on the march, what recollections of home did they not carry with them, the lengthening chain that time nor distance ever breaks. During the summer they became well drilled. They believed they were the best drilled corps in the army—in either army—in any army for that matter, for the Marylander never loses anything by diffidence or self-depreciation. He always thinks as well of himself as any one ever thinks of him. Beauregard said they marched like Frenchmen. This set them up; but more knowledge would have restrained their self-conceit, for no Frenchmen have ever marched or moved as brightly as they did. Beauregard's compliment was to his own people, not to ours.

Joseph E. Johnston's wife was a Maryland woman, and he, tough old soldier as he was, had a tender spot in his heart for Marylanders, and whenever they passed him at review or on the march, he always had a pleasant word to say about them. It is due to the truth of history to say that during the summer and fall of 1861 the first Maryland regiment became as conceited a set of young blades as ever faced a battery or charged a line of battle.

Variety is a virtue in a soldier. Beauregard wanted a line of Yankee posts along the Potomac overlooking Alexandria seized. It required dash, quickness, unfailing nerve. J. E. B. Stuart and some troops of cavalry and the First Maryland were sent to do it. Of course they did it, and for a month or two they watched the dome of the Capitol and the marchings up and down of McClellan, in front of Alexandria. Peaches were ripe. They liked peaches. The Yanks held a fine peach orchard in front, so they drove them out, and ate their peaches. The Yanks had some fine beef cattle. The Marylanders drove in their pickets, went inside their lines and got their cattle out and ate them. There was also an assortment of sows and little pigs over there. They went over and got them and had roast pig. In August and September roasting ears are very fine, but require selection to get the tender kind. Just beyond Mason's hill, between the lines, was a cornfield of probably an hundred acres. The Federals held one side, the Marylanders the other, and every morning when the foragers started out to find chickens, ducks, tomatoes, for their messes, the whole command would turn out, deploy themselves as skirmishers, sweep the cornfield, drive in the gentlemen in blue, and pick their roasting ears at their ease. The picket at Munson's and Mason's hills was a picnic, and when their tour of duty—three days—was out, they would petition to be allowed to take the place of their relief and serve double time. Such a curious request was always granted. But the service was good for them. It taught them alertness, promptness, obedience and coolness, for their little skirmishes were not always bloodless and always were spliced with danger. On a dash on Munson's hill—a mile from their post at Mason's—they struck a more obstinate antagonist than usual, who killed Fountain, of Company I, and wounded Hugh Mitchell, first lieutenant of the same company, like Achilles in the heel, and lamed him for life. But the Marylanders, like Colonel Washington at Fort Necessity, thought "there is something charming in the sound of a bullet," and they delighted in that daily music.

After the seizure of Maryland by the Union troops, the process of manacling her went on with celerity and efficiently. A Union regiment, the First Maryland, was recruited with John R. Kenly as colonel. Colonel Kenly had been major of the Maryland-District of Columbia battalion in the Mexican war, and had served with honor to himself, his command and to his State. At Monterey, where Colonel Watson commanding was killed, Major Kenly brought out the shattered remnants of the battalion with great coolness and courage, and no man of his rank came out of that war with more reputation than Major Kenly. He had experience, he had gallantry, he had ability, and he was devoted to the Union. But with this devotion he was above narrow bigotry, which refuses to recognize sincerity, honesty, or unselfishness in his opponent. With a heart absolutely devoid of self-seeking, ignorant of dishonor, or dishonesty, Colonel Kenly furnished as pure a character and as high a type of patriotism as served on either side in that war. He believed it his duty to stand by the Union. He did so like a soldier, like a man of honor, like a patriot, but no act of his ever stained his career, and he left no spot on his escutcheon. He was truly "without fear and without stain." But in pressing the policy initiated by Ben Butler toward Maryland, the Federal authorities promptly carried out the latter's ideas. The "State" of Maryland, where religious liberty and free thought were born in this world, was converted by a general order from headquarters at Washington into "the Department of Annapolis" and Gen. N. P. Banks was assigned to command it vice Cadwallader, relieved, with headquarters at Baltimore. Banks assumed command on June 10th. On the 27th he arrested George P. Kane, marshal of police, and confined him in Fort McHenry.

The police commissioners "protested" against this violation of law, and Banks arrested them and sent them to join Kane. They sent a memorial to Congress and Congress laid it on the table. They applied to the Presi-

dent, and Banks put them on a steamer July 28th and
sent them to Fort Lafayette in the harbor of New York.
On August 6th Judge Garrison, of a State court in Brooklyn, issued his habeas corpus to Colonel Burke, then com-
mandant of the fort, to produce them in court. Colonel
Burke defied the writ, under the orders of Lieutenant-
General Scott. Attachment for contempt was then issued
against him, and he snapped his fingers at that and
booted the marshal out of his presence. Judge Garrison
dismissed the proceedings, "submitting to inevitable
necessity." So habeas corpus was suspended in the
loyal State of New York as well as in the "Department
of Annapolis." General Banks appointed Col. John R.
Kenly marshal of police, who promptly assumed command of the force in the city of Baltimore, the Union
thus assuming control of a city police. The Congress
subsequently appropriated money to pay their wages.

On August 7th the legislature passed more eloquent
resolutions, protesting against the unconstitutional and
illegal acts of President Lincoln, but they are not worth
the room it would take to record them. The time for
"protests" was past, if it ever had existed, and as the
scolding of the Maryland legislature became annoying
to the authorities, they determined to suppress the one
and thus silence the other. On September 12, 1861,
Major-General Dix, commanding in Baltimore, ordered
the arrest of the members of the legislature from Baltimore City and the mayor and other obnoxious persons
who annoyed him with talk, to-wit: George William
Brown, Coleman Yellott, Senator Stephen P. Dennis,
Charles H. Pitts, Andrew A. Lynch, Lawrence Langston,
H. M. Morfit, Ross Winans, J. Hanson Thomas, W. G.
Harrison, John C. Brune, Robert M. Denison, Leonard
D. Quinlan, Thomas W. Renshaw, Henry May, member
of Congress from the Fourth congressional district,
Frank Key Howard, editor of the "Baltimore Ex-
change," and Thomas W. Hall, editor of the "South."
The arrests were made with great secrecy, and it was

intended to send them to the Dry Tortugas, but there being no steamer fit for the voyage in Hampton Roads, they were dispatched to Fort Warren in Boston harbor. Liberty of the press as well as free speech had gone after the privilege of the writ of habeas corpus.

On the 11th of September Simon Cameron, secretary of war, had issued an order to General Banks that the passage of an ordinance of secession by the legislature, which was to assemble at Frederick on September 17th, must be prevented, even if the arrest of the legislature was necessary to accomplish this end. Maj.-Gen. George B. McClellan, then commanding the army of the Potomac, issued his order to General Banks to have everything prepared to arrest the whole party when they assembled. General Banks sent his aide, R. Morris Copeland, to attend to this business, and he accomplished it very successfully, "greatly assisted by several citizens of the place," says the chronicler. Both houses were called to order on the 17th, at 1 p. m., but no quorum appearing, they adjourned until the next day. The climate of Frederick was disagreeable to many of the protesters at that particular season. But Major Copeland was equal to the emergency. He closely picketed the town and held everybody in who was in, and took everybody in who wanted to go out. On the 18th he arrested Milton Y. Kidd, the chief clerk of the house, and his assistant, Thomas H. Moore; William Kilgour, secretary of the senate, and his assistant, L. P. Carmark, and John M. Brewer, reading clerk of the senate, and William E. Salmon, Elbridge G. Kilbourne, Thomas J. Claggett, Philip F. Raisin, Andrew Kessler, Josiah H. Gordon, James W. Maxwell, R. C. McCubbin, George W. Landing, Dr. Bernard Mills, William R. Miller, Clark J. Durant, John I. Heckart and J. Lawrence Jones, members of the house; E. Riley, printer of the house and editor of the "Annapolis Republican," and a number of citizens of Frederick pointed out by the "citizens of the place who were greatly assisting."

CHAPTER VI.

MARYLANDERS IN 1862 UNDER GENERALS JOSEPH E.
JOHNSTON AND STONEWALL JACKSON.

IN November, 1861, Gen. Joseph E. Johnston, then in
command of the Confederate army of the Potomac,
withdrew from the posts of Mason's and Munson's
Hills, established by Beauregard, having information that
McClellan was about to sweep them in. Beauregard had
established a capital secret service, and his spies in Washington, in the departments and in McClellan's headquarters, kept his headquarters perfectly advised of the intentions of General McClellan. They had reported in time
McDowell's projected movement on Bull Run, which
resulted in the first battle of Manassas. In November
Johnston withdrew from the line of Fairfax Court House
to Centreville, in front of Bull Run, and in a month fell
back to Bull Run, where he put his troops in camp for
the winter. He made his men cover themselves in log
huts, which were comfortable, but too warm and ill-venti-
lated for troops in the field.

During all this period the Marylanders furnished a singular exception to the rest of the army. The soldiers in
the Southern regiments were suffering from mumps,
measles and whooping cough, which became epidemic
with them; the Thirteenth North Carolina, for instance,
which came up after the battle of Manassas thirteen hundred rank and file for duty, became so reduced by these
diseases that it could not parade enough men for camp
guard, and was sent to the mountains to recruit its sick.
But the First Maryland had none of these diseases. It
lost a few men, not ten in all, by typhoid fever, but it
was exempt from the numerous complaints that afflicted

the troops from further south.   Its camp was established on Bull Run just above Union Mills, and it served during the winter with the other regiments of the Fourth brigade, the Tenth and Thirteenth Virginia and the Third Tennessee, picketing the front from Wolf Run Shoals by Burke's Station up toward Fairfax Court House.   It was hard service.   The men were taken out of warm huts and sent on tours of three days' duty in the open fields or in the woods without shelter   Their huts had been occupied during their absence and they never saw them again.   Sleeping on the wet ground in sleet, snow and hail of necessity produced pneumonia and rheumatism.   Nevertheless they never lost their gay spirit. Their march to picket and their return were always marked by shouts and yells and songs.

The song of " Maryland " was too solemn for these spirited boys.   Its movement was too slow.   It was more like a dirge.   It had been introduced to them in the most picturesque way.   During the summer at Fairfax Station, Hetty, Jenny and Constance Carey, who had run the blockade from Baltimore, came up to visit the regiment.   It was full of their brothers, their cousins and their beaux, and these beautiful young women in camp produced an effect on the mercurial Marylanders that can only be imagined, not described.   The boys and the officers were on their heads.   The young ladies were quartered in the field officers' tents, where they held court for several days.   One night the glee club of the regiment was serenading them, when the fly of Colonel Steuart's tent was thrown open and all three appeared, Jenny Carey in the center and her sister Hetty on one side and cousin Constance on the other.   Their pure voices rang through the summer night with the words and air of " My Maryland," and no such audience ever inspired songsters before or since.   The boys were carried away.   Silence, then cheers, then silence, then suppressed and not unmanly sobs attested the power of the

sentiment of love for home. But "Maryland" touched
too deeply the feeling of the heart to do for camp or
march. "Gay and Happy" was the air that thrilled
souls, and it rang like the drum-beat of the assembly or
the bugle sound to the charge. So the march of the
Marylanders was announced by the ringing song of
"Gay and Happy."

Johnston understood perfectly that as soon as the
spring sun dried up the roads and the fields of Virginia,
McClellan must move on him. The latter had two hundred thousand men, Johnston forty thousand, so for more
than a month he was clearing out his camp and sending
impedimenta to the rear. Early in March, 1862, he received notice from his spies in Washington that McClellan
was about to strike. On the 8th he began his retrograde
to the line of the Rappahannock, still keeping his pickets
out on their usual posts, to present the appearance of
being in the same position and to prevent intelligence
leaking through to the Union commander. Early on the
morning of the 9th the first battalion of the First Maryland, four companies, under Lieutenant-Colonel Johnson moved out to Burke's Station to relieve the
Thirteenth Virginia, whose term of picket had expired.
They reached Burke's before noon and Johnson reported
to Walker of the Thirteenth that he was ready to relieve
him. The two officers rode along the line, posting the
reliefs and sending the Virginians back to their camp,
when all at once on the opposite line of hills appeared a
line of skirmishers, and simultaneously a squadron of
cavalry rattled down the road. Company F, First Lieut.
William D. Hough in command, had been posted on a
hill, just below the road, in front of a wood and a fence.
As soon as Hough saw the cavalry coming, he very properly made for the fence, for he had no bayonets. But
the horsemen, a squadron of the Eighth Illinois, were on
him before he got there. He turned and made a gallant
fight. Second Lieut. Joseph H. Stewart jerked a rifle

Md 9

from one of his men, shot the leader of the charge, a captain or lieutenant, knocked the horse's front legs from under him with his clubbed rifle and was cut down by the sabre. Nine men, including Stewart, were captured. Company H, under the gallant captain, Wm. H. Murray, came running up as soon as they heard the firing. The remnant of Company F got behind the fence and gave the charging party a volley, and Murray from the nearest hill gave them another, and they went back faster than they came. But the advancing line of skirmishers were sweeping the front as far as the eye could reach on each side, and it was clear that an advance in force was present. Colonel Johnson, therefore, drew in his command. Walker had formed and waited for him a mile to the rear They joined forces and marched comfortably back to Union Mills, where they arrived after dark. The bridge was on fire, the army had gone and Colonel Nicholls, of the Louisiana regiment, since Governor Nicholls, was holding the place for them until they got through. Crossing Bull Run they marched on the rear guard of the army and the next day reached the Rappahannock. Maj.-Gen. Richard S. Ewell, who was in command of the division, was posted there by Johnston to hold the enemy back while Johnston got his trains out of the way. He held the position for several weeks, until during the last of April he moved to Gordonsville, thence to Somerset and thence by Swift Run Gap and across the Blue Ridge to Conrad's store in the valley of Virginia.

After First Manassas George B. McClellan was put in command of all the Union armies when Winfield Scott resigned, superannuated. General McClellan had come out of the Mexican war with a first-rate reputation, and in 1861 made a brilliant campaign in West Virginia, the American Switzerland, against Wise, Floyd and Robert E. Lee. He was, therefore, with reason regarded as the first soldier on his side. During the winter of 1861-62 he prepared a plan of a grand campaign, of which Rich-

mond was to be the objective, and which was to be carried
but by the army of the Potomac under his personal
direction, in conjunction with an army in West Virginia
under General Milroy, and another in the valley of Virginia under General Banks.   While McClellan trans-
ported his great army of the Potomac by water to York
river, whence he could move on the flank of Richmond,
Milroy was to march down west of the Alleghanies, and
Banks was to move directly up the valley,—the latter two
uniting at Staunton to march on Lynchburg, where they
would cut the communication between Richmond and
the southwestern States of the Confederacy.   Maj.-Gen.
Thomas J. Jackson (Stonewall) was in the valley with
8,000 men to observe and check this concentration.
Ewell was on the Rappahannock with 7,000 to watch Mc-
Clellan's move by that route, while Johnston had taken
the main part of his army to the peninsula between the
York and James rivers, to confront McClellan, whose
move in that direction had become fully developed.

Jackson required more men.   Banks in front had more
than four times his number, and his force could not cover
the ground.   The story at the time was that he applied
to Richmond for " more men and fewer orders."   Ewell
was ordered to report to him and reached Conrad's Store
on the first days of May.   To his astonishment and per-
plexity he found the embers of Jackson's camp fires and
no orders.   Jackson had vanished in a night, without a
word, without a trace.   So Ewell impatiently waited a
week for directions and at length came the telegram from
" Stonewall "—" McDowell, May 9th:—God has given
us a victory at McDowell to-day."   That was all, but it
was sufficient.

Without stopping to take breath, Jackson sped back to
Staunton, moved swiftly on Banks, who had got to Strasburg, and ordered Ewell to meet him at New Market.
Thence they recrossed the Massanutten range and raced
swiftly down the Luray valley.   This march was like the

tiger's approach, stealthy, silent until within striking distance, then one leap on his prey. The army of the Valley marched ten to twelve miles a day, then twenty, then thirty, and it was on Banks before he knew Jackson had left McDowell.

Colonel Steuart had been promoted brigadier-general on March 28th; Lieutenant-Colonel Johnson colonel, and Major Dorsey, lieutenant-colonel. General Steuart was ordered to organize the Maryland Line, consisting of the First Maryland and the Baltimore Light artillery as a nucleus, but was temporarily assigned to command a brigade of cavalry, being an old cavalry soldier. Colonel Johnson was thus left in command of the Maryland Line. They marched to the quarters of General Elzey, between whom and themselves there had always existed the tenderest affection, though Elzey had never been in command of the regiment, having been assigned to a brigade as soon as he joined. But they loved him. His brusque, prompt manner, his gallant bearing, his generous heart, made him dear to them. In battle Elzey's look was like the blast of a bugle; in camp he was careful of his men, though he scolded them from start to finish and they always deserved it. The parting, therefore, was more than usually touching.

In the First Maryland, matters at this time were in a very unsatisfactory condition. The Richmond companies had been mustered into the army of Virginia for twelve months, that being the term of enlistment in that service. The Harper's Ferry companies had been mustered by Lieutenant-Colonel Deas into the army of the Confederate States for the war. But during the year they had got it into their hearts that they, too, ought to have been mustered for only twelve months, and that if their muster rolls showed differently, they had been deceived. There was not the slightest doubt that they were mistaken, but this idea naturally breeded great discontent. Companies A and B had been mustered at the Point of Rocks for twelve months, as their muster rolls showed. On May 18th Company C's time expired and they were mustered out by Colonel Johnson, who expostulated with them to no effect. They wanted their rights, they wanted to go into the cavalry, they were tired of trudging. So off they went. They had no idea of going home, or abandoning the fight. The rest, except Companies A and B, being absent on detached service, were nearly in a state of mutiny as they neared the enemy. At length, on May 22d, when twelve months from the muster at Harper's Ferry expired, the large majority of them stacked their arms and refused to do duty. This was mutiny, and the colonel promptly had the arms packed in the wagons and the men put under a guard with loaded guns. He sent for Color-Sergeant Doyle, as good a soldier as ever bore musket, and showed him how impossible it was to have any discussion in the presence of the enemy, and directed him to find out how many men were willing to go on and defer the decision of their claims and complaints until after the campaign. Doyle reported that about half the command were willing to stand by the colors in any event. The army was then within an easy march of Front Royal, where Banks had stationed a force to protect his flank. The next morning, the 23d, the march was begun, the First Maryland in the worst possible condition—one-half under arrest for mutiny, the rest disgusted with the service, and the colonel disgusted with them. A halt was made for rest about five miles from Front Royal, and during it an aide brought this order: "Colonel Johnson will move the First Maryland to the front and attack the enemy at Front Royal. The army will halt until you pass. JACKSON." The colonel turned on his regiment: "You have heard this personal order from General Jackson and you are in a pretty condition to obey it. You are the sole hope of Maryland. You carry with you her honor and her pride. Shame on you— shame on you. I shall return this order to General Jackson with the endorsement, ' The First Maryland refuses to face the enemy,' for I will not trust the honor of the glorious old State to discontented, dissatisfied men. I won't lead men who have no heart. Every man who is discontented must fall out of ranks—step to the rear and march with the guard. If I can get ten good men, I'll take the Maryland colors with them and will stand for home and honor; but never again call yourselves Marylanders! No Marylander ever threw down his arms and deserted his colors in the presence of the enemy—and those arms and those colors given you by a woman! Go!'' This appeal settled it. The men in ranks cheered and yelled, '' Forward, we'll show you!'' The men under guard pleaded with tears to be allowed to return to duty, ran back miles to the wagons, got their guns and rejoined their regiment by the time it attacked at Front Royal. The Marylanders marched forward, rejuvenated, reinvigorated, restored! The army halted. As they went by they could hear time and again, '' There they go. Look at the ' game cocks.' '' The Louisiana brigade, Gen. Dick Taylor, came to a front and presented arms. The Marylanders trod on air, for no men are so susceptible to praise or enjoy flattery more.

Clear of the column, they debouched from the wooded road into the open, where there was a long stretch of fields between them and the village of Front Royal. A squad of cavalry charged down the road. Captain Nicholas and Company G were deployed as skirmishers on each side of it. A mile distant, by the side of a fence was a blanket stretched from two fence rails as a shelter. A man got up, looked at the strange sight coming out of the woods, sheltered his eyes from the sun, then made a grab for his musket, but before he could fire, the cavalry was on him, and that picket was gobbled up. There were three men on post, but they did not have time to give the alarm. A cavalry man, with cocked carbine, trotted them to the rear. General Ewell, General Steuart and Colonel Johnson were riding at the head of the column. "What regiment do you belong to?" was the colonel's eager inquiry. " First Maryland," was the response of the Dutchman. " There's the First Maryland," cried the Confederate, pointing behind. Great Heavens! was such good fortune ever given to a soldier? The Federal First Maryland had been recruited under the gallant Kenly, but it was largely composed of foreigners, and the Marylanders had always refused to recognize it as representing their State. They were the only simon-pure, genuine Marylanders, and if ever they got a chance they would show them! Here was the chance. As the news flew back through the ranks, shoulders were straightened, chests thrown out, and every man thanked God he was a Marylander and was there!

As they approached the town, a hot musketry fire broke out from the doors and windows of a large building to the left, probably four or five hundred yards distant. " Colonel, can you take that building?" said General Ewell. " Yes, sir, in five minutes." " Men, you see that house? You are to take it. Forward, double quick charge!" And the Marylanders went at it like a charge of canister. " Excuse me, Colonel," said Adjutant Frank Ward, touching his cap as he dashed by on his pony. Capt. Billy Murray and Lieut. George Thomas broke from their proper places and ran in front, and the building was taken in half the time promised. Gathering the command together it was rushed into the town with Wheat's battalion on the left, then through the town, where the enemy was discovered on the crest of some hills with a battery in position at his center, and a force of cavalry, probably a squadron, on his right. Wheat with the Louisianians took the left, the Marylanders the front and center and moved across the open to attack. A shell exploded in the ground under the color guard, and the colors fell; but Lieut. Dick Gilmor had them before they touched the ground. The Louisianians worked their way from cover to cover, until they nearly enveloped Kenly's right. But the Marylanders could make no further progress. They were in the open with no cover. Lines of stone fences running parallel to Kenly's front gave secure protection to his skirmishers, so that when, after hours' work, one line was dislodged and forced back on its reserves, another was promptly formed and reinforced by Kenly, who handled his command with gallant skill and coolness. He had 800 infantry, a battery, and probably eighty cavalry. The First Maryland paraded that day 375 rifles and Wheat had 200, and Kenly could see every man of his antagonists.

Jackson, adhering to his persistent strategy of mystery, kept his army concealed in the woods several miles off, and left the Louisianians and Marylanders to fight their fight out, without assistance. Company F, Capt. J. Louis Smith, was sent by his colonel into a skirt of woods on the right to work his way up to Kenly's left, which he succeeded in doing during the afternoon, and began firing down Kenly's line. At length Kenly began to move. His cavalry came down the hill and deployed in the field and came forward in a trot to charge the Marylanders and cover Kenly's withdrawal. The fire of his battery also became very active, but the Baltimore light artillery quieted that in a few minutes. Kenly had discovered from his elevated position two regiments of Virginia cavalry moving round his left to get in his rear, though unknown to the Louisianians and Marylanders. As soon as Kenly's move was understood, the whole line was moved forward. The skirmishers under Lieutenant-Colonel Dorsey advanced into a charge as soon as they got within reach. This expedited Kenly's retreat, so that he was unable to burn the bridge over the Shenandoah. He set it on fire, but the Louisianians and Marylanders put it out before any harm was done, and the Sixth Virginia cavalry pressed over it in single file in hot pursuit. Jackson, Ewell and Steuart joined the leading squadron as soon as the enemy was well started and the cavalry on them. Jackson and Ewell then returned to their proper places with the infantry and Steuart pushed on all night, picking up nearly every man of Kenly's command. It was a fight between First Maryland and First Maryland, creating great amusement in the army, for among the prisoners were many brothers, cousins, uncles, and some fathers of the Confederates. Such a scene was never witnessed before in war as the meeting between the two regiments after the Union Marylanders were brought in as prisoners by the cavalry. It was amusing and even jovial, for one side was glad to see somebody from home, and the other that it had fallen into the hands of relatives and kindred, although technically they were enemies. Kenly fought his men with indomitable gallantry, intelligence and good sense. He made all out of it that was possible, and he might have held his position had it not been for the flanking movement of the cavalry. He was wounded by saber cut and pistol ball. His adjutant, Tarr, was also badly wounded.

The next morning Colonel Johnson and staff called on Colonel Kenly and staff and tendered any courtesies that it was proper for the one to receive or the other to offer. But Kenly was sore in body and spirit and refused any favors of any kind at the hands of his conqueror. The ill humor of the gallant soldier was condoned on account of his misfortune, and no one thought the worse of him for his bitterness. Kenly performed an inestimable service to Banks. He held Jackson back for twelve hours, and thus gave Banks opportunity to fall back from Strasburg to Winchester.

On the 24th Ewell moved up within reach of Winchester, Jackson marching by Strasburg and the valley pike. By daylight they were in line of battle, Jackson's right

almost touching Ewell's left, both together forming a
semi-circle round the town.   Before day the line moved
forward, First Maryland on Ewell's left with orders to
watch out for Jackson in the pike, and get in touch of
him as soon as possible.   Skirmishers were out; but
nothing could be seen, for a dense fog enveloped everything.   Feeling their way slowly and carefully forward,
at last the skirmishers were withdrawn and Colonel
Johnson made a dash forward at a stone wall, which could
be dimly discerned ahead.   To their surprise they went
over it without a shot and were halted in an apple
orchard, some distance inside the wall.   It appeared that
they had penetrated Banks' center, between his right and
left wing, and were behind his line.   It was uncertain
whether they were prisoners in a big army, or had
achieved a grand tactical movement and exploit.   The
colonel sent back Adjutant Ward to report the situation
to General Ewell with the suggestion that as soon as
Ewell attacked in front, the First Maryland would charge
down behind the Union lines and sweep them away from
the front attack.   The fog was thick and dark.   Ward
was gone, and the Marylanders waited for the fire from
the front.   The Union bugles sounded "cease firing!"
The fog rolled up like the curtain at the theater and the
Federal line was disclosed, wheeling by companies into
column and marching to the left.   On the extreme
Union right, Dick Taylor's Louisiana brigade swept up
the hill, like a steel-tipped wave—over the earth-works,
over the guns, over the line of battle, and the fields were
filled with Banks' fugitives.   The Maryland colonel
brought his men to attention, wheeled into column and
said, "Men, this regiment is to be first at the Taylor
House!"   They cheered and started with quickened
pace to the center of Winchester.   They went down the
main street just as the sun of that May morning was gild-
ing the steeples and housetops.   Doors and windows
flew open.   Women in dishabille, in nightdress, filled

the windows and the streets, crying and screaming in ecstasy, and the Marylanders *were* the first at the Taylor House. They had policed the town, seized the warehouses and magazines of supplies and put guards over them before others got up, so that when Ewell's commissary came up, an immense quantity of everything useful to an army was turned over to him intact, except of course some things retained by the Marylanders, who were entitled to salvage and took it! Lieut.-Col. Edwin R. Dorsey was wounded as he charged singly and alone a squad of Union soldiers in a side street. He was the only man of the command hit during the day.

The Marylanders went into camp four miles north of the town on the valley pike, and next day, the 26th, marched into Martinsburg. There they were engaged for two or three days collecting stores left by Banks, and then rejoined the main army near Charlestown. While there General Steuart with the First Maryland and two batteries drove the enemy from Bolivar Heights, which he occupied, but evacuated after a few hours and went into camp at Halltown. The next morning at daylight the army took the retrograde. Gen. Charles S. Winder, the Marylander, had been sent to the other side of the Shenandoah to take Loudoun Heights and demonstrate from there on Harper's Ferry, which he did. Everything was done to make the enemy understand that the Confederates proposed crossing the Potomac at Harper's Ferry, and moving down in the rear to take Washington. When Winder recrossed to join the army, then in retreat, he found the First Maryland alone just moving out of camp, having received no order of march. It had no brigade. Winder at once directed Colonel Johnson to report to him and gave him the position of honor, the rear guard, and thus they moved up the valley—the Stonewall brigade the rear guard of the army, the First Maryland the rear guard of the Stonewall brigade.

Jackson's movement had accomplished Lee's object in ordering it.   It deranged and temporarily broke up Mc-Clellan's campaign on Richmond.   It was plain that no grand strategy could be carried out with such an erratic, eccentric, unaccountable, uncontrollable character as Stonewall interfering, intercepting, and meddling all the time.

While Jackson was at Charlestown, Harry Gilmor, the most daring of scouts, operating in Hardy county west of the Alleghanies, reported to him that Fremont with a large army was moving rapidly south, with the evident intention of cutting him off at Strasburg.   Scouts from east of the Blue Ridge kept him fully advised of the movements of Shields, who was hurrying by forced marches to Front Royal.   Front Royal is about twelve miles from Strasburg.   Through this gap between Fremont and Shields, Jackson was to make his escape.   He had five thousand prisoners and three thousand captured wagons, making a column ten miles long.   He pushed his spoils ahead, and when he reached Strasburg Fremont was three miles to his right and Shields twelve miles to his left at Front Royal.   In fact, Shields' cavalry was on the road parallel to the pike and only three miles distant.   Jackson hurried Charles Winder and the Stonewall brigade up to meet Fremont.   Winder sent orders to Colonel Johnson that if charged by cavalry he must take to the fences on the sides of the pike.   The Maryland rear guard covered that critical movement and were the last to cross the burning bridges.   Clear of his flanking enemies, with all of them behind him, Jackson stretched himself up the valley in a seventy-mile race, Fremont closing in behind, and Shields pushing up the Luray, or Page valley on the east, parallel to Jackson's line of march.   If the two Federal armies could out-march Jackson and throw themselves across the Confederate retreat, Jackson must be ground up between Fremont with forty thousand men and Shields with eight thousand.   Fremont was a dashing and imprudent soldier and Shields a headlong Irishman. Fremont's cavalry was commanded by Sir Percy Wyndham, an Englishman, a soldier of fortune, who had served under Garibaldi with Maj. Robideau Wheat of Wheat's battalion.

Fremont mounted a considerable force of infantry in wagons, and with them supporting his cavalry pushed and harassed Jackson day and night. The Union cavalry became very bold. They rode over the Confederate guns and over Confederate cavalry when it pleased them. Ashby and Steuart were in command of the cavalry, and they determined to give Sir Percy a lesson. On the 5th of June, Jackson turned from the main turnpike, south to Stanton, toward Port Republic, east of the Shenandoah and west of the Blue Ridge, where he could head off both Fremont and Shields, and if necessary, dodge through a gap in the mountains and hold the gap against their combined force. During the next day, the 6th, Sir Percy pressed on the Confederate cavalry rear, but Ashby, as crafty as an Indian, drew him into an ambuscade, and captured him and his leading squadron, dispersing the rest. This taught the Union general some caution, and he began to perceive that Jackson's retreat was not a flight, but was strategy.

Late in the afternoon Ashby in person reported to General Ewell that the wagon brigade had pushed far ahead of the infantry, and if the general would give him a few regiments, he would capture the whole gang of this four-wheeled cavalry. Ewell gave him the First Maryland, the Forty-fourth and Fifty-eighth Virginia. The First Maryland was, as usual, in the rear, and, therefore, when the command was faced about, was entitled to the right of the line. "Always next the enemy," they claimed— "in front going toward him, behind going trom him." When, therefore, by countermarching they were thrown in the rear, they lost their post of honor. Colonel Johnson that morning had dressed himself in a new uniform, little worn, glittering with gold lace and the three stars of

his rank and had ridden ahead to talk to General Jackson
about the condition of his command and apply for some
detached service, where he could rest and receive recruits
from the Marylanders then flocking to Virginia. He
was reduced to seven companies and two hundred and
seventy-five rifles. The time of two companies had expired and that of a third, Company C, would expire on
June 17th. Jackson heard all this and assented to it
cordially, and then said, "Colonel, I can't let you go on
detached service at this time. Go and select a good
camp, drill your men three times a day, and you'll draw
recruits as soon as they know where to find you." All
this was incontrovertible, but Jackson's drill did not
tend to replenish depleted ranks. He drilled that regiment in three battles in the next three days and in ten in
the next thirty! Colonel Johnson, however, galloped
back to his command as fast as he could, and on his
arrival found it moving rearward, First Maryland far-
thest from the enemy, in the rear.

It was about sundown, and as they moved across an
open field, he broke from his place in column and pushed
on to get parallel to the Fifty-eighth Virginia, the leading
regiment, the Forty-fourth Virginia next. Ewell and
Ashby were riding at the head of the Fifty-eighth, Ashby's
dark face afire with enthusiasm. His hair and head
were as black as a crow and his beard grew close up to
his black eyes, until he looked like a Bedouin chief. He
was pointing out the positions and topography, swinging
his arm right and left. " Look at Ashby enjoying himself," said the Maryland colonel to Adjutant Ward riding
by his side. They pushed across the open field and entered the wood. The evening sun was shooting its hori-
zontal arrows through the June foliage. The wood was
open, with little undergrowth and the timber well grown
and large. Ewell sent over to the First Maryland for
skirmishers. Company G, Captain Nicholas, and Company D, Captain Herbert, were sent to him. They were

deployed in front of the two columns, Virginians on the right, Marylanders on the left, and the whole pressed on into the darkening wood.   Soon the dropping fire of the skirmishers on the right showed that they had found the enemy, and Ashby moved the Virginians in line straight to the firing.   Ewell remained with the Marylanders and threw them into line and marched them straight forward, Ewell and Johnson riding on the right.   All at once the skirmish fire deepened, a volley roared out, and in a second the Virginians on the right were thrown into confusion.   The dusk, the surprise, the sudden death to so many shocked them into momentary panic.   They were as brave men as were in that army and proved their valor on every battlefield of the army of Northern Virginia but the shock had unnerved them for a moment.   Colonel Johnson, springing in front of his regiment, ordered, "Halt! Steady battalion! Stand fast, First Maryland!" and swinging his saber in a circle round his head, "Rally, Virginians! Rally! Form behind that wall!" pointing to the staunch ranks of the First Maryland. This recalled every one to his duty, and when Ewell gave the order to charge, the men moved forward as if in review.   They reached the edge of the wood and found on the farther side of a field a six-gun battery and a regiment, apparently of cavalry.

At this time the fire on the right, where Ashby was, had become hot—and growing every second.   Ewell dashed up — "Charge, colonel!" he cried.   "Attention battalion," was the order, "by the right flank, march." The regiment moved by the flank towards the fire.   As soon as it arrived at the top of the hill, the head of the column was turned to the right, and when the colors came in "by the left flank, charge!" was the order.   The right battalion swung into line and charged in a run.   The left battalion jumped into place and went along.   There is no such movement or order in any tactics, but it was sufficient.   The enemy, thirty yards off, was lying be-

hind a worm fence and, as the Marylanders came into line,
a volley from the fence swept down Colonel Johnson,
Captain Robertson, Lieutenant Snowden, Sergeant
Doyle, and twenty of the men in ranks.   The colonel's
new uniform procured him especial attention.   Three
bullets, tearing off the pommel of his saddle and cutting
down his horse, dismounted him, but he was on his feet
in a moment and with his regiment at the fence.   Their
opponents, the Pennsylvania Bucktails, broke, and as
they ran across the open field, the Marylanders pelted
them with great comfort and satisfaction.   Few escaped,
the Bucktails were nearly annihilated, and Colonel Kane
captured.   The Maryland colors went down time and
again but never touched the ground.   All the color guard
were killed or wounded.

From this place Jackson moved to Cross Keys, on the
Shenandoah, where, with Shields and the river in his
rear, he offered battle to Fremont against odds of three
to one.   Fremont attacked early on the 8th, and as the
Marylanders were moving up to their place in line, Ewell
said to Colonel Johnson, "Colonel, you must carry a
bucktail in your colors as your trophy, for you won it on
Friday."   Many of the men were wearing bucktails in
their caps, which had attracted Ewell's attention.   Company D was passing at the moment, and Colonel Johnson
called out to William H. Ryan, a tall, long-legged boy,
who had one, "Here, Ryan, give me that bucktail."
Ryan brought it.   "Now you tie it to the head of the
colors yourself and your trophy shall be the trophy of the
regiment."   That is the way the bucktail got to be the
cognizance of the First Maryland regiment.

The Marylanders held Ewell's right from sunrise until
four o'clock, when their rifles having become so hot and
so foul they could no longer be loaded or fired, they were
withdrawn to a branch in rear to clean their guns.

The Baltimore light artillery held the center of the
line, which was commanded by Elzey.   The right was

Charge of the First Maryland Regiment, near Harrisonburg, June 6, 1862, at the time of the death of General Ashby, defeating the Pennsylvania Bucktail Regiment.

commanded by Trimble and the left by Steuart, and Elzey selected the line on which the battle was to be fought. The Marylanders, therefore, always claimed Cross Keys as a Maryland battle and a Maryland triumph.

But while Fremont's guns were thundering at Cross Keys, Shields was plunging up the other side of the river to strike Jackson's rear and drive him back on Fremont. He got there twelve hours too late. Jackson's troops slept in line on the night of the 8th, but next morning before the sun was up they were over the river in Shields' front, and made right at his throat. The Marylanders, after their hand-to-hand fight on the evening of the 6th, had not had half rations during the next day, for they had to bury their dead at Cross Keys church. On the 8th they had not a mouthful, for their wagons had been sent off. On crossing the river by sunrise of the 9th Colonel Johnson gained Ewell's permission to stop and get something to eat. The fire of the Louisianians at Port Republic, two miles off, abbreviated their breakfast and they pushed on to the fight. They got there only in time to act as reserve to their old comrades, the Stonewall brigade, but enjoyed none of the joys of the charge, as the Louisianians had done, and none of the glory which the gallant soldiers of Dick Taylor and their general had gathered in such abundance.

Ewell decorated the First Maryland by a general order and honored them in his report, as follows:

" Headquarters, Third Division.
General Order No. 30.

In commemoration of the gallant conduct of the First Maryland regiment, on the 6th of June, when, led by Col. Bradley T. Johnson, they drove back with loss the Pennsylvania Bucktail rifles in the engagement near Harrisonburg, Rockingham Co., Va., authority is given to have one of the captured Bucktails, the insignia of the Federal regiment, appended to the color staff of the First Maryland regiment.

By order of Major-General Ewell:
                            JAMES BARBOUR, A. A. G. "

Md 11

From General Ewell's report of the Valley campaign:

"The history of the First Maryland regiment, gallantly commanded by Col. Bradley T. Johnson during the campaign of the Valley, would be the history of every action from Front Royal to Cross Keys. On the 6th, near Harrisonburg, the Fifty-eighth Virginia regiment was engaged with the Pennsylvania Bucktails, the fighting being close and bloody. Colonel Johnson came up with his regiment in the hottest period, and by a dashing charge in flank, drove the enemy off with heavy loss, capturing Lieutenant-Colonel Kane commanding. In commemoration of this gallant conduct, I ordered one of the captured Bucktails to be appended as a trophy to their flag. This action is worthy of acknowledgment from a higher source, more particularly as they avenged the death of the gallant General Ashby, who fell at the same time. Four color bearers were shot down in succession, but each time the colors were caught before reaching the ground and were finally borne by Corporal Daniel Shanks to the close of the action.

"On the 8th inst. at Cross Keys they were opposed to three of the enemy's regiments in succession."

General Jackson in his report says:—

"Apprehending that the Federals would make a more serious attack, Ashby called for an infantry support. The brigade of Gen. Geo. H. Steuart was accordingly ordered forward. In a short time the Fifty-eighth Virginia became engaged with a Pennsylvania regiment called the Bucktails, when Colonel Johnson of the First Maryland regiment, coming up in the hottest period of fire, charged gallantly into its flank and drove the enemy with heavy loss from the field, capturing Lieutenant-Colonel Kane commanding. In this skirmish, our infantry loss was seventeen killed, fifty wounded and three missing. In this affair Gen. Turner Ashby was killed."

It is a curious commentary on official reports and historical records that both these reports from the highest authorities state that the Marylanders charged in flank, while in fact they charged full in front of the enemy, and received his fire from the front of his line of battle.

CHAPTER VII.

MARYLANDERS IN 1862 UNDER GEN. ROBERT E. LEE.

AFTER Cross Keys and Port Republic, when Fremont and Shields were sent whirling down the valley, Jackson made a feint of pursuit, and pushed his cavalry some marches after them. He ordered the First Maryland to Staunton to recruit, where, during the next ten days, Company I was mustered out on June 17th, its time having expired. These men left the regiment with the respect of the whole command and the love of their colonel. Their captain, Michael Stone Robertson, belonged to an historic family in Charles county and was a descendant of Col. John H. Stone, colonel of the First regiment of the Maryland Line of the Revolution. His words as he fell were, "Go on, boys, don't mind me," and he died at his next breath. Lieut. Nicholas Snowden, of Company D, who died at the same time, had been captain of a cavalry company in Prince George's in 1860-61, and had joined Captain Herbert, his cousin, at Harper's Ferry, early in May, 1861. He was as honest, gallant and high-minded a gentleman as ever lived. The blood that Maryland poured out on that evening of June 6th was as precious and as glorious as any she has ever given in all her history, at Long Island, at Monterey, or in the army of Northern Virginia.

At Staunton the regiment was reinforced with a new company under Capt. John H. Barry, which was designated Company G. About June 24th Jackson made a sudden disappearance from the front of Fremont, and reappeared on Lee's left on the Chickahominy. He picked up the First Maryland at Staunton, and moved by

83

train.   On the 25th he reached Ashland on the Richmond, Fredericksburg and Potomac railroad, fifteen miles north of Richmond, and at daylight of the 26th moved east toward Lee's left. By three o'clock he got in touch with the enemy's pickets at Pole Green church in Hanover county, and the First Maryland was ordered forward (they held the right of Jackson's column) to drive them in.   This was done, and they forced them back to Beaver Dam creek, on the farther side of which they made a stand, and the Marylanders could not move them.   General Jackson, riding up, asked Johnson, " Colonel, what have you stopped for?" "I can't get those fellows there out of the woods!" "Give them some shell!" and the colonel ordered up the Baltimore light artillery, which soon quieted the fire on the other side.   It was then dark and the command lay down in line of battle.   At daylight they moved forward toward Old Cold Harbor, and by noon were ordered to support artillery.   They remained in this position until nearly sundown.   The battle had been raging for hours on the right.   The roll of musketry surged on like the surf of the ocean—until it breaks and then recedes.   The battle on the right made no progress.

All the infantry had been sent in until the Maryland regiment was left alone with the batteries. General Jackson, riding by, said, " Colonel, take your command in." "What shall I do with the batteries?" "The cavalry must take care of them." "General, when I park them, which way shall I move?" "That way!" said Jackson, swinging his right arm to the right.   Colonel Johnson immediately obeyed the order and moved forward by the right flank, until bursting shell and whizzing balls and wounded, limping men showed that they were approaching the point at issue.   Just at the edge of a ditch they were halted, fronted and dressed carefully.   The ground was impassable and the horses of the field officers and staff were sent back.   The colonel

First Maryland Regiment at Cold Harbor, June 27, 1862, on dress parade and going through the manual of arms, under fire of the Federal batteries.

said, " Men, we alone represent Maryland here. We are few in number, and for that reason our duty to our State is greater. We must do her honor.'' The command moved as quickly as a deep morass and heavy undergrowth would permit, and, emerging on open ground, reformed and lay down until every man got over. They were just then near the crest of a hill, on the side of a wide field, with no obstruction in front for nearly half a mile. The farther side was covered with a thick curtain of smoke, rolling backward and forward, in which only incessant, lurid flashes could be seen. Occasionally a small group would emerge, bearing a wounded man, or a frightened soldier would run back. Some distance to the left a large battery was sweeping the plateau. From the front came an incessant rain of bullets. Directly to the left the most tremendous roar of small arms announced a desperate struggle. "Up, men!" was the order. "Shoulder arms, right-shoulder-shift arms. Forward march!" The regiment moved forward as it never moved on drill, as steady and straight as a line. On it went, over that dreadful plain, strewed with dead and dying, every officer in place; the hospital detail, with the surgeons, Drs. Johnson and Latimer, thirty paces in rear. Shot and shell tore through the ranks. Not a man fell out. The wounded men were picked up by the hospital detail and attended to on the spot by our gallant medical officers, who in every action were as close to us as the line of field officers. Wishing to change direction, the order was given, " Battalion right wheel!" and it swung round like an arm. Coming to a small rise which would shelter the men, they were halted, brought to a "shoulder," then an "order," then "lie down." Colonel Johnson went forward to reconnoiter, and returning quickly commanded, " Up, men, and forward!"

Just then Capt. McHenry Howard of General Winder's staff rode up and said, " General Winder thinks you are not strong enough to take those batteries. He directs

that you wait until he can bring up the Stonewall brigade
to your support!" In a minute the Stonewall brigade
was found on the right, and General Winder directed
Colonel Johnson to take direction of the line and charge.
As they rose the crest, the batteries became visible near
the McGee house, the orchard and sunken road between
us and the McGee house being filled with Yankees, who
were covered by the road and a breastwork of knapsacks.
Just then a disorderly crowd, composed of parts of some
regiments broken in this desperate charge, recoiled past
the Stonewall brigade and Marylanders. "Steady, men!
Steady!" were the words with which the line was held
firm. Then while the canister screamed above them,
they were reformed and put through the manual of arms
by Colonel Johnson as deliberately as if on dress parade.
His object was to distract the attention of the men from
the terrible fire and death around them, and make them
look alone toward their commanding officer.

The charge was now made with the old-time cheer.
Over everything they went, pell-mell into the road, over
the fence, through the orchard, by the house. But the
batteries were gone. They found two guns in the road
that night. No further stand was made by the enemy,
and the battle of Cold Harbor was won. It is proper to
put on record a contemporaneous account of the manual
of arms, written that night by Orderly-Sergeant Robert
Cushing, of the First Maryland regiment. He was killed
at Gettysburg, July 3, 1863.

"Friday, June 27th (1862), battle of Cold Harbor.
Our regiment on reserve marched and countermarched
all day; about half-past five moved forward, got under
enemy's fire before six. Shells flew thick and fast—got
where the minie-balls occasionally would reach. Colonel
Johnson got blood up, said, 'Men, I have offered to lead
forward the line that never yet broke—never can be
broken. Forward, quick march, guide center!' The
old regiment marched proudly forward. 'Halt, order
arms!' and the lines were dressed, and guns ordered like

on dress parade. Other regiments were brought forward, and formed on us at last. ' Forward march,' and on the line of battle moved until with a yell, we charged, and took the field, sleeping on it. Our regiment has reason to be proud of its action and of its colonel.''

The next morning Ewell moved rapidly to Dispatch Station on the York River railroad in McClellan's rear, the First Maryland on the right. It was sent forward to drive off the picket at the Station, and McClellan was cut off from his base on York river at West Point. For a day or two Ewell's division remained at Dispatch Station until on McClellan's retiring toward James river it rejoined the army and pressed on in pursuit. It was not engaged until Malvern Hill, where the First Maryland lay all the afternoon under the fire of McClellan's seventy guns on his right and his gun boats on his left. After dark, the Maryland regiment joined General Winder, who had the fragment of the Stonewall brigade, which had been badly cut up. Winder ordered Colonel Johnson forward to cover and hold as much of the field as possible until daylight while he supported him. This was done satisfactorily, and the next morning Lee followed McClellan to Westover, where he left him, satisfied that any forward movement by the beaten Federal commander was improbable.

After Westover the Marylanders were sent to Charlottesville to recruit, where they remained a month, and were then ordered to Gordonsville to guard the depot of supplies and the railroad junction there. They were in camp while Jackson moved swiftly by and on August 9th sprang on Pope at Cedar Mountain in Culpeper.

On August 16th a special order from the adjutant-general of the Confederate States to the colonel of the First Maryland was received by him, ordering him to muster the regiment out of service without delay. The regiment could not parade more than two hundred and fifty rifles for duty, but its officers were as efficient, gallant,

well-instructed a set of young soldiers as were in either
army. They were in this summary manner dismissed
f~om the service, without charges, without notice and
without a hearing. This extraordinary proceeding was
heard of with regret by the army and with acute anger by
the regiment itself. Colonel Johnson mustered them out
on the 17th, the men presented their flag and their
bucktail to Mrs. Johnson and then dispersed, grieved
and offended. Generals Jackson and Ewell sent Colonel
Johnson letters of regard and sympathy and also recom-
mendations to the President of the Confederate States,
that he be made brigadier-general. Colonel Johnson
declined to go to Richmond, or become an applicant for
a place he had won by hard service, and Jackson assigned
him to command the Second brigade, Jackson's division,
Second corps—Jackson's own.

A new regiment was soon brought together, of which
James R. Herbert became lieutenant-colonel, and William
W. Goldsborough, major. But the disbanding of the
gallant First regiment, although another was so soon
formed, was attended by some unfortunate results.

It will be noted that when the army crossed the Potomac in September, 1862, after the second battle of
Manassas, it carried with it no Maryland regiment bearing the Maryland flag, and thus there was no nucleus on
which recruits could rally. The First Maryland artillery,
under the gallant Dement, and the Baltimore light artillery, with Griffin, were there, but detached batteries operating in different commands gave no points of rendezvous
for raw recruits seeking an association in an army. General Lee and the Confederacy were much disappointed at
the failure of Maryland to rise, but this disappointment
was without adequate reason. Lee crossed the Potomac
on September 5th and the next day, the 6th, camped
around Frederick. The population of that section of
Maryland was strongly Union, fully one-half of it being
adherents of that side. On September 10th Lee moved

from Frederick to Hagerstown and the next week was taken up in operations which culminated in the battle of Sharpsburg on September 17th. McClellan moved from Washington on the 6th, his columns covering the whole country between Lee's army and southern Maryland, where the chief strength of the Confederates lay. So Lee was only stationary four days, and at no time was the country open for Confederate sympathizers to join him. He issued this proclamation:

" Headquarters Army N. Va.

Near Fredericktown, September 8, 1862.

To the People of Maryland:

It is right that you should know the purpose that has brought the army under my command within the limits of your State, so far as that purpose concerns yourselves.

The people of the Confederate States have long watched with the deepest sympathy the wrongs and outrages that have been inflicted upon the citizens of a commonwealth, allied to the States of the South by the strongest social, political and commercial ties. They have seen with profound indignation their sister State deprived of every right, and reduced to the position of a conquered province. Under the pretense of supporting the Constitution, but in violation of its most valuable provisions, your citizens have been arrested and imprisoned upon no charge and contrary to all forms of law. The faithful and manly protest against this outrage made by the venerable and illustrious Marylander, to whom in better days no citizen appealed for right in vain, was treated with scorn and contempt. The government of your chief city has been usurped by armed strangers: your legislature has been dissolved by the unlawful arrest of its members: freedom of the press and of speech has been suppressed: words have been declared offenses by an arbitrary decree of the Federal executive, and citizens ordered to be tried by a military commission for what they may dare to speak.

Believing that the people of Maryland possessed a spirit too lofty to submit to such a government, the people of the South have long wished to aid you in throwing off the foreign yoke, to enable you again to enjoy the inalienable rights of freemen and restore independence and sovereignty to your State.

Md 12

In obedience to this wish, our army has come among you, and is prepared to assist you with the power of its arms, in regaining the rights, of which you have been despoiled.

This, citizens of Maryland, is our mission so far as you are concerned: no restraint on your free will is intended: no intimidation will be allowed. Within the limits of this army at least, Marylanders shall once more enjoy their ancient freedom of thought and speech. We know no enemies among you and will protect all, of every opinion. It is for you to decide your destiny, freely and without constraint. This army will respect your choice, whatever it may be, and while the Southern people will rejoice to welcome you to your natural position among them, they will only welcome you when you come of your own free will.

R. E. LEE, General Commanding.''

Colonel Johnson, whose Second brigade was camped at the barracks on the suburbs of the town, and who had policed the town with Capt. Lewis N. Randolph, of the Irish battalion, as provost marshal, sent out the following appeal:

"To the People of Maryland:

After sixteen months of oppression more galling than the Austrian tyranny, the victorious army of the South brings freedom to your doors. Its standards now wave from the Potomac to Mason and Dixon's line. The men of Maryland, who during the last long months have been crushed under the heel of this terrible despotism, now have the opportunity for working out their own redemption, for which they have so long waited and suffered and hoped. The government of the Confederate States is pledged by the unanimous vote of its Congress, by the distinct declaration of its President, the soldier and statesman Davis, never to cease this war until Maryland has the opportunity to decide for herself, her own fate, untrammeled and free from Federal bayonets. The people of the South, with unanimity unparalleled, have given their hearts to our native State, and hundreds of thousands of her sons have sworn with arms in their hands that you shall be free.

You must now do your part. We have the arms here for you. I am authorized immediately to muster in for the war, companies and regiments, the companies of one hundred men each, and the regiments of ten companies. Come, all who wish to strike for their liberties and homes! Let each man provide himself with a stout pair of shoes, a good blanket and a tin cup. Jackson's men have no baggage.

Officers are in Frederick to receive recruits, and all companies formed will be armed as soon as mustered in. Rise at once. Remember the cells of Fort McHenry! Remember the dungeons of Fort Lafayette and Fort Warren! the insults to your wives and daughters! the arrest! the midnight searches of your houses! Remember these wrongs! and rise at once in arms, and strike for liberty and right.

> BRADLEY T. JOHNSON, Colonel C. S. A."

Frederick, September 8, 1862.

A few companies reported to Colonel Johnson under this call. Just at the time, Gen. J. R. Jones, who had been wounded in battle before Richmond, came up and reported for duty and resumed command of the Second brigade, and Johnson had no location in the army. He rode with Jackson's staff, but it was impossible to care for green volunteers in the rapid evolutions of the army of Northern Virginia from September 10 to 18, 1862. The new recruits merely followed along after the army and dispersed after the battle of Sharpsburg. It is probable that if a strong regiment of Marylanders under the Maryland flag had marched with Lee at that time it might have been made the rallying point of a new division.

CHAPTER VIII.

MARYLAND UNDER FEDERAL MILITARY POWER.

GOVERNOR HICKS did not respond to the first call of the President of the United States for troops until he had delivered the State over to the Federal authorities, securely tied, handcuffed and gagged, and when habeas corpus was defied, freedom of speech made a crime, liberty of the press suppressed, trial by jury abolished, Butler holding down Baltimore under the prisons of Federal Hill and throttling the State government at Annapolis. Governor Hicks, who, at the meeting in Monument Square in the afternoon of April 10th, prayed his God to wither his right arm if ever he raised it against a sister Southern State, against Virginia and the South, had not complied with President Lincoln's first call for troops, but Butler's guns and the Federal control of the city recovered him from the panic into which he had been precipitated by the paving stones of Pratt St., and on the 14th of May, the day of Ross Winans' arrest, he issued a proclamation calling for four regiments of volunteers to serve for three months, " within the limits of Maryland, or for the defense of the capital of the United States, and not to serve beyond the limits aforesaid." In consequence of the delay, the short term of service and the ridiculous terms proposed for enlistment, the government refused to accept the home guards, guaranteed " never to leave the State except in case of invasion."

On the 2d of May President Lincoln had called for forty-two thousand and thirty-four regulars to serve for three years, and a large number of men who had volunteered under the first call enlisted under the second.

James Cooper, Esq., who was a native of Carroll county, Maryland, but had lived all his life in Pennsylvania and had served that State in the Senate of the United States with honor to himself and distinction to his State, was commissioned brigadier-general by the Federal authority, and assigned to the duty of raising and organizing the militia of the State of Maryland for Federal service. The governor and State authority were thus superseded by the Federal government, as the legislature was shortly afterward dispersed, imprisoned and disbanded, the judges ignored and the courts trampled under foot. The Constitution of the United States as well as that of Maryland was thus suspended and another instance given, as has been done since history began, that "inter arma silent leges"—in time of war paper guarantees and written agreements have no force. It was freely asserted by the great legal authorities, by learned lawyers and great judges, supporting the Union side, that "constitutions are not made for war times!"

Patterson's army, after retiring from Virginia, on the expiration of the time of its ninety-day men, was camped at Williamsport, where during the summer it was reinforced by new recruits. Maj.-Gen. N. P. Banks was assigned to command this army and picketed the Potomac from Georgetown to Harper's Ferry. Maj.-Gen. Joseph Hooker with a division was posted in southern Maryland, and picketed the Potomac from Washington to its mouth. Forty thousand men were thus occupied in guarding Maryland along the line of the Potomac alone.

Another division was posted in Baltimore with garrisons at every county town in the State. The November election of 1861 was considered of great consequence to the Union side in that State. Governor Hicks, in his zeal not to raise his arm against a sister Southern State, applied to General Banks to work into the Maryland election so that "a killing majority shall be rolled up against secessionism. General McClellan issued an order to General Banks, calling his attention to the alleged "apprehension among Union citizens in many parts of Maryland, of an attempt at interference with their rights of suffrage by disunion citizens." The wolves clearly perceived the intention of the lambs below them to muddy the stream. He directed Banks to garrison the polls, and see "that no disunionists are allowed to intimidate them, or in any way interfere with their rights." Also to arrest all persons who have recently returned from Virginia and who show themselves at the polls. General Dix, governing in Baltimore, directed the United States marshal and the provost marshal to arrest all disloyal persons and to hold them securely. Col. John W. Geary, of the Twenty-eighth Pennsylvania regiment, reported from Point of Rocks, Maryland, November 8, 1861, to Capt. R. Morris Copeland, assistant adjutant-general on Banks' staff:

"Previous to the election a number of enemies to the Union in this State *preliminated* schemes for disturbing the peace of the various precincts. I had several of the most prominent actors in this, among whom was a candidate for senator, arrested before election and held until to-day. I had *detailments* from various companies of my regiment, with proper officers, stationed in Sandy Hook, Petersville, Jefferson, Urbana, New Market, Buckeyetown, Frederick City and other places where the polls were held. Owing to the presence of the troops everything progressed quietly and I am happy to report a Union victory in every place in my jurisdiction."

These arbitrary arrests caused Lord Lyons, the English minister at Washington, to remonstrate with Mr. Lincoln. On November 4th he wrote Earl Russell that he had told Mr. Seward that "while the English people did not enter far into abstract questions of national dignity, they felt very strongly on the subject of the treatment of their fellow citizens abroad: nothing inspired them with so strong or lasting a resentment as injuries or indignities inflicted by foreign governments on her majesty's subjects.'' Mr. Seward replied that "the recent arrests had all been made in view of the Maryland elections, that those elections would be over in a week's time, and that he hoped then to be able to set at liberty all the British subjects now under military arrest.'' In another dispatch of September 16, 1861, Lord Lyons says: "A war has been made at Baltimore upon particular articles of dress, particular colors, portraits of Southern leaders and other supposed symptoms of supposed disaffection. The violent measures which have been resorted to have gone far to establish the fact that Maryland is retained in the Union only by military force. They have undoubtedly increased the dislike of the people to their Northern ruler.''

Augustus W. Bradford was the candidate of the Union party, Benjamin C. Howard, of the Democratic party. The Union soldiers voted everywhere "freely without hindrance, and fully without denial, and speedily without delay,'' as much and as often as they chose. Bradford was declared elected by a majority of over 30,000. He could just as well have had a recorded majority of 300,000.

The marshal of police, George P. Kane, the police commissioners, and the mayor of Baltimore had been arrested in July and imprisoned at Fort Lafayette. Thus, at the beginning of the year 1862, the Federal army of occupation was commanded by Major-General Dix in Baltimore; Hooker in Charles county, and along the Potomac, south of Washington, Generals McClellan, Keyes and Casey; in and around Washington, General Stone at Poolesville, and Banks at Darnestown, up to Williamsport, General Kelly at Cumberland, where he was relieved early in January by General Lander. It had elected Augustus W. Bradford governor, and a subservient legislature in November, 1861. The judiciary was deposed and dragged from the bench. Judge Robert B. Carmichael, illustrious for a long life of private virtue and public service, was seized on the bench in his court house at Easton in Talbot county, knocked senseless with a revolver on the very seat of justice, incarcerated in the negro jail in Baltimore, and thence sent to Fort Lafayette and there held.   Hon. James L. Bartol, of the court of appeals, was imprisoned in Fort McHenry.   As General Lee said in his proclamation to the people of Maryland: "Words have been declared offenses, by an arbitrary decree of the Federal executive, and citizens ordered to be tried by a military commission for what they may dare to speak."   Lord Lyons, therefore, well said, "that the violent measures which have been resorted to have gone far to establish the fact that Maryland is retained in the Union only by military force."

The legislature was convened by Hicks on December 3, 1861, and promptly passed resolutions of thanks to Col. John R. Kenly, of the First Maryland regiment, "for his early, prompt and distinguished services in the cause of his country."

But the lot of the Maryland Unionists was not a happy one.   They had harnessed themselves to the car of the radical revolution, and they began to see, when too late, whither they were being driven.   In March, 1862, the legislature passed a resolution that "The general assembly of Maryland have seen with concern, certain indications at the seat of the general government, of an interference with the institution of slavery—in the slave-holding States—and cannot hesitate to express their sentiments, and those of the people they represent, in regard to a policy so unwise and mischievous.   This war is prosecuted by the nation with one object, that, namely, of a restoration of the Union, just as it was before the rebellion broke out.   The rebellious States are to be brought back to their places in the Union without change or diminution of their constitutional rights, etc., etc."

They further resolved frequently and copiously against the secessionists and in favor of the Union.   Nevertheless and notwithstanding this outcry, in April, 1862, Congress passed a law for the abolition of slavery in the District of Columbia. The legislature of Maryland passed a " treason law," which denounced the penalty of death against any one convicted of levying war against this State, or who shall adhere to the enemies thereof, whether foreign or domestic, giving them aid or comfort within this State or elsewhere. Punishments were also denounced for breaking railroads or canals; for belonging to any secret club intended to encourage the secession of the State from the Union; for displaying secession flags, encouraging any minor to go South and join in the rebellion, or furnishing any minor or any other person with money, clothes, provisions or conveyance to aid in such an object. It also appropriated $7,000 for the relief of the families of those soldiers of the Sixth Massachusetts regiment who were killed in the riot of April 19, 1861. It made no provision for the families of those citizens of Maryland who were killed by the soldiers. Loyalty could not further go.

When President Lincoln, on the 14th of April, 1861, called for seventy-five thousand volunteers to suppress the rebellion, he required Maryland to furnish four regiments of four hundred and eighty men each as her quota. But on the 20th, the day after the Baltimore attack on the Massachusetts troops, Governor Hicks wrote him that " he thought it prudent (for the present) to decline responding affirmatively to the requisition." About the last of April, as has been noted, the Federal government commissioned Hon. James Cooper of Frederick to raise a brigade. Recruiting was at once begun in Baltimore by J. C. McConnell, and other companies were raised in different parts of the State, and before the first of June, 1861, the First regiment Maryland volunteers was mustered into the service of the United States, and John R. Kenly commissioned colonel, and Nathan T. Dushane lieutenant-colonel. The Second regiment was mustered in about the middle of September under Colonel Summers and Lieutenant-Colonel Duryea. The Third Maryland was recruited by foreigners in Baltimore City and western Maryland and was commanded by Colonel DeWitt. The Fourth regiment, commanded by Colonel Sudburgh, was composed of Germans. The First and Second Maryland artillery companies were commanded by Captains Hampton and Thomson, and the First Maryland cavalry by Lieutenant-Colonel Miller.

These first forces raised for the Union in Maryland were, with the exception of the First regiment, mainly composed of foreigners, aliens by birth and aliens to the institutions, ideals and motives that for nine generations had formed the character of Marylanders. They were good men, but they were not Marylanders. They were devoted to the Union, but they had no conception of the force and duty of "courage and chivalry." The First Maryland under Kenly was the only Maryland regiment on the Union side. The Confederate Marylanders, on the other hand, embodied the faith and pride of the State. Not a historic family of Maryland but was represented in the Maryland Line. Five grandsons of John Eager Howard, of the Cowpens, carried sword or musket in the First Maryland regiment. A grandson of Charles Carroll of Carrollton rode as a private in Company K, First Virginia cavalry. Colonel Johnson, of the Maryland Line, rode at the head of seventy-two kinsmen, descendants of soldiers of the Revolution, his own flesh and blood!

In the summer of 1862 the First and Second Eastern Shore regiments were raised under Colonels Wallace and Wilkins; the First and Second regiments Potomac home brigade under Colonels Maulsby and Johns; and the Purnell Legion of one regiment infantry, Col. William Louis Schley, one company of artillery and two troops of cavalry; the First Maryland artillery, Captain Alexander, and the Fourth, Sixth, Seventh and Eighth regiments of infantry.   There was also a battalion of artillery, Maj. E. R. Petherbridge, Battery A, Capt. I. W. Wolcott, with eight three-inch rifle 10-pounders, and Battery B, Capt. A. Snow, with six of the same as Battery A.

Colonel Kenly was promoted brigadier-general on the 22d of August, 1862, "for gallant conduct at the battle of Front Royal."   On September 8th he was assigned to command a brigade to consist of the First, Fourth, Sixth, Seventh and Eighth regiments of Maryland volunteers with Alexander's battery of light artillery.   The First regiment, as we have seen, served with distinction in the valley under Banks in 1862.   The Second was with Burnside at New Bern, N. C.   There they received the following decoration from their commanding general:

"Headquarters Department of North Carolina.
New Bern, May 22, 1862.
Lieut.-Col. Eugene Duryea,
Commanding Second regiment Maryland Volunteers:
Sir:—The commanding general desires me to express his gratification at the skillful and soldierly manner in which your movement on Pollocksville was executed on the 14th and 17th instant, and high appreciation of the fortitude and perseverance with which the obstacles presented by the elements were borne and overcome by yourself and your command.

I have the honor to be, colonel,
Very respectfully, your obedient servant,
LEWIS RICHMOND, A. A. G."

The move on Pollocksville consisted of a march of sixty miles in seventy-two hours in the face of an active enemy, through deep mud and in a drenching rain, maintaining their position for two days against heavy odds, repelling repeated assaults and performing their work effectually, and then safely returning to the army notwithstanding a vigorous pursuit!

The Second Maryland returned with Burnside to Virginia, where it joined Pope and did good service at Second Manassas.   Maryland is not entitled to merit for this gallant command.   Its colonel, Duryea, was not connected by blood or in any way with the State, and most of the enlisted men were foreigners.

The Third regiment, under Colonel DeWitt, was hotly engaged at Cedar Run, and lost heavily. Major Kennedy and over one hundred men were killed and wounded. They also lost over thirty-three per cent of the command at Sharpsburg, killed and wounded.

The First regiment of cavalry, Lieutenant-Colonel Miller and Maj. James M. Deems, served under Generals Buford and Sigel in the army of the Potomac, in 1862.

The Potomac home brigade, Col. William P. Maulsby, and the Purnell Legion, were enlisted and organized as home guards for home service and never to leave the State. Colonel Maulsby, of the First regiment, and commanding the Potomac home brigade, was as high spirited and as chivalric a knight as ever set lance in rest for the rescue of the Holy Sepulcher, for he was a Marylander by descent, by tradition and in every fiber of his being. Therefore, when the army of the Potomac moved toward its enemy, Maulsby's Potomac home brigade moved with it, on its own ardent demand. Its muskets would have marched had there been no men to carry them, for the spirit of the commander permeates and electrifies all under him, and the fire of the head and heart heats all the members.

The Maryland artillery battalion, under Maj. Edward R. Petherbridge, was before Richmond in the artillery reserve under Colonel Hunt. At the New Bridge over the Chickahominy, Battery B once had an artillery duel with the First Maryland artillery, Confederate, in which it fired over six hundred shots, doing considerable damage.

CHAPTER IX.

MARYLAND ARTILLERY—SECOND MARYLAND REGI-
MENT INFANTRY—FIRST MARYLAND CAVALRY.

THE First Maryland artillery was organized at
Richmond, Va., in July, 1861, with Richard
Snowden Andrews as captain, William F. Dement
first-lieutenant, and Charles Snowden Couter second-
lieutenant. The captain, Andrews, was the son of Colonel Andrews of the United States army and had peculiar
qualifications for the profession of arms. He had been
born and reared in the military and impressed with the
traditions of the "Old Army," which for deep convic-
tions of duty, devotion to ideals of high chivalry, purity
of motive, entire unselfishness, patriotism, valor and
genius for war has never been excelled by any army
that ever marched under any flag. Snowden Andrews
was the ideal of a young gentleman formed by such influences—intellectual, well-informed on army matters,
firm, persistent, indefatigable. No man went into service better equipped on either side. Believing himself
better qualified for the scientific service of the artillery,
he left his home and young wife in Bath, with the delib-
erate purpose of creating a battery, of which he intended
to be commander. He procured from the department of
war in Washington drawings of the most approved models
of guns for the army. At Richmond he recruited his
battery with indomitable energy. He selected his assist-
ants, his lieutenants, with unerring judgment, for no
better or braver men ever directed a gun than Dement
and Couter. He submitted his drawings to the Confederate war department, secured its official endorsement,
and by authority had the ordnance manufactured at the

Tredegar works in Richmond, as far as the resources of that establishment could go. So that when the First Maryland artillery took the field, it might have been said that the whole of it, men and guns, harness and wheels, was the creation of the head and heart, the mind and will of its captain. It occupied a position on the extreme right of the Confederate line, at Shipping Point on the Potomac, where its fire effectually blockaded that river until March, 1862, when Johnston withdrew from Manassas and the line of the Potomac. In the Seven Days' battles it was attached to the division of Maj.-Gen. A. P. Hill. When Lee began his movement around McClellan's right on June 26, 1862, the First Maryland artillery fired the first shots at Mechanicsville, just as the First Maryland regiment had fired the first shots against McClellan's pickets at Hundley's Corner an hour before. It was attached to Pender's North Carolina brigade, and Captain Andrews was slightly wounded. General Pender in his report says: " The section of Andrews' battery was under Lieutenant Dement, who did fine service. Captain Andrews as usual was present, chafing for a fight."

After that campaign he was promoted major "for gallant and meritorious conduct displayed in the battles before Richmond," and a battalion was formed for him consisting of the First Maryland; the Chesapeake, Captain William D. Brown—afterward known in the Maryland Line as the Third Maryland; and several Virginia batteries.

In the movement on Pope in August, 1862, Major Andrews commanded the artillery of Winder's division, originally Jackson's. On the 9th of August Pope moved from Culpeper Court House on Jackson at Slaughter's Mountain, half a march distant. Charles Winder, though too sick for duty, insisted on commanding his division in action. His place was the left of Jackson's line and with him was Andrews' battalion of artillery.

The Federals struck Winder on his exposed flank, doubled up his two left brigades, the First and Second, and sent them back behind the right of the division. Just at that minute a Federal line of battle was marching straight across the open fields against Winder's right and, with the broken brigades and Federals in the rear and the attack in front, they would have been crushed and Jackson ruined. Andrews, without waiting for orders, took his old battery, the First Maryland, across the front of the two brigades in a sweeping gallop, whirled them into battery on a hillock five hundred yards from the charging line of battle and opened on it with grape and canister with such bitterness, vigor and intensity, that human nature could not stand it, and in three minutes the charge became a rout and the field was filled with fugitives. It is the only case on record of a line of battle being charged by a battery of artillery. But though the service was the most brilliant and valuable done that day, it was more than paid for. As Winder was attempting to rally his broken brigades, a shell knocked him from his horse dead, and as Andrews rode at the head of his battery, he was nearly cut in two by a shell which laid open the anterior covering of his abdomen. It was useless to harass a dying man, it was thought by the surgeons; so he was left on the field with his devoted friend and faithful surgeon, Grafton Tyler of the First Maryland.

Maryland lost one of her most distinguished sons when Charles Winder fell, and nearly lost another as good a man when Snowden Andrews was so badly wounded. He ought to have died by all the rules of anatomy and experience of surgery, but he was of fiber too tough to be killed merely by one Yankee shell. His indomitable will and his unflinching courage pulled him through, and he lives to-day, vigorous in mind and body, just as obstinate as ever, and as faithful to friends as in the days when he was left lying on the field of Culpeper, with his head on Grafton Tyler's lap, insisting that he wouldn't die when everybody said he must die. He was promoted lieutenant-colonel for this. Col. A. R. Courtney, chief of artillery of the Third division, in his report said, "The officers and men of Captain Dement's First Maryland battery, the only one which had been in action before, showed more coolness and deliberation." Colonel Crutchfield, chief of artillery of the Second corps, in his report said: "These two batteries were capitally handled and evidently damaged the enemy severely." He also "calls special attention to the gallantry displayed by Maj. R. S. Andrews in this action." General Jackson said, "Special credit is due Major Andrews for the success and gallantry with which his guns were directed, until he was severely wounded and taken from the field."

After the battle of Slaughter's Mountain the First Maryland was foremost in every skirmish and affair in which the army of Northern Virginia was engaged in its transfer from the front of McClellan on the James to the rear of Pope at Manassas. On the 22d of August Early's brigade of Ewell's division crossed the Rappahannock at the White Sulphur Springs by the ford, the bridge having been broken. Early had with him the Thirteenth Georgia and the two Maryland batteries. Pope believed that this was Lee's advance over the river and forthwith concentrated a large force (Early says, "his whole force") to attack it. During the night a tremendous rain fell and the river rose six feet and the bridge was impassable This little force, therefore, was cut off on the northern side of the river. During the entire day Early made a great show by marching and countermarching his regiments, and that stood off the Federals until dark. Then they made a move in heavy force to crush the small body in front of them and they charged with cheers, but Dement opened on them with canister at very short range, repulsed them and saved the command. When Jackson moved around Pope's flank and got in his rear at Bristoe Station on the 26th of August, 1862, Ewell's division was left at Bristoe, while Hill and Taliaferro (who had succeeded Charles Winder in command of the First division) were sent to Manassas Junction. In the afternoon Pope's advance came up in heavy force, but Dement's guns stopped them until Ewell got out comfortably to Manassas. At Manassas in the battle of August 28, 29, 30, 1862, the three Maryland batteries —the First, Captain Dement; the Second, Baltimore light, Captain Brockenbrough; the Third, Chesapeake, Captain Brown, performed distinguished services. On the last day the First Maryland having exhausted all its long range projectiles of shot and shell, was moved up closer so as to shorten the range and increase the efficiency of canister.

Upon the investment of Harper's Ferry, during the night of September 14th, Colonel Crutchfield, Jackson's chief of artillery, took two guns each from the batteries of Dement, Brown, Latimer and Garber, and moved them across the Shenandoah, so as to flank and enfilade the Federal lines. This was the key of the position. Crutchfield was ordered to open at daylight, but the work of cutting a road along the mountain delayed him. At dawn the Confederate batteries of Pegram, McIntosh, Davidson and Braxton of A. P. Hill's division opened on the Federal right. General Miles, the Federal commander, began to form to charge them, when Crutchfield broke out in a tremendous fire which silenced the Federal battery on the left and drove the Federal infantry from their entrenchments. As the circle of fire from mountain to mountain closed around General Miles, he put up the white flag and surrendered. At Sharpsburg the Maryland batteries were on the Confederate left operating with Maj.-Gen. J. E. B. Stuart and his cavalry. At Fredericksburg, the Chesapeake artillery, under Lieutenant Plater, at Hamilton's Crossing did excellent service, said Early. At the battle of

Md 14

Chancellorsville, the First Maryland and the Chesapeake artillery defended an important position in Early's line against Sedgwick on the 2d, and on the 3d was on Marye's Hill. Both batteries lost heavily in these engagements and received distinctive notice from General Early in his report.

The Second Maryland infantry* was organized at Winchester, Va., in the fall of 1862, of companies recruited in Richmond by officers of the First Maryland and some Marylanders who had come to Virginia after the battle of Sharpsburg. Those most active and influential in recruiting new companies were Captains Herbert, Goldsborough, Lieutenant George Thomas, Corporal Clapham Murray, Private W. P. Zollinger, late of the First Maryland, and Captains J. Parran Crane, Ferdinand C. Duvall, Jos. L. McAleer, John W. Torsch, Gwynn and Stewart, who were generally new men, except Torsch, who had commanded a company in a Virginia regiment for the preceding year. The regiment was organized as follows:

Lieutenant-Colonel, James R. Herbert.
Major, William W. Goldsborough.
Adjutant, J. Winder Laird.
Acting Adjutant, Lieut. George Thomas.
Quartermaster, Maj. Charles W. Harding.
Commissary of Subsistence, Capt. John Eager Howard.
Surgeon, Richard P. Johnson.
Assistant Surgeon, De Wilton Snowden.
Sergeant Major, William R. McCullough.
Quartermaster Sergeant, Edwin James.
Ordnance Sergeant, Francis L. Higdon.
Chief Musician, Michael A. Quinn.
Company A: Captain, William H. Murray. Lieutenants, Geo. Thomas, Clapham Murray, William P. Zollinger.

---

*Major W. W. Goldsborough, of the Second Maryland, has a graphic account of the regiment in his "Maryland Line, C. S. A.," which has been freely drawn on in this chapter.

Company B: Captain, J. Parran Crane. Lieutenants, J. H. Stone, Chas. B. Wise, James H. Wilson.

Company C: Captain, Ferdinand C. Duvall. Lieutenants, Charles W. Hodges, Joseph W. Barber, Thomas H. Tolson.

Company D: Captain, Joseph L. McAleer. Lieutenants, James S. Franklin, J. T. Bussey, S. T. McCullough.

Company E: Captain, John W. Torsch. Lieutenants, William J. Broadfoot, Wm. R. Byus, Joseph P. Quinn.

Company F: Captain, A. J. Gwynn. Lieutenants, John W. Polk, David C. Forrest, John G. Hyland.

Company G: Captain, Thomas R. Stewart. Lieutenants, G. G. Guillette, George Brighthaupt, William C. Wrighttor.

Company H: Captain, J. Thomas Bussey.

Col. Bradley T. Johnson had first been unanimously elected by the officers of the battalion to be lieutenant-colonel. Colonel Johnson was at that time on the military court at Richmond and had not contributed to the organization of the new command. He declined the proffered commission on the ground that it was due to Herbert as the senior officer of those who had got together, armed, equipped, drilled and instructed the Second Maryland. They had done the work and should have the honors. So Captain Herbert was elected lieutenant-colonel and Captain Goldsborough major.

The Second Maryland was employed during the winter and spring of 1863 at New Market, Harrisonburg and various other points along the Valley pike, sometimes on picket, sometimes in scouting. They several times accompanied Gen. Wm. E. Jones, who was in command of the valley, with his brigade of Virginia cavalry, the Second Maryland infantry and the Baltimore light artillery, on raids and long and arduous marches over the mountains of West Virginia, to disable the Baltimore & Ohio railroad by tearing up its track and burning its bridges.

In June, 1863, when General Lee commenced his move

on Pennsylvania by pushing Ewell's corps from Culpeper over the mountains to attack Milroy at Winchester, Jones' command was moved down the valley to make a junction with Ewell.   At Kernstown, a few miles from Winchester, three companies of the Second Maryland, under Major Goldsborough, were out as skirmishers. They soon struck the enemy and drove him steadily back into the town of Winchester.   They passed the night half a mile from the town and before sunrise next morning the Marylanders charged into the town, but were withdrawn by order of Gen. John B. Gordon, who had his brigade near them.   The next day was occupied in Ewell's preparations to assault the fortifications around the town, into which Milroy had collected his army, but at daylight next morning the Maryland skirmishers entered the town and found everything had been evacuated during the night and Milroy had marched out toward Harper's Ferry.   Ewell, however, had prepared for that movement and captured almost his entire command, though Milroy himself escaped.   The loss of the Second Maryland in this affair was nine wounded and one captured.*

The curious part of this affair was that the Confederate Marylanders for the two days were fighting their own friends and kinsmen, the Fifth Maryland Federal, in which Major Goldsborough's brother was surgeon. The major captured his own brother.   The regiment, the morning after the battle of Winchester, was attached to the brigade of Gen. George H. Steuart, former colonel of the First Maryland.   It was composed of Virginia and North Carolina regiments, in Maj.-Gen. Edward Johnson's division of Ewell's corps.

From Winchester they marched with the army to Gettysburg.   On the evening of the first of July, 1863, Johnson's division being on the left of Ewell's corps,

*See appendix A, for losses of the regiment in this and subsequent engagements.

which was the left of the army, moved about nightfall to attack Culp's Hill. After a bitter struggle they took the position with a loss of three hundred in Steuart's brigade, including one hundred in the Second Maryland. In this attack Lieutenant-Colonel Herbert was severely wounded by three balls, it was believed mortally. They held their place all night, and at daylight next morning Steuart's brigade was formed at right angles to the works they had taken the night before, and charged down them at a line held by the enemy two hundred yards in front, with an open field between. As the brigade emerged into the open, it was swept by the fire in front and a tenfold more destructive one from the left, where a large force of the enemy had been concentrated during the night. Major Goldsborough was shot down and Captain Murray killed, and the Second Maryland annihilated. It had carried five hundred men into battle the night before. Two hundred reported the morning after. Almost all the remainder were killed and wounded, for none were captured except five men tending wounded or dying comrades. After Gettysburg the Second Maryland marched with the army to Orange Court House in Virginia, where in November it was detached from Steuart's brigade and ordered to report to Col. Bradley T. Johnson, commanding the Maryland Line at Hanover Junction.

On June 2, 1864, the Second Maryland was held in reserve to Echols' brigade of Virginians, who occupied a line of works in front of McGehee's house at Cold Harbor, on the same ground over which the battle of Cold Harbor had been fought June 27, 1862. At daylight of June 3d Hancock's corps made a sudden rush at the works, ran over them, and the first thing the Marylanders knew the Union flag was right over them and the Union troops ramming canister in the captured guns in the fortification, to open them on their late owners. Without waiting for orders, officers and men rushed straight at the enemy with the naked bayonet, and in the

twinkling of an eye hurled them back the way they had
come and turned the guns they had shotted on the routed
mass.   It was a most brilliant exploit, for it saved
Lee's line and probably a serious disaster, for Grant had
massed troops to pour them through the opening made
by Hancock.   Their loss was severe.

From that date the Second Maryland was engaged in
every combat of Ewell's corps.   They were first assigned
to Walker's brigade and then to Archer's brigade of
Heth's division.   On the 13th of June they had a severe
fight at White Oak Swamp and continual skirmishes followed up to August 25th.   On August 18th General Mahone made an attack on Ream's Station on the Petersburg and Weldon railroad, south of Petersburg,
Archer's brigade being part of his force. The fighting here
was extremely bloody and the loss heavy on both sides.
At Pegram's Farm, September 30, 1864, Heth's division
had another severe fight.   The Second Maryland lost out
of one hundred and forty-nine men who went into the
fight, fifty-three killed and wounded.   At that time there
were only six commissioned officers left with the regiment.
All the rest had been killed or wounded.   On October
1st they had another bloody fight on the Squirrel Level
road and lost heavily.

From that day they were constantly fighting in the
trenches until April 2, 1865, when they made their last
gallant stand in the lines of Petersburg. General Archer
having been wounded, the brigade command devolved
on Brigadier-General McComb, of Tennessee.   General
McComb held his place on the line until nearly sur-
rounded, and then fell back to Hatcher's Run.   From
there they marched with the army to Appomattox Court
House, where they were inscribed on the roll of honor of
those who were paroled with Lee.*

The First Maryland cavalry was organized at Win-

---

*Appendix G.

chester, Va., on the 25th of November, 1862, with—
Major, Ridgely Brown.

Adjutant, George W. Booth.

Assistant Quartermaster, Capt. Ignatius Dorsey.

Surgeon, Wilbur R. McKnew.

Sergeant-Major, Edward Johnson.

Quartermaster Sergeant, Charles I. Tregner.

Company A: Captain, Frank A. Bond. First-Lieutenant, Thomas Griffith. Second-Lieutenant, J. A. V. Pue, Edward Beatty.

Company B: Captain, George M. Emack. Lieutenants, Mason E. McKnew, Adolphus Cook, Henry C. Blackiston.

Company C: Captain, Robert C. Smith. Lieutenants, George Howard, J. Jeff. Smith, Groeme Turnbull.

Company D: Captain, Warner G. Welsh. Lieutenants, William H. H. Dorsey, Stephen D. Lawrence, Milton Welsh.

Subsequently the battalion was joined by—

Company E: Captain, William J. Raisin. Lieutenants, John B. Burroughs, Nathaniel Chapman, Joseph K. Roberts.

Company F: Captain, Augustus F. Schwartz. Lieutenants, C. Irving Ditty, Fielder C. Slinghoff, Samuel G. Bond.

Thereupon Major Brown was promoted lieutenant-colonel, and Capt. Robert Carter Smith major.

In July, 1864, Capt. Gustavus W. Dorsey joined the battalion with Company K of the First Virginia cavalry as Company H: Captain, Gustavus W. Dorsey. Lieutenants, N. C. Hobbs, Edward Pugh. Second Lieutenant, Mr. Quinn. (Rudolphus Cecil had been killed in battle.)

The battalion served in the valley of Virginia in the brigade of Wm. E. Jones, as a constituent part of the Maryland Line, consisting of the First Maryland infantry, the First Maryland cavalry and the Second Maryland or Baltimore light artillery.

The winter of 1862-63 was employed in picketing and scouting General Jones' front and accompanying the command on various raids on the Baltimore & Ohio railroad and to collect provisions and horses. In the latter part of April, 1863, General Jones went through Moorefield and western Maryland, having numerous skirmishes at the villages of that region and collecting much spoil. On their way to Oakland in Maryland, at Greenland Gap, a pass in the mountain range, necessary to go through in order to reach their destination, they encountered a strong blockhouse of logs, garrisoned with one hundred and fifty infantry, which commanded the way. The Seventh Virginia, Col. Richard H. Dulany, was first ordered in, but was repulsed, its colonel badly and supposed mortally wounded. The First Maryland was then sent forward. The position was almost impregnable. The strong log house was crenelated and the garrison poured through its crevices a constant and devouring fire. Its only approach was by a path, along which only two could charge abreast. Brown took charge and with his adjutant, Booth, led the forlorn hope. With a small number of men they got up to the side of the house, and by sticking close to the wall and firing through the crevices with their revolvers, managed for some moments to live. Brown was shouting for fire, when both he and Booth were shot through the leg from muskets poked through the cracks at them. But the fire was got up and the house set in flames and then the garrison surrendered. Maj. Robert Carter Smith and Lieutenants Pue and Beatty of Company A were severely wounded. The First Maryland lost several in its rank and file. All the field and staff were wounded. After a few days Colonel Brown's, Major Smith's and Captain Booth's wounds became so bad that they had to be sent to the rear, when Capt. Frank A. Bond was assigned to the command.

In the movement on Pennsylvania in June, 1863, the First Maryland was assigned to the command of Brig.-

Gen. Albert G. Jenkins, who had been ordered to the valley with his cavalry brigade.   With Jenkins' brigade the First Maryland made the Gettysburg campaign and participated in all the raids, foragings and skirmishes of that command, General Jenkins being in the advance in Lee's forward movement.   When Lee withdrew from Gettysburg, Jenkins was sent with his brigade to protect the trains which were forwarded ahead of the infantry. Meade detached Kilpatrick's division down through Maryland to strike Lee's trains in the mountains, and at midnight it attacked them at Monterey, on the dividing line between Maryland and Pennsylvania—Mason and Dixon's line.   Emack's and Welsh's squadrons were at the point of attack.   They were thrown behind the stone fences, part held mounted, and as Kilpatrick's advance charged in the pitch dark, the Marylanders sent them whirling back, and charged them mounted.   These two squadrons held back Kilpatrick's division from midnight until dawn, when Jenkins got up, it having been impossible to pass the wagon train in the dark.   They saved Ewell's train, his ammunition and his ambulances with his wounded.   Passing on down the mountain, they again met the enemy's cavalry at Hagerstown, where a desperate hand-to-hand mêlée took place in the streets, and Maj. Ulric Dahlgren lost his leg.   Captain Bond also received a wound which lamed him for life.

After the army returned to Virginia the First cavalry served in Jenkins' brigade, and then in the brigades of Gens. Fitz Lee and Lomax until November, 1863, when it was ordered to report to Col. Bradley T. Johnson, commanding the Maryland Line.

CHAPTER X.

THE MARYLAND LINE.

AFTER the First regiment was mustered out of service August, 1862, and the army of Northern Virginia returned from Sharpsburg, the hope of Maryland seemed dead. The Second regiment and the First cavalry in the valley were ordered to report to Brig.-Gen. William E. Jones, commanding the Valley district. Steuart was brigadier, Elzey was major-general, and Johnson was colonel on a military court organized under an act of the Confederate Congress to sit as permanent general court-martial for each corps in the army. The Marylanders were more dispersed than ever.

When the campaign of 1863 opened, the Second Maryland led Ewell's advance on Winchester, and established its reputation for drill, for gallantry and for esprit, in the army. From Winchester Lee crossed the Potomac and moved into Pennsylvania. Johnson, chafing at being in the rear when the army was advancing, convinced Hon. James A. Seddon, secretary of war, that it was legal to constitute a regiment by consolidating the infantry and cavalry battalions, and he was commissioned colonel of the First regiment, Maryland Line. He was ordered to take command of all the Maryland battalions and companies in the army of Northern Virginia, and authorized to organize regiments and appoint officers for them and report to Maj.-Gen. Isaac R. Trimble. He left Richmond, took horse at Charlottesville, and rode rapidly through the country to Gettysburg, where he arrived on the evening of July 2d. He reported his orders to Trimble, who reported them to Ewell. Ewell had succeeded Jackson in command of the Second corps,

114

and knew Johnson well. He said in his crisp, brusque way, "This is no time to be swapping horses." The battle was then raging in his front. The next day, the 3d, Ewell assigned Johnson to the command of his old brigade, and he remained in command of the Second brigade until November, 1863, when at last the order assigning him to the Maryland Line was executed. General Lee ordered him to take the Second infantry, the First cavalry and the Baltimore light artillery (the Second Maryland) to Hanover Junction, where the Richmond, Fredericksburg & Potomac railroad crossed the Virginia Central and where five long, high bridges over the North Anna, the South Anna and the Middle river made the safety of the position essential to the transportation of Lee's army. Here then at last, after more than two years' effort and struggle, was the Maryland Line organized. During the winter it was reinforced by Maryland commands and Marylanders, until there were assembled more than fifteen hundred Marylanders under the Maryland flag, the largest number that was ever collected in war: more than Lord Sterling commanded at Long Island, or under DeKalb fell and died in front of Camden, or under Otho Williams swept the field at Eutaw, or by Howard's order charged at Cowpens, or broke the Grenadier Guards at Guilford.

It was composed of the élite of the State, young men charged with devotion to duty, honor, country, liberty, justice and right. Their gallantry in battle became an ideal of the army of Northern Virginia all through their service.

The commands assembled were: First Maryland cavalry, Lieut.-Col. Ridgely Brown; Maj. Robert Couter Smith; Adjutants George W. Booth, Tom Eager Howard Post.

Second Maryland infantry: Captain J. Parran Crane commanding; Lieut.-Col. Jos. R. Herbert and Maj. W. W. Goldsborough, both absent, wounded at Gettysburg.

First Maryland artillery, Capt. Wm. F. Dement.

Second Maryland artillery, Baltimore light, Capt. Wm. H. Griffin.

Fourth Maryland artillery, Chesapeake, Capt. Walter S. Chew.

The organizations of the batteries were as follows:

First Maryland: Captain, William F. Dement. Lieutenants, Charles S. Couter, John Gayle, Wm. J. Hill.

Second Maryland, Baltimore light artillery: Captain, William H. Griffin. Lieutenants, William B. Bean, John McNulty, J. W. Goodman.

Fourth Maryland, Chesapeake artillery: Captain, Walter S. Chew. Lieutenants, John E. Plater, Benjamin G. Roberts.

The field and staff consisted of: Bradley T. Johnson, colonel commanding; George W. Booth, captain and A. A. G.; Wilson Carey Nicholas, captain and A. I. G.; George H. Kyle, major and C. S.; Charles W. Harding, major and Q. M.; Richard P. Johnson, surgeon and medical director; Thos. S. Latimer, assistant surgeon; Rev. Thomas Duncan, chaplain· Andrew C. Trippe, lieutenant and ordnance officer.

During the winter General Lee conceived the plan of sending the Maryland Line, the cavalry minus their horses and the artillery minus their guns, across the Potomac in open boats to attack Point Lookout, where there were 15,000 Confederate prisoners with a strong guard of infantry and artillery. This forlorn hope was broken up by Federal movements around Hanover Junction, which rendered the Maryland Line more essential there than in any desperate forays against gunboats or fortified places and heavy artillery to rescue prisoners of war. About the 1st of March, 1864, Colonel Johnson was informed by telegram from army headquarters that a heavy force of cavalry had passed by the right flank of the Confederate army and was making its way for Hanover Junction, presumably to burn the bridges, and he was directed to protect them at every cost. He at once dispatched most of his cavalry in an expanding circle of scouts north and northeast, until after midnight he located the enemy moving by Frederick's Hall toward Ground Squirrel Bridge over the South Anna, five miles east of the railroad bridges. Posting all his infantry at the bridges, Colonel Johnson with the remnant of the First cavalry and the Baltimore light artillery pushed out toward the enemy. A mile from camp he struck a Federal picket approaching the bridges. A couple of shells and a rattling charge sent the raiders whirling whence they came. Johnson then moved along a parallel road to get between them and Richmond if possible. He had sixty sabers and four guns. At Ashland a party charged into the village, but were driven back, and the Marylanders pushed on to Yellow Tavern, where the road they were on ran into and joined the road by which the Federal Cavalry were pushing on to Richmond. Arriving at the point after his enemy, Johnson concealed his force behind a barn on the roadside and posted a picket on the Brooktown pike, just in front, along which the Federal cavalry were advancing. The advance of the Federals were thundering away with their artillery at the outside fortifications of Richmond. In a few minutes five horsemen in blue dashed up to the pickets, who were clad in Federal uniforms captured that morning. Two were killed and three captured. Among the captured was a lieutenant, staff officer of Colonel Dahlgren. From the prisoners was extracted with difficulty and by force the information that the enemy in front, attacking, was under Maj.-Gen. Judson Kilpatrick, with 3,000 sabers, and that Colonel Dahlgren with 500 more was on the river road and that this dispatch was to inform Kilpatrick of his whereabouts, and that he intended to charge into the city at dusk and expected General Kilpatrick to assist by charging at the same time. Thus, knowing his enemy's hand Colonel Johnson promptly trumped it. He picked up his sixty sabers and hurled them against Kilpatrick's rear guard on the Brook pike. He ran them in on Kilpatrick, who was shelling the Richmond defenses. That officer, seeing he was between the upper and the nether mill-stone, took horse and got out toward the Chickahominy, which he crossed, and went into camp at the Meadow Bridges, the Marylanders being on the side nearest Richmond. During the night Hampton came down on him with the First and Second North Carolina cavalry and ran him out of his camp. He stood not on the order of his going, but went at once, and at daylight Johnson and the Marylanders struck his trail. During the whole day they incessantly charged his rear guard and delayed and hindered his march. The ferry boats on the Pamunkey had all been sunk by Colonel Johnson's order as soon as he was notified of the movement of the enemy's cavalry by General Lee, the river was nowhere fordable, and Kilpatrick's only escape was by the peninsula to Fortress Monroe, or to a force sent thence to relieve and rescue him. At Old Church he was obliged to turn and fight. He put his 3,000 men and six guns in line of battle and sent one regiment out to charge his pursuers. He hadn't an idea of who or what they were. They might be Hampton with the whole of the Confederate cavalry pushing to gobble him up. The Federal charge drove the Marylanders back a mile with a loss of two men killed and one prisoner. As they were reforming to renew their attacks on Kilpatrick's rear guard, a courier reported that a heavy column was moving rapidly up on Colonel Johnson's rear and was then less than half a mile distant. Johnson had just time to dismount his men and rush them into the woods on each side of the road, but had not time to get his led horses out of the way when the Federals charged. They went through and the remnant rejoined Kilpatrick a mile distant, but the Marylanders killed, wounded and captured over a hundred men. This last detachment was a part of Dahlgren's command. Colonel Dahlgren, his communi-cation with Kilpatrick having been cut off by the capture of his dispatch at Yellow Tavern, had taken one hundred men and gone off to find him.   He had crossed the Pamunkey at Dabney's Ferry by swimming his horses and carrying his men and ammunition over in the sunken ferry boat, which he had found and raised, and was making his way back to the Union lines when he was killed in King and Queen county, the very night after the day the other part of his command cut its way through the Marylanders and escaped to Kilpatrick.

After this little episode the Marylanders stuck to Kilpatrick until he reached the railroad at Tunstall's Station, where he was received by an escort sent up for him by Major-General Butler from Fortress Monroe.   General Hampton reported that the exploits of the Maryland Line had saved Richmond, for, he said, Kilpatrick would certainly have ridden into Richmond if Colonel Johnson's attack in his rear had not paralyzed and delayed him so much that an infantry division could be brought up from the lines and set out to confront him.   He complimented Colonel Johnson by presenting him with a saber, the only other patterns of which were borne by Lieutenant-General Hampton and President Jefferson Davis. Major-General Elzey, commanding the district of Richmond, reported that Colonel Johnson and his command, the Maryland Line, had saved the city of Richmond, and issued a general order complimenting him and them.

On the 9th of May, 1864, Maj.-Gen. Phil. Sheridan passed by the right flank of the army of Northern Virginia.   Colonel Johnson was absent from the headquarters of the Maryland Line at the Junction, on a scout down the peninsula, leaving Colonel Brown in command.   In the afternoon Colonel Brown had information of the Federal movement and proceeded promptly to put himself in front of it, and before Richmond, with one hundred and fifty sabers. He came in contact with the enemy at about eleven o'clock that night about a mile from Beaver Dam Station on the Virginia Central railroad, now the

Chesapeake & Ohio railroad. The enemy was tearing up and destroying the railroad ties. Colonel Brown dismounted his command, about ninety men, the rest left as horse holders and as reserve. He himself got up close to them and saw their position. Returning to his command, he attacked and moved forward, driving in pickets and skirmishers sent out to stop him. He pressed them back on the line of Sheridan's command formed to receive him. Thirteen thousand to one hundred and fifty was odds. The Marylander was obliged to decline and Brown withdrew. The next morning, in obedience to a dispatch from Gen. J. E. B. Stuart to attack and delay them until he could get up, he stood against this overwhelming force all the morning, constantly forcing them to form line of battle and move forward in order. Stuart was thus able to get to Yellow Tavern just after Sheridan had passed that point and was about to attack Richmond. The Maryland Line paid dearly for the honor won that day. Capt. Schwartz, Company F, and Lieut. J. A. Ventris Pue, Company A, were badly wounded, and died on being carried off by the Federals to Washington. They did not die from wounds, but from maltreatment in being borne over bad roads in a rough ambulance. The ride killed them, not the bullets.

In the latter part of May Lee's army fell back to the line of the North Anna, and Grant as usual moved by his right and crossed the Pamunkey at Dabney's Ferry. Colonel Johnson and the cavalry of the Line happened to be near there watching for such a movement. Colonel Baker of North Carolina was there with Gordon's North Carolina brigade, and he attacked the party which had crossed the river and driven off the Confederate pickets. Gen. Fitzhugh Lee, to whom Colonel Johnson was temporarily reporting, directed him to go to the assistance of Baker. After a conference Johnson agreed that if Baker could hold the Federals while he, Johnson, could get around them, they two would capture the whole party. So Baker kept up a brisk skirmish, and Johnson moved up a side road to the right. He had not gone a mile when he met Baker's pickets coming back with the Federals at their heels, pressing so close that Johnson hardly had time to leave the narrow road and deploy in an open field before the enemy was on him. They killed Colonel Johnson's horse and shot his saber clean from his side. By the time he got out into the field a column of blue cavalry was going by his left flank and into his rear. So he attempted to withdraw decently and in order. But this was impossible. The Marylanders made repeated charges to get relief, to be as frequently driven back, until at last the only order of going was "*sauve qui peut.*" Out of two hundred and fifty men carried in they left seventy killed, wounded or missing. There was a larger percentage of killed than is usual in battle, for the fighting, as Jackson said about the Bucktail fight, "was close and bloody." Some of the finest young men of the Maryland Line lost their lives that day. Alexander Young, private in Company D, son of a former comptroller of the treasury of the United States under Buchanan's administration, was a model of manly beauty, of chivalry and grace, of courage and accomplishment. Beautiful as he was brave, refined as highly educated; intellectually, physically and morally he was a pattern gentleman. He died in his tracks, dismounted on the skirmish line, holding his place against a charge of mounted cavalry. This was known in the traditions of the Maryland Line as the fight at Pollard's Farm on May 27, 1864.

On the 1st of June following a force of Federal cavalry drove the First Maryland out of Hanover Court House over the Richmond & Fredericksburg railroad at Wickham's Crossing, back to the Virginia Central railroad not far north of Ashland. The bridges of the first road had ceased to be important, for Lee had fallen back between them and Richmond, but the Virginia Central

Md 16

bridges were very valuable, for they gave the only way by rail to the valley of Virginia. Colonel Johnson with his forces fought the enemy from hill-top to hill-top all the way from Wickham's back to the Virginia Central bridges, in hopes that reinforcements would be sent and thus the bridges saved, for he kept General Lee advised of his movements all day and he knew the conditions accurately. But no reinforcements came. At the very last effort, a desperate charge, Ridgely Brown was shot through the middle of the forehead and died without speaking a word. He was the bravest, the purest, the gentlest man from Maryland who died for liberty in that four years' war. His commanding officer recorded the estimation in which he was held by officers and men in these appropriate terms:

" Headquarters Maryland Line, June 6, 1864. General Order No. 26.

Lieut.-Col. Ridgely Brown, commanding First Maryland cavalry, fell in battle on the 1st instant near the South Anna. He died as a soldier prefers to die, leading a victorious charge.

As an officer, kind and careful; as a soldier, brave and true; as a gentleman, chivalrous; as a Christian, gentle and modest; no one in the Confederate army surpassed him in the hold he had on the hearts of his men and the place in the esteem of his superiors. Of the rich blood that Maryland has lavished on every battle field, none is more precious than his and that of our other brave comrades in arms who fell in the four days previous, on the hill sides of Hanover. His command has lost a friend most steadfast, but his commanding officer is deprived of an assistant invaluable. To the first he was ever as careful as a father, to the latter as true as a brother.

In token of respect for his memory the colors of the different regiments of this command will be draped and the officers wear the usual badge of military mourning for thirty days.

By order of Col. Bradley T. Johnson,

GEORGE W. BOOTH, A. A. G."

The Maryland cavalry under Colonel Johnson took a

conspicuous and useful part in the battle at Trevilian's on June 12th between the Confederate cavalry, 4,500 sabers under Hampton, and the Federal cavalry, 13,000 sabers under Sheridan. When Custer in a dashing charge rode through a vacant place in Hampton's center, Rosser from the left with his own brigade and the Maryland Line cavalry charged Custer's flank, and in turn rode through him, cutting him in two. The Marylanders captured over one hundred good horses and men completely armed and equipped.

After this engagement at Trevilian's, Colonel Johnson obtained permission from General Hampton to undertake an expedition he had been preparing for all the preceding winter at Hanover Junction. He proposed to pick two hundred men and horses, proceed by roads he knew well on the east foot of the Blue Ridge to the Potomac, within twenty miles of Washington, cross at a well-known ford and ride swiftly to the Soldiers' Home, twelve miles off, where Lincoln was in the habit of spending the summer nights, guarded by a small picket of cavalry, disperse that, mount the President on a strong horse behind an officer, and send him back into Virginia with five men. Johnson with the rest of the command was to strike west for Frederick, cut the way between Washington and Baltimore, isolate Frederick east and west, and try to cross the Potomac at Point of Rocks, at Shepherdstown or Williamsport, whichever should be found most practicable, or if pressed get beyond Cumberland and escape to the Virginia mountains by that route. But if they should be cut off entirely from Virginia, he intended to ride through Pennsylvania to Niagara and cross then into the British possessions. He believed that everything would be in such confusion on the disappearance of the President, who could not be heard of in less than two or three days, that he would have that much start and would easily get off. At any rate the prize was worth the risk, and the game the candle. So he left Hampton to ride his raid and was busily engaged near Gordonsville shoeing his horses and getting up his disunited men.

One day General Early came along with his corps to head off Hunter, then rapidly approaching Lynchburg. Colonel Johnson felt himself bound to disclose to General Early his projected raid, for he would unexpectedly be operating within the sphere of Early's movements, and the latter promptly prohibited it. " I want to make that expedition myself, and I want you and your cavalry to assist me in it. You go to Waynesboro in the valley and watch there, guarding my rear until I dispose of Mr. Hunter. As soon as I've smashed his little tea party, I'll come back and we'll go into Maryland together and see what we can do."

So instead of "riding his raid" Johnson marched to Waynesboro and waited with what patience nature had given him until Early's corps had returned to Staunton. Then Early assigned him to the command of Wm. E. Jones' cavalry brigade, Jones having been killed at New Hope church below Staunton on Hunter's advance up the valley. The First Maryland cavalry and the Baltimore light artillery were added to the command. In a few days Colonel Johnson received his commission of brigadier-general. He made Capt. George W. Booth assistant adjutant-general of brigade, Booth having been his adjutant with the First Maryland infantry and with the Maryland Line at Hanover Junction, and for gallantry, for intelligence, for industry, for zeal, for self control and cool courage being unexcelled by any man high or low in the army of Northern Virginia.

General Johnson, in charge of the advance, moved rapidly through Winchester, marching on Shepherdstown. At Leetown, south of Martinsburg and northwest of Harper's Ferry, he encountered General Mulligan with 3,000 infantry and a six-gun battery to stop him. He promptly attacked Mulligan, and after more than half a day's fight drove him away. Johnson's cavalry brigade consisted of 8oo mounted men, one four-gun battery, and a number of dismounted men who had lost their horses in the preceding thirty days, fighting Hunter, and were now following their command to take the chances of a horse turning up. Like the Welshman, if somebody would furnish them with a bridle, they would find a horse. From Leetown Johnson crossed the Potomac at Shepherdstown, passed rapidly through Sharpsburg to Boonsboro, on the 4th of July, leaving a large infantry force on Maryland Heights on his right and rear, depending on Early's infantry to take care of them. From Boonsboro he pressed down the National road through Middletown on Frederick. At Middletown he ran into a regiment of Federal cavalry, the Eighth Illinois, and Alexander's Maryland battery. Pushing them back and over the mountain, he drove them to the suburbs of Frederick, where he found a large force of infantry deployed in front of the town. He sent Lieutenant-Colonel Dunn with his Virginia regiment over to the Harper's Ferry road, while he proposed to move by the reservoir road into the opposite end of the town. Frederick was his native place and he was hourly informed of the condition of things and the troops defending the place. He was convinced that a simultaneous charge by Colonel Dunn at one end and by himself at the other would result in the capture of the town and all the troops in it. It was crammed with a wagon train escaping from Harper's Ferry, whence Gordon, of Early's command, had driven them.

Just as he got in motion for this attack, Maj.-Gen. Robert Ransom, commanding Early's cavalry, came up, and being informed of what was proposed, countermanded it and ordered Johnson back to the mountain at Hagan's on the top of it. He said that General Johnson was too enthusiastic and sanguine to get home, and that he would be cut to pieces. That night General Early gave General Johnson his orders, just received from General Lee by Robert E. Lee, his son. General Lee had singular tenacity and persistency of mind. He had formed the plan the preceding winter to send Johnson and the Maryland Line across the Potomac in boats to release the prisoners at Point Lookout. That plan had been frustrated by the movements of Kilpatrick and Sheridan, and now he recurred to it as soon as there was a possibility of accomplishing it. He directed General Early to detach Johnson with orders to move around the north of Baltimore, burn the bridges on the railroads leading north and cut the wires; then, circling round, to break the communication between Washington and Baltimore; then move on Point Lookout and attack at daylight on the 12th of July, when an attack would be made from the water side by Capt. John Taylor Wood, who would run out of Wilmington and by Fortress Monroe in a Confederate gun-boat. When the prisoners, some 15,000, were released, Johnson was to assume command and march them to Bladensburg, where General Early was to wait for them, when Washington was to be carried, communication established across the Potomac, and Grant's army forced to release Richmond and come back to recover Washington.

Johnson showed the commanding general that the time allowed was entirely insufficient. It was then the 8th of July and he was ordered to be at Point Lookout on the morning of the 12th, three days and three nights to make a march of two hundred and fifty miles. Horse flesh couldn't do it. However, it was orders, and no more was to be said. The explanation was made to account for the inevitable result. The next morning at daylight he started, rode through Westminster to Reisterstown and Cockeysville, where he arrived on the morning of Sunday, July 10th. At that point he detached Lieut.-Col. Harry Gilmor, who with the Second Maryland cavalry had been attached to his command on the march down the valley, with orders to move on to the railroad connecting Baltimore and Philadelphia, burn the bridges over the Gunpowder and Bush rivers and then report to him in the neighborhood of Washington, where he would be by the 14th. Gilmor accomplished the object of his expedition, burned the bridges, captured a passenger train on which was Major-General Franklin of the Federal army, who subsequently escaped during the night, and reported as per orders on the 14th, at Poolesville. Johnson, after burning the bridge at Cockeysville, turned round and rode rapidly around north of Baltimore. When five miles from that city, it was reported to him that the home of Governor Bradford, governor of Maryland, was only a short distance down the road. He at once detailed Lieutenant Blackstone, Company B, First Maryland cavalry, with a detail of a few men and written orders to burn the house, in retaliation for the burning of the home of Governor Letcher of Virginia by General Hunter at Lexington within the preceding thirty days. Such debts require prompt payment, and this was paid in thirty days without grace.

From Cockeysville he had dispatched a friend into Baltimore to find out the condition of the transportation on the Baltimore & Ohio railroad, and he left two men at Hayfields, John Merryman's place, to bring him the report of his scout about midnight. He stopped at the Caves, the place of John Canon, Esq., about midnight, to feed. While there his couriers from Hayfields got up and reported that the Nineteenth corps, General Emory, had arrived in transports and was at Locust Point and was being landed on the trains of the Baltimore & Ohio and hurried to Washington. Johnson sent this information to Early by an officer and five men, with orders to ride at speed, seizing horses as fast as theirs gave out. Thence he rode across Montgomery and Howard counties to Beltsville on the Baltimore & Ohio railroad to Washington, where he struck a thousand Federal cavalry and drove them

helter-skelter into Bladensburg. After cutting the railroad he started for Point Lookout, distant eighty miles,
with seventeen hours to make it. He sent couriers
ahead to tell the people he was coming, and that they
must have their horses on the roadside ready to be exchanged for his broken-down ones. They would have
done it, for they were all ardent Southerners. Just as
his column got in motion, he received an order from General Early to report to him at once. Turning the head
of the column toward Washington, he caught Early that
night near Blair's house at Silver Spring and, as usual,
took the rear guard. At Rockville there was a halt to
feed, when a regiment of Federal cavalry charged them,
but was driven back with loss. The Marylanders,
however, did not escape unscathed. Capt. Wilson Carey
Nicholas, acting inspector-general of the Maryland Line,
leading the charge of the 'first squadron, had his horse
shot and was himself shot and taken prisoner. He was
as good a soldier and as gallant a gentleman as ever
rode a horse in that war.

From Rockville, still covering the rear, Johnson's brigade followed the army to Poolesville, where during half
the day it covered Early, recrossing the Potomac. His
trains were long, piled with plunder, and his herds of
cattle and horses very large. The Federals pressed
down on the rear guard with pertinacity and in force,
but the cavalry held them until dark, and the Baltimore
light artillery fired the last shots, as the First cavalry
were the last troops that crossed the Potomac, on Early's
withdrawal from Maryland in 1864. He had received
Johnson's dispatch from the Caves, reporting the arrival
of the Nineteenth corps, just in time to countermand the
order for an assault at daylight next morning on the
apparently deserted Federal fortification. The morning
revealed those same works crammed with troops, and
Johnson's dispatch, therefore, probably saved him from a
great disaster, for the works were impregnable to assault

when fully manned. This ride from July 9th to July 13th was probably the longest ride taken during the war. It was one hundred and twenty hours in which the men never dismounted except to unsaddle and feed once every twenty-four hours, and of course they ate what they could pick up on the roadside, and slept in their saddles.

After crossing the river, Johnson's brigade followed Early to Winchester, and in a short time to Martinsburg. From that point General Early dispatched Gen. John McCausland with his own and Johnson's brigade to demand a contribution from Chambersburg, Pa., in retaliation for the burning of the houses of Hon. Alexander R. Boteler, Andrew Hunter and Edmund Lee at Shepherdstown and Charlestown a short time before. He sent a written demand on the authorities of Chambersburg for $100,000 in gold and $500,000 in greenbacks for the purpose of indemnifying these losers from Hunter's barbarities, or, in default of payment, he ordered the town to be burned. The expedition started on July 29th and reached Chambersburg on the 30th. McCausland then sought the town authorities, but they had fled. He then caused the court house bell to be rung to call together a town meeting to make his demand known to them. But the panic-stricken people would trust themselves in no conference with the "rebels." They did not believe, and they were not chary in saying so, that the rebels would never dare to burn their town; they were afraid to do so. This was really the tone assumed by the people of Chambersburg that morning. Finding delay useless and dangerous, McCausland set fire to the court house, which made a flaming beacon of fast-coming disaster, and in five minutes the whole town was in a blaze from twenty different points.

The Confederates were withdrawn from the burning town and started for Virginia. They moved up to Cumberland, but finding General Kelly there with a force too strong for them, turned off and recrossed the Potomac at

Old Town, in Hampshire county, now West Virginia. Thence they moved on the Baltimore & Ohio railroad at New Creek, and finding that heavily fortified and defended, proceeded to Moorefield in Hardy county, where they camped on the 6th of August. The First and Second Maryland had been placed under command of Lieut.-Col. Harry Gilmor and were camped up the Romney road. The lines were made, the camps pitched and the pickets posted according to the orders of Brigadier-General McCausland, the commanding officer of the expedition, and Brigadier-General Johnson obeyed his orders. Next morning before day Averell surprised Johnson's picket on the Romney road, captured the reserve, and then rode over the camps of the two Maryland battalions. Johnson just escaped capture and endeavored to rally his brigade. But the surprise was too nerve-shattering. The Twenty-first Virginia, Col. William E. Peters, was the only regiment that could be held in hand. Peters was a man of iron resolution and imperturbable courage. He couldn't be shaken. Earthquakes, tornadoes, electric storms couldn't move him. He would have stopped and asked, " What next? " if the earth were opening beneath him and the mountains falling on him. Johnson set him to hold Averell, while he brought the rest of the brigade to his support. But the Federal rush, the élan of success, was too strong. It carried off the Twenty-first Virginia like chaff before the whirlwind, leaving Peters shot through the body, mortally wounded, if any wound can be mortal. But human will triumphs over human anatomy and surgical skill, and Peters survives to this day as indomitable in his Latin professorship as he was that drear morning at Moorefield.

After the return from Chambersburg, the Maryland Line in Johnson's cavalry brigade was actively engaged in all the operations of Early in the valley. There was not a fight in which the Marylanders were not in front. Like the clan McDonald, which refused to charge at

Culloden because it had been placed on the left of the line of battle, and McDonald since Bannockburn had always held the right of the clans, they always were in front, whether posted there or not.   They took it, and held it!

After Early was expelled from the valley by the overwhelming force of Sheridan, the Maryland Line cavalry and artillery were attached to Davidson's brigade, afterward commanded by Gen. Wm. L. Jackson.   There they served in Lomax's cavalry division during the winter until March, 1865, when the remnant of Early's command was dispersed by Sheridan at Waynesboro.   As Sheridan pursued Early across the mountains toward Richmond, the Marylanders hung on his flank and annoyed him as flies worry a horse, but could do no harm.

In the latter part of March, 1865, they were ordered to report to General Fitz Lee at Stony Creek.   Reaching Richmond the evening of April 1st they camped there, and next day, Sunday, April 2d, saw the evacuation of the capital of the Confederacy.   The Marylanders had then been reduced to less than one hundred.   At Stony Creek they found General Lee had moved, and they received orders to cover the rear of Mahone's division, the rear guard of the army.   On the 4th of April, Colonel Dorsey, commanding the First Maryland, joined Gen. Fitzhugh Lee and was assigned to Gen. Wm. H. Payne's brigade.   General Payne was wounded at Amelia Springs and was succeeded by Gen. Thos. T. Munford. Under him, the Marylanders, like the McDonalds, always nearest the enemy, kept the enemy pursuing them in check.   On the 9th of April a heavy force of the Federal cavalry was seen moving along Munford's front, parallel to it.   Dorsey mounted his men and, pulling down a fence in his front, was moving through the gaps in it toward the enemy.   As soon as his first section had passed through, they saw the Federals in full charge at them not a hundred yards off.   " We must charge them," said Capt. William J. Raisin, "that's our only chance."

" Draw saber, gallop, charge!" was Dorsey's order, and the Marylanders hurled themselves on the advancing foe and drove him back. This was the last cavalry charge made in the army of Northern Virginia. William C. Price, Company E, was killed. His was the last blood shed in the war in Virginia. As General Munford well said in his farewell address to the Marylanders, " You spilled the first blood of the war in Baltimore and you shed the last in Virginia."

Munford did not surrender at Appomattox. None of the cavalry did. They marched away to Lynchburg. In ten days Colonel Dorsey got an order to move up the valley to Salem. When they arrived at Cloverdale in Botetourt county, they received this parting address from Munford, " the bravest of the brave."

" Cloverdale, Botetourt Co., Va., April 28, 1865.
Lieutenant-Colonel Dorsey,
        Commanding First Maryland Cavalry:
I have just learned from Captain Emack that your gallant band was moving up the valley in response to my call. I am deeply pained to say that our army cannot be reached, as I have learned it has capitulated. It is sad indeed to think that our country's future is all shrouded in gloom. But for you and your command there is the consolation of having faithfully done your duty. Three years ago the chivalric Brown joined my old regiment with twenty-three Maryland volunteers, with light hearts and full of fight. I soon learned to respect, admire and love them for all those qualities which endear soldiers to their officers. They recruited rapidly, and as they increased in numbers, so did their reputation and friends increase; and they were soon able to take a position of their own.

Need I say when I see that position so high and almost alone among soldiers, that my heart swells with pride to think that a record so bright and glorious is in some part linked with mine? Would that I could see the mothers and sisters of every member of your battalion, that I might tell them how nobly you have represented your State and maintained our cause.

But you will not be forgotten. The fame you have

won will be guarded by Virginia with all the pride she feels in her own true sons, and the ties which have linked us together, memory will preserve.

You who struck the first blow in Baltimore and *the last in Virginia* have done all that could be asked of you. Had the rest of our officers and men adhered to our cause with the same devotion, to-day we should have been free from Yankee thralldom. I have ordered the brigade to return to their homes, and it behooves us now to separate.

With my warmest wishes for your welfare, and a hearty God bless you, I bid you farewell.

THOMAS T. MUNFORD,
Brigadier-General Commanding Division.''

And so closes the record of the Maryland Line in the army of the Confederate States. It is inscribed on the pages of the history of the army of Northern Virginia. It fired the first gun in the Seven Days' battles. It fired the first gun in Early's advance into Maryland in 1864, when he crossed the Potomac at Shepherdstown, and the last, when he recrossed at Poolesville. It struck the first blow and shed the first blood of the revolution in Baltimore on the 19th of April, 1861, and made the last charge at Appomattox, April 9, 1865. Future generations of Marylanders will be proud of its achievements, and in the South I hope its memory will be honored and loved.

ROSTER OF MARYLAND LINE.*

PROVISIONAL ARMY OF THE CONFEDERATE STATES.

FIRST MARYLAND INFANTRY.

FIELD AND STAFF.

Colonels—Arnold Elzey, June 17, 1861; promoted brigadier-general July 21, 1861, major-general December 4, 1862. George H. Steuart, July 21, 1861; promoted brigadier-general March 18, 1862. Bradley T. Johnson, March 18, 1862; promoted brigadier-general June 28, 1864.

Lieutenant-Colonels—George H. Steuart, June 17, 1861; Bradley T. Johnson, July 21, 1861; E. R. Dorsey, March 18, 1862.

Majors—Bradley T. Johnson, June 17, 1861; E. R. Dorsey, July 21, 1861.

Acting—Adjutants, Lieutenant Frank X. Ward, Company H; Lieutenant George W. Booth, Company D. Surgeons, E. T. Galliard, R. P. Johnson. Assistant-Surgeons, Styles Kennedy, Thos. S. Latimer. Captain and A. Q. M., Grafton D. Spurrier, Chas. W. Harding, Septimus H. Stewart. Captain and A. C. S., John E. Howard. Chaplain, Stephen J. Cameron. Sergeant-Major, George W. Bishop, Philip L. Moore. Quarter-master-Sergeant, Chas. J. Wegner. Chief Musician, Alex. Hubbard. Drum Major, Hosea Pitt.

LINE.

Company A—Captain, Bradley T. Johnson, Wm. W. Goldsborough. First-Lieutenant, George K. Shellman.

---

* NOTE.—This is not presented as a complete roster. It is compiled from such muster rolls as have been found in the War Records Office at Washington, with additions from memory.

Second-Lieutenant, Chas. W. Blair, Geo. M. E. Shearer, W. H. B. Dorsey, John F. Groshon. Sergeants, John T. Smith, George Tyler, D. Windsor Kessler, W. H. Pope. Corporals, Francis T. Bender, Wm. Ritter, Perry McDowell, James Abbott. Musician, Alex J. Hubbard.

Company B—Captain, Chas. C. Edelin. First-Lieutenant, James Mullen. Second-Lieutenant, Thomas Costello, Jos. Griffin. First-Sergeant, Peter Boyle. Sergeants, George Moog, Daniel Dougherty, Jas. Lemates. Corporals, George Bates, Wm. Haffey, Dennis O'Brien, George Probest. Musician, Joseph Smith.

Company C—Captain, Robert C. Smith, E. R. Dorsey. First-Lieutenant, Septimus H. Stewart. Second-Lieutenant, Wm. P. Thomas. First-Sergeant, Wm. Smyth. Sergeants, Sterling Murray, John B. Berryman, John H. Uhlhorn. Corporals, Chas. A. Arnold, John O'Loughlin, Frank S. Price, Henry C. Scott. Musician, Hosea Pitt.

Company D — Captain, James R. Herbert. First-Lieutenant, Geo. W. Booth. Second-Lieutenant, Wm. Key Howard, Nicholas Snowden. First-Sergeant, Geo. F. Ruff. Sergeants, Chas. J. Wegner, Wm. H. Slingluff, Edward L. King, Mason E. McKnew. Corporals, Edward Selvage, Jos. Wranck, Washington Hands, Wm. Weber. Musician, Chas. Tuttle, Jas. M. Ruley.

Company E—Captain, Edmund O'Brien, Harry McCoy. First-Lieutenant, John J. Lutts. Second-Lieutenant, John Cushing, Jr., Jos. G. W. Marriott. First-Sergeant, Geo. G. Raborg. Sergeants, Napoleon Camper, Green H. Barton, Wm. T. Wallis, Robert H. Cushing. Corporals, Patrick H. Williams, Thos. H. Davidson, Joseph T. Doyle, Alfred Pearce. Musician, Wm. Gannon, Michael Quinn.

Company F—Captain, J. Louis Smith. First-Lieutenant, Wm. D. Hough. Second-Lieutenant, Wm. J. Broadfoot, Joseph H. Stewart. First-Sergeant, Geo. W. Foos. Sergeants, John Marny, John Morris, Samuel A. Kennedy.   Corporals, John Ryan, Michael McCourt, Edward Sheehan, Owen Callen.   Musician, Francis Farr.

Company G—Captain, Wilson C. Nicholas.   First-Lieutenant, Alexander Cross.   Second-Lieutenant, Edward Deppish.   First-Sergeant, John J. Platt.   Sergeants, James Farrell, Louis Neidhammer, James Shields.   Corporals, George Ross, Eli Fishpan, Samuel Kirk, Charles Fercoit.   Musician, Andrew Myers.

Company H—Captain, Wm. H. Murray.   First-Lieutenant, George Thomas.   Second-Lieutenant, Francis X. Ward, Richard T. Gilmor, W. P. Dollinger.   First-Sergeant, John H. Sullivan.   Sergeants, McHenry Howard, James Lyon, Chapman B. Briscoe.   Corporals, Edward Johnson, Richard C. Mackall, Clapham Murray, Wm. S. Lemmon.

Company I—Captain, Michael S. Robertson.   First-Lieutenant, Hugh Mitchell.   Second-Lieutenant, Hezekiah H. Bean, Eugene Diggs.   First-Sergeant, John J. Brawner.   Sergeants, John H. Stone, F. L. Higdon, Wm. H. Rison, Warren W. Ward.   Corporals, Z. Francis Freeman, Francis L. Higdon, Thomas I. Green, Thomas L. Hannon.

Company C (Second)—Captain, Edmund Barry.   First-Lieutenant, John Marshall.   Second-Lieutenant, Wm. H. Edelin, Tom Washington Smith.   First-Sergeant, Albert Tolson.   Sergeants, Richard Brown, William Barry. (This company was enlisted in Richmond and united with the regiment.   No muster roll of this company has been found in the war records.)

Battles and actions in which the First Maryland infantry was engaged: Manassas, Mason's Hill, Munson's Hill, Rappahannock River, Front Royal, Winchester, Harrisonburg, Cross Keys, Mechanicsville, Gaines' Mill, Dispatch Station, Malvern Hill, Harrison Landing.

SECOND MARYLAND INFANTRY.

FIELD AND STAFF.

Lieutenant-Colonel, James R. Herbert; Major, Wm. W. Goldsborough; Surgeon, Richard P. Johnson; Assistant-Surgeon, DeWilton Snowden; A. Q. M., John E. Howard; Adjutant, J. Winder Laird; Sergeant-Major, Wm. R. McCullough; Q. M. Sergeant, Edwin James; Ordnance-Sergeant, Francis L. Higdon; Chief Musician, Michael A. Quinn.

LINE.

Company A — Captain, Wm. H. Murray, George Thomas. First-Lieutenant, Clapham Murray. Second-Lieutenant, Wm. P. Zollinger. First-Sergeant, Wm. L. Blackiston. Sergeants, Jas. F. Pearson, Jas. W. Thomas, Ezekiel S. Dorsey, Wm. H. Smith. Corporals, Willis Brancock, Chas. E. Maguire, George Denton, Lawrence K. Thomas. Musician, Wm. Gannon.

Company B—Captain, J. Parran Crane. First-Lieutenant, J. H. Stone. Second-Lieutenant, Chas. B. Wise, Jas. H. Wilson. First-Sergeant, Philip T. Reeder. Sergeants, John G. Barber, Francis Z. Freeman, Wittingham Hammett. Corporals, Thomas Simms, Wm. F. Wheatley, John Z. Downing, Albert Fenwick. Musician, Chas. T. Drury.

Company C—Captain, Ferdinand Duvall. First-Lieutenant, Chas. W. Hodges. Second-Lieutenant, Thomas H. Tolson, Joseph W. Barber. First-Sergeant, Wm. T. Outten. Sergeants, Robert T. Hodges, George Probest, Wm. Ritter, Thos. D. Barron. Corporals, Edward A. Welch, Beale D. Mullikin, John W. Collins, Chas. Clayton.

Company D—Captain, Jas. L. McAleer. First-Lieutenant, Jas. S. Franklin. Second-Lieutenant, Samuel T. McCullough. First-Sergeant, Thos. C. Butler. Sergeants, Wm. Jenkins, J. Wm. Proudt, Isaac Sherwood, Edwin

Gover.   Corporals, Geo. W. McAtee, Alfred Riddlemoser, John McCready.

Company E—Captain, John W. Torsch.   First-Lieutenant, Wm. J. Broadfoot.   Second-Lieutenant, Wm. R. Byus, Jos. P. Quinn.   First-Sergeant, Samuel Kirk. Sergeants, Geo. L. Ross, Wilbur Ritter, Wm. Heaphy. Corporals, John Cain, Lewis P. Staylor, Jas. Reddie, Benj. F. Amos.   Musician, Joseph Smith, Jas. L. Aubrey.

Company F—Captain, A. J. Gwynn.   First-Lieutenant, John W. Polk.   Second-Lieutenant, David C. Forrest, John G. Hyland.   First-Sergeant, Nicholas J. Mills. Sergeants, Walter J. Randall, Philip T. Muirhead, Thos. O. Hodges, Joseph O. Wagner.   Corporals, Jas. H. Dixon, Jas. T. Brown, Washington Martin.

Company G—Captain, Thos. R. Stewart.   First-Lieutenant, G. G. Guillette, James A. Davis.   Second-Lieutenant, Geo. Brighthaupt, Wm. C. Wrightson.   First-Sergeant, Daniel A. Fenton.   Sergeants, Geo. W. Manning, Michael C. Holohan, Algernon Henry, Patrick O'Connell. Corporals, Jas. E. Briddle, Henry A. Mumford, Wm. Lord, Benj. F. Twilley.

Company H—Captain, J. Thos. Bussey.   First-Sergeant, Thos. O'Brien.   Sergeants, John J. Powers.   Corporals, Patrick Keenan, John J. Ward.

Battles in which the Second Maryland regiment· infantry was engaged: Winchester, Gettysburg, Cold Harbor, White Oak Swamp, Weldon Railroad, Squirrel Level Road, Hatcher's Run, Pegram's Farm, Appomattox, Petersburg.   Steuart's brigade, to which the Second Maryland was assigned, assaulted Culp's Hill at Gettysburg, July 2, 1863, and took the line of Federal works, occupying the same through the night.   On the following morning a further advance movement was attempted, which, however, failed, and after a desperate conflict the Confederate line was retired to the position on Rock Creek.   The Second Maryland has commemorated this service by the erection of a monument which stands on the Federal line of works. The regiment carried into action about 400 muskets, of which force more than one-half were killed or wounded.

FIRST MARYLAND CAVALRY.

FIELD AND STAFF.

Lieutenant-Colonels—Ridgely Brown, Robert Carter Smith, Gus. W. Dorsey.

Majors—Ridgely Brown, Robert Carter Smith.

Adjutants—Geo. W. Booth, John E. H. Post.

Assistant-Surgeon—Wilbur R. McKnew; A. Q. M., Ignatius W. Dorsey; Sergeant-Majors, Edward Johnson, John E. H. Post, Arthur Bond; Quartermaster-Sergeant, Chas. J. Wegner; Orderly-Sergeant, Edward Johnson.

LINE.

Company A—Captain, Frank A. Bond. First-Lieutenant, Thomas Griffith. Second-Lieutenant, J. A. V. Pue, Edward Beatty. First-Sergeant, John H. Scholl. Sergeants, Hammond Dorsey, Frank Griffith, Joshua Riggs, Chas. R. Cockey. Corporals, Wm. Wilson, Bazil Clark, Arthur Bond, John Harding.

Company B—Captain, Geo. M. Emack. First-Lieutenant, Mason E. McKnew. Second-Lieutenant, Adolphus Cook, Henry C. Blackiston. First-Sergeant, S. B. Spencer. Sergeants, W. A. Wilson, W. H. W. Guyther, D. M. Turner, O. H. Perry. Corporals, G. M. Serpell, J. J. Spear, Pembroke Jones, J. R. H. Deakins, Robert Carvell.

Company C—Captain, Robert C. Smith. First-Lieutenant, Geo. Howard. Second-Lieutenant, T. Jeff Smith, T. J. Green, Graeme Turnbull, Jas. D. Walters. First-Sergeant, Illinois Carruthers. Sergeants, Geo. Smith Norris, E. Clarence Neale, Wm. F. Dorsey, Hamilton Lefevre. Corporals, Richard Knox, Richard C. Smith, LaFayette Hause.

Company D—Captain, Warner G. Welch. First-Lieu.

tenant, Wm. H. Dorsey. Second-Lieutenant, Stephen D. Lawrence, Milton Welch. First-Sergeant, Phineas I. Davis. Sergeants, Upton L. Dorsey, Thomas G. Worthington, Albert Jones, Lewis W. Trail. Corporals, Geo. R. Simpson, Edwin Selvage, Geo. R. Cather, Rich H. Norris.

Company E—Captain, Wm. J. Raisin. First-Lieutenant, S. B. Burroughs. Second-Lieutenant, Nathaniel Chapman, Jos. K. Roberts, Jr. First-Sergeant, Townley Robey. Sergeants, John Savage, Solomon Wright, Thos. H. Gemmill. Corporals, Geo. T. Hollyday, Benj. J. Turton, Henry C. Wallis, John W. Slaven.

Company F—Captain, Aug. F. Schwartz. First-Lieutenant, C. Irving Ditty. Second-Lieutenant, Fielder C. Slingluff, Samuel G. Bond. First-Sergeant, Josiah H. Slingluff. Sergeants, Howard H. Kinsey, Henry A. Wile. Corporals, Wilbur J. Rolph, John W. Latham, Jos. C. Shorb.

Company K—Captain, 'Geo. R. Gaither, Gus. W. Dorsey, N. C. Hobbs. First-Lieutenant, Rudolphus Cecil, George Howard. Second-Lieutenant, E. H. D. Pue, Samuel W. Dorsey, George Howard, Ridgely Brown, Thomas Griffith, Frank A. Bond. First-Sergeant, Robert Floyd. Sergeants, W. H. Wright, Geo. Buckingham, Ira Albaugh, W. W. Burgess. Corporals, F. Leo Wills, William Barnes, B. H. Morgan, Robert Bruce, James Oliver.

Some of the actions in which the First Maryland cavalry was engaged: Kernstown, Maurytown, Greenland Gap, Oakland, Morgantown, Bridgeport, Cairo, Middletown, Winchester, Hagerstown, Morton's Ford, Brandy Station, Auburn or Cedar Creek, Buckland, Gainesville, Taylorsville, Pollard's Farm, Old Church, Beaver Dam, Dabney's Ferry, Ashland, Trevilian's Station, Leetown, Bladensburg, Rockville, Poolesville, Gettysburg, Martinsburg, Charlestown, Bunker Hill, Fisher's Hill, Madison C. H., Liberty Mills, High Bridge, Appomattox.

SECOND MARYLAND CAVALRY.

No official muster rolls of this command having been found, a partial list is given from various sources.

FIELD AND STAFF.

Lieutenant-Colonel, Harry Gilmor; Adjutant, Herman F. Keidel; Quartermaster, N. W. Owings; Sergeant-Major, Edward Williams; Quartermaster-Sergeant, Wm. Allen.

LINE.

Company A—Captain, Nicholas Burke. First-Lieutenant, W. W. McKaig. Second-Lieutenant, John B. Wells. Second Lieutenant, Meredith Gilmor. First-Sergeant, Jos. Stansbury. Second-Sergeant, Alonzo Travers.

Company B—Captain, Eugene Diggs. First-Lieutenant, Harrison. Second-Lieutenant, J. C. Holmes.

Company C—Captain, David M. Ross. First-Lieutenant, Richard T. Gilmor. Second-Lieutenant, Geo. Forney, Wm. H. Kemp. First-Sergeant, Frederick Baker. Sergeants, M. Todd, Fields, John Bosley. Corporals, W. H. Todd, John Emmerick, Henry Bushbaum.

Company D—Captain, J. R. Burke. First-Lieutenant, Polk Burke.

Company E—Captain, J. E. Sudler. First-Lieutenant, Geo. Ratcliffe. Sergeant, J. C. Holmes.

Company F—Captain, Jas. L. Clark. First-Lieutenant, W. H. Richardson. Second-Lieutenant, Wm. Dorsey, E. Hurst, Jas. McAleese. First-Sergeant, J. A. Stine. Sergeants, J. Sprigg, L. McMullin, R. Hahn, Robert Kemp, T. Kidd. Corporals, J. Andre, C. J. Stewart, S. C. Magraw.

FIRST MARYLAND ARTILLERY.

"MARYLAND."

Captain, R. Snowden Andrews, W. F. Dement. First-Lieutenant, Chas. S. Couter. Second-Lieutenant, John

Gale, Frederick Y. Dabney, W. J. Hill, J. H. Stonestreet.
First-Sergeant, De Wilton Snowden, J. Harris Forbes,
Gratial C. Thompson.   Corporals, F. W. Bollinger,
Theodore Jenkins, Geo. T. Scott, E. C. Moncure, P. A.
L. Couter, J. G. Harris, John F. Ransom.

Battles and actions of the First Maryland Artillery:
Chickahominy, Evansport, Mechanicsville, Cedar Moun-
tain, Gaines' Mill, 2nd Manassas, Malvern Hill, Harper's
Ferry, 1st Cold Harbor, 2nd Cold Harbor, Sharpsburg,
Hamilton's Crossing, 1st Fredericksburg, 2nd Fredericks-
burg, Winchester, Mine Run, Gettysburg, Turkey Ridge,
Petersburg, White Sulphur Springs, Squirrel Level
Road.

SECOND MARYLAND ARTILLERY.

"BALTIMORE LIGHT."

Captain, John B. Brockenbrough, Wm. H. Griffin.
First-Lieutenant, Wm. B. Bean, John McNulty.
Second-Lieutenant, Jas. T. Wilhelm, J. W. Goodman.
First-Sergeant, W. Wirt Robinson. Sergeants, W. Y.
Glenn, George Poindexter, John F. Hayden, John
Powers, Andrew J. Byrne, J. H. Smith. Corporals,
Wm. C. Dunn, Patrick Kirby, Lewis F. Talbott, Wm.
H. Kendrick, Jas. O'Grady.

Some of the battles and actions of the Baltimore Light
Artillery: Rappahannock, Front Royal, Winchester,
Bolivar Heights, Fishers' Hill, Harrisonburg, Cross Keys,
Gaines' Mill, Dispatch Station, Malvern Hill, Second
Manassas, Harpers' Ferry, Moorfield, Sharpsburg, Kern-
stown, Carlisle, Pa., Gettysburg, Hagerstown, Mine
Run, Brandy Station, Old Town, Yellow Tavern, Mar-
tinsville, Poolesville, Maurytown.

THIRD MARYLAND ARTILLERY.

Captain, Henry B. Latrobe, Ferd. O. Claiborne, John
B. Rowan, Wm. L. Ritter. Lieutenants, Ferdinand O.
Claiborne, W. Thompson Patten, Holmes Erwin, T. D.

Giles, J. W. Doncaster. Assistant-Surgeon, Thos. J. Rogers. First-Sergeant, Rufus McCeeney. Quartermaster, A. T. Emory. Sergeants, Jas. M. Buchanan, Jr., John P. Hooper, E. H. Langley, Joseph Lackey, L. W. Frazier, J.W. Smith, Wm. Fleming, Daniel Toomey, Edw. Wynn, A. J. Davis. Corporals, B. F. Weaver, S. G. W. Gerding, Jos. Edgar, M. H. I'Connell, W. H. Erwin, G. W. Hancock, T. H. Jones, J. C. Pendley, V. P. Herron, A. G. Cox, Wm. T. Sykes, W. Pirkle, B. Sanchez, S. Hylton, M. L. Welsh, Jackson Simmons, S. R. Sheppard, Wm. Buckner, John Light, Baldwin Bradford. Bugler, Frederick Geiger. Blacksmith, Nicholas Powers. Artificer, Patrick McCann, Jos. G. Fletcher. Farrier, W. B. P. Mills. The Third Maryland artillery was mustered into the service of the Confederate States January 14, 1862, at Richmond, Va., and immediately sent to Knoxville, Tenn. Served under E. Kirby Smith in the campaigns in Tennessee and Kentucky, being the advance battery from Lexington, Ky., to within three and one-half miles of Covington. After the retreat from Kentucky was sent to Vicksburg, under General Stevenson. One section, commanded by Lieut. W. T. Patten, manned the guns of the ram Queen of the West, when the Indianola was captured, and all except four were lost when the Queen was burned. Another detachment under Lieut. Wm. L. Ritter served under Col. G. W. Ferguson on Deer Creek, assisted in capturing a large Federal transport, and was afterwards under General Johnston in the battle before Jackson, Miss. The rest of the battery remained with Pemberton, participated in the battle of Baker's Creek, fought on the Vicksburg lines and were there surrendered. Seventy-seven were paroled, and furloughed after being exchanged. Reorganized in September, 1863; went to the front at Sweetwater, Tenn., served at Lookout mountain, Missionary Ridge, and on the retreat to Dalton, Ga. Under the title of the Stephens (Georgia) light artillery, it participated in the Atlanta campaign and Hood's campaign in Tennessee. At Nashville the battery suffered heavy loss and Captain Rowan was killed by a shell on the morning of December 16th. The company's last muster was at Meridian, Miss., May 10, 1865.

FOURTH MARYLAND ARTILLERY.

" CHESAPEAKE."

Captain, William Brown, Walter S. Chew. First-Lieutenant, John E. Plater. Second-Lieutenant, Benj. G. Roberts. First-Sergeant, Jas. D. Wall. Sergeants, Robert A. Crowley, Philip H. H. Brown, John P. Hickey, Jos. H. Ennis, Henry C. Buckmaster. Corporals, Thos. W. Mummey, Geo. A. Smith, Henry Baker, Isaac J. Blunt, Geo. C. Philip, Thos. G. Jackson, F. M. Fairbanks. Bugler, Daniel A. Wilkinson. Artificer, Michael H. Brady, A. J. Covington.

Some of the engagements of the Fourth Maryland Artillery: Fredericksburg, Seven Pines, Gettysburg, Second Manassas, Hanover Junction, Cedar Mountain, Seven Days around Richmond, Frederick's Hall, Sharpsburg, Harper's Ferry, Winchester, Yellow Tavern, Petersburg.

APPENDIX A.

LOSSES OF SECOND MARYLAND INFANTRY.

At Winchester, Va., June, 1863.

Company A, wounded—Sergt. E. S. Dorsey; Privates Somervell Sollers, John Wilson. Company B, wounded—Privates J. E. Joy, mortally; H. Cony, Wm. Herbert. Company C, wounded—Capt. Ferdinand Duvall, severely. Company D, wounded—John Devres, mortally. Company E, wounded—Lieut. W. R. Byers; captured, Joseph P. Quinn. Total, 9 wounded and 1 captured.

At Gettysburg, July 3, 1863.

Wounded—Col. James R. Herbert, Maj. W. W. Goldsborough.

Company A, killed—Capt. W. H. Murray; Privates Wm. Bruce, John W. Hardesty, James Iglehart, Jr., Arthur Kennedy, C. T. Lloyd, Geo. W. McIntire, Wilbur Morrison, McCormick, Herman Nicholai, George C. Starlings, John H. Windolph. Wounded—John Bond, Philip Barry, Wm. H. Bowly, mortally; Chas. S. Braddock, Wallace Bolling, Thos. B. Bolling, James E. Cavey, Wm. S. J. Chandler, mortally; Moses Clayville, Jacob N. Davis, Wm. J. Edelin, Bernard Freeman, Alex. Fulton, Wm. F. Gardiner, Samuel T. Glenn, Notley Hanson, Samuel J. Hopkins, D. Ridgely Howard, Lamar Hollyday, Leonard Ives, mortally; T. A. Kleinkiewiez, W. T. V. Loane, W. E. Lowe, Wm. H. Laird, Craig Lake, John Marney, Philip Pindell, mortally; Frank H. Sanderson, mortally; A. J. Sollers, Charles H. Steele, Wm. T. Thelin, Charles M. Trail, Andrew C. Trippe, John P. Williams, Jacob E. Zollinger. Captured—Albert Emory, Bernard

Hubball, David H. Luchesi, James A. Peregoy, Tillard Smith.

Company B, Capt. J. Parran Crane commanding. Killed—Sergt. Thomas S. Freeman, Private Warren F. Moore. Wounded—Second Lieut. James H. Wilson, Sergt. Francis L. Freeman, Corp. George Hayden, mortally, Corp. Thomas Simms, Corp. William F. Wheatley; Privates James P. Alvey, John H. Chum, Edgar Combs, Thomas J. Delozier, Albert Fenwick, Henry Ford, John A. Hayden, James H. Keech, Thomas F. Magill, Joseph H. Milstead, Wm. H. Simms, Henry Turner, Wm. L. Turner, James R. Webster, John W. Wills, James A. Wills.

Company C, First Lieut. Charles W. Hodges commanding. Killed—First Sergt. Robert H. Cushing; Privates Daniel Duval, Michael Davis, Jeremiah Dulaney, Bernard Kenney, Benj. L. Lanham, James McWilliams, John T. O'Byrn, Benjamin Payne. Wounded—Second Lieut. Joseph W. Barber, mortally, Second Lieut. Thomas H. Tolson, Sergt. George Probest, Corp. Beall D. Hamilton, mortally, Corp. James A. Lawson, mortally; Privates Samuel Anderson, mortally, Robert H. Clough, Tobias Duvall, Thomas Edgar, mortally, Samuel H. Hamilton, Edgar Hammond, mortally, Charles Hammond, John McGenna, W. V. McCann, James Nash, mortally, Wm. L. Nicholas, mortally, Frank K. Steele, Wm. K. Skinner, Wm. A. Shipley, John G. White. Captured—Corp. Edward A. Welch; Privates Robert M. Dawson, Walter Mullikin, Francis E. Storm, Justus Schultz.

Company D, Capt. Joseph L. McAleer commanding. Killed—Privates James A. Brown, Cornelius Kerns. Wounded—Sergt. Wm. Jenkins, Corp. Joshua Owings, mortally, Corp. Emmett W. Webb, mortally; Privates Lewis Green, John Hays, Thos. J. Hines, Richard G. Killman, Philip Lipscomb, James H. O'Brien, John H. Septer, Wm. Watts. Captured—Privates Wm. Hogarty, John Lamb.

Company E, Capt. John W. Torsch, commanding. Wounded—First Lieut. Wm. J. Broadfoot, mortally, Sergt. P. M. Moore, mortally, Corp. John Cain, Corp. James Reddie; privates, Michael Barry, Charles E. Byus, John Brown, Alex. Brandt, James Fallon, Edward Fallis, J. S. Halbig, James Lemates, John N. Martin, Wm. P. Moran, Daniel McGee, Frank Roberts, Herman H. Radeke, John Sullivan, Wm. A. Wilkinson. Captured—Michael Burke.

Company F, Captain Andrew J. Gwynn, commanding. Killed—Henry G. Taylor. Wounded—Capt. Andrew J. Gwynn, Second-Lieut. John G. Hyland, First-Sergt. Nicholas J. Mills, Sergt. Joseph S. Wayner; privates, Andrew Leroy, Geo. H. Clagett, J. W. Clagett, Philip Doyle, Lemuel Dunnington, Benj. F. Dement, Benj. Hodges, Robert Holden, Minion F. Knott, Alex. V. Keepers, Samuel Polk, John W. Thompson, R. Wagner.

Company G, Capt. Thomas R. Stewart, commanding. Killed—Second-Lieut. William C. Wrightson, privates, J. S. Littleford, J. N. Gossman, W. R. Cator. Wounded—Capt. Thomas R. Stewart, First-Lieut. James A. Davis, Corp. J. Edwin Briddel; privates, James Abbott, S. E. Adkins, E. W. Breslin, mortally, Daniel Boyles, Charles A. Clarke, J. R Fentswait, mortally, W. B. Fountain, mortally, William Robbins, Benjamin F. Twilly, D. B. P. Tingle, W. A. Vickers, J. L. Woolford. Captured—privates, L. H. Weaver, Ross Messick.

AT COLD HARBOR, JUNE 3, 1864.

Capt. I. Parran Crane, commanding.

Company A, Capt. George Thomas. Killed—privates, Wm. H. Holliday, Henry C. Owens. Wounded—Thomas O'Brien, Alexander Fulton, mortally, Thomas D. Harrison, Frederick Heiston, Ivan C. Henry, Wm. Hoffman. Company B, First-Lieut. John H. Stone. Wounded—First Lieut. John H. Stone; privates, James R.

Herbert, A. W. .Neale, Rinaldo I. Moran.   Company C, Capt. Ferdinand Duvall.   Wounded—Second Lieut. Morris H. Tolson; Privates Wm. H. Claggett, C. S. Ford, Henry Loughran, R. B. Willis.   Company D, First Lieut. James S. Franklin.   Killed—Private James Henley. Wounded—Second Lieut. S. Thomas McCullough, First Sergt. Thomas E. Butler, Abram Philip.

WELDON RAILROAD, UP TO REAMS' STATION.

Company C, wounded—Private Richard T. Anderson. Company G, wounded—Privates James Abbott, Thomas Brannock, George Langford.   Company H, wounded— Corp. John I. Ward, Private John Parker.

AT REAMS' STATION, AUGUST 19, 1864.

Capt. J. Parran Crane, commanding, received a severe contusion.   Adjt. J. Winder Laird, killed.

Company A, First Lieut. Clapham Murray.   Killed— Private Jacob W. Davis.   Wounded—Lieut. W. P. Zollinger, Corp. Willis Brannock; Privates J. E. Fitzgerald, John C. Henry, N. Heenur, D. Ridgely Howard, Joseph I. Joy, George W. Marden, Somervell Sollers, Richard C. Tilghman.   Captured—First Lieut. Clapham Murray, First Sergt. James F. Pearson, Sergt. James W. Thomas; Privates William Adair, Charles S. Brannock, William J. Edelin, H. L. Gallagher, Theophilus N. Neale, I. R. Phelps, James S. Raley.

Company B, First Sergt. C. Craig Page commanding. Killed—First Sergt. C. Craig Page.   Wounded—Sergt. P. T. Rudar, Corp. J. Z. Downing; Privates Dionysius Ball, John H. Chum, J. J. Delogier, J. Mann Freeman, Washington Page, Henry Turner.   Captured—Sergt. F. Z. Freeman, Corp. W. F. Wheatley; Private James S. Keech.

Company C, First Lieut. Charles W. Hodges.   Killed —Sergt. Robert T. Hodges.   Wounded—Privates H. H. Crawford, Daniel Duvall, John G. White.   Captured—

Corp. Edward A. Welch; Privates Theodore Cookery, W. C. Gibson, John C. Millen, Robert H. Welch.

Company D, First Lieut. J. S. Franklin. Wounded —Privates John Johnson, C. C. Leitch, Philip Lipscomb, Thomas McCready. Captured—First Lieut. J. S. Franklin, Sergt. William Jenkins; Privates William Killman, John Lynch.

Company E, First Lieut. William R. Byus. Wounded —Lieutenant Byus; Privates Elisha Bitter, S. M. Byus, James Hanly, Thomas McLaughlin. Captured—Sergt. George L. Ross, Corp. John Cain, Privates James Applegarth, John Cantrell, John Grant, James Lemates, John L. Stansbury.

Company F, First Lieut. John W. Polk. Wounded— Private Josiah T. Boswell.

Company E, Capt. John W. Torsch. Killed—Private Charles E. Byus. Wounded—Captain Torsch, First Sergt. Samuel Kirk; Privates Levi G. Dawson, Joseph Smith, William Wilkinson, mortally.

Company F, Capt. A. J. Gwynne. Killed—Lemuel Dunnington. Wounded—Captain Gwynne, Sergt. R. F. Muirhead; Privates Andrew Cretin, Hillary Cretin, Bernard Dorsey, Alexis V. Keepes.

Company G, First Lieut. G. G. Guillette. Killed—Wm. S. Reid. Wounded—Private Michael Hines.

Company H, Capt. J. Thomas Bussey. Wounded— William Hardy, Maurice Nair.

At White Oak Swamp, June 13, 1864.

Company A, killed—Private John G. Wagner. Company C, killed—Private Lewis H. Vrit. Company G, killed—Private William H. Calhoun. Captured—Sergt. Joseph L. Wagner; Corporals J. T. Brown, James H. Dixon. Company G, killed—Francis D. Edelin. Wounded—Private Martin L. Rider. Captured—Lieut. G. G. Guillette; Sergeants Daniel A. Fenton, Algernon Henry, George W. Manning; Corp. Benjamin F. Twilly;

Privates William L. Brannock, W. L. Etchison, Levi Wheatly. Company H, wounded—Capt. J. E. T. Bussey; Private Julian Harzy.

At Pegram's Farm, September 30, 1864.

Wounded—Capt. Ferdinand Duvall, commanding battalion.

Company A, Capt. George Thomas, commanding. Killed—Corp. S. Pinkney Gill, George Deaton. Wounded —Capt. George Thomas, Second-Lieut. Wm. F. Zollinger; Privates John Goodwin, Wm. A. Hance, Frederick Heister. Missing—Wm. H. Hubbard, supposed killed.

Company B, Second-Lieut. Charles B. Wise, commanding. Killed—Private John H. Junger. Wounded—Sergeants John B. Barber, Whittingham Hammett; Privates Robert Beal, Charles J. Foxwell.

Company C, Sergt. George Roberts, commanding. Killed—Private Richard T. Guion. Wounded—Sergt. George Roberts; Privates Wm. Grace, Thomas L. Mitchell. Captured, John T. White.

Company D, Sergt. Isaac Sherwood, commanding. Wounded—Privates David Hammett, Beale W. Owens, John Spence. Missing—Philip Lipscomb.

Company E, Sergt. William Heaply, commanding. Wounded—Corp. Benjamin F. Amos, Privates John Keppleman, Michael Noonan. Captured—Private Martin G. Hallon.

Company F, Capt. A. J. Gwynne, commanding. Killed —Private Abel Hurley. Wounded—Captain Gwynne; Privates J. H. Claggett, John W. Claggett, Hillary Cretin, Thomas J. Webb.

Company G, Second-Lieut. George Brighthaupt, commanding. Wounded—Lieut. George Brighthaupt, mortally; Corp. William Lord; Private Robert Mumford. Captured—Sergt. Hallohan; Privates Michael Eligett, Jesse Waters.

Company H, Corp. Patrick Heenan commanding. Wounded—Edward Welch.

At Battle of Squirrel Level Road, Oct. 1, 1864.

Capt. John W. Torsch commanding.

Company A, Sergt. Charles E. McGuire commanding. Wounded—Private William T. Bailey. Company B, Second Lieut. Charles B. Wise commanding. Wounded— Private Wm. Herbert, mortally. Company C, Corp. C. M. Clayton commanding. Wounded—John W. Blumendeur, Charles Hammond, Frank Wheatley, mortally. Company D, Sergt. Isaac Sherwood commanding. Wounded—Sergt. Isaac Sherwood. Company E, Sergt. Samuel Kirk commanding. Wounded—Private John Brown, Wm. Gwynne. Company F, Sergt. John W. Pold commanding. Wounded—Charles A. Hoge, mortally. Company H, wounded—Private James Powers.

APPENDIX B.

List of officers and men of the Second Maryland infantry, surrendered at Appomattox Court House, April 9, 1865:

John W. Torsch commanding; Wm. R. McCullough, adjutant; DeWilton Snowden, assistant surgeon; Edwin James, quartermaster-sergeant; Frank Dement, sergeant-major; F. L. Higdon, ordnance sergeant; M. A. Quinn, chief musician; Charles F. Drewry, Joseph E. Smith, musicians.

Company A, Corp. H. William Smith; Privates William J. Edelin, Bernard Freeman, Henry Holliday, John J. Hunter, William H. Laird, William E. Lowe, John W. McDaniel, Alex. Murray, Edward O'Donovan, James A. Peregoy, Andrew T. Miller.

Company B, Sergt. Philip T. Raeder; Privates Henry Ford, Thomas Magill, William G. Matthews, John C. Mills, A. W. Neale, F. X. Lemans, James A. Wills, Walter Wood.

Company C, Corp. B. D. Mullikin; Privates J. W. Blumenar, Wm. H. Claggett, Evans Duvall, Franklin Duvall, William Grace, Thomas Mitchell, James R. Moog, Peter Ore, Joshua Watts.

Company D, Sergeants Thomas C. Butler, Isaac N. Sherwood; Privates William F. Brawner, James Gardner, William Gavin, Edward Lawn, Joseph Ridgel, Elisha R. Rutter, William Unkel.

Company F, Privates G. W. Claggett, G. N. Guy, John O. Hill, A. V. Keepers.

Company G, Sergt. Daniel F. Fenton; Privates John Callahan, Joseph Manly, William R. Mumford, William Pickel.

Company H, John Parker.

BIOGRAPHICAL

MARYLANDERS IN THE MILITARY AND NAVAL SERVICE OF THE CONFEDERATE STATES.

IT is generally estimated in Maryland that twenty thousand men from that State served in the armies of the Confederacy. There are no data by which an approximate estimate can be made of the number furnished, but the above conjecture is reasonable and probable. It is certain that there was no neighborhood in Maryland from Mason and Dixon's line to the seashore, from which all the young men of the better class did not go to military service in Virginia, and an examination now will show Maryland Confederate soldiers still living all over the State. Frederick county, which was a Union stronghold, shows a list of over one thousand Confederates. The Marylanders were scattered throughout the armies of the Confederacy. In Virginia, in Georgia, in Mississippi, in Arkansas, they were found serving in the ranks of their regiments, or as commissioned officers from captain to brigadier-general. A large percentage, the majority, of the officers in the army and navy of the United States from Maryland, resigned their commissions, and entered the service of the Confederacy.

Captain Franklin Buchanan, United States navy, became Admiral Buchanan in the Confederate service. He commanded the iron-clad Virginia when he sank in Hampton Roads the Congress and the Cumberland, two of the best men-of-war in the navy of the United States, and was prevented from sinking all transports and gunboats in that anchorage only by the accidental and timely arrival of the Monitor, a newly invented ironclad, constructed by Ericsson. Admiral Buchanan was wounded at Hampton Roads. As soon as he again reported for duty, he was assigned to the command of Mobile harbor, with all the vessels and gunboats there. He defended his post with gallantry and skill the most distinguished, against the Federal fleet under Admiral Farragut, until he was wounded and taken prisoner in August, 1864.

Captain Raphael Semmes served in the United States navy with distinction during the Mexican war, and was aide to General Worth. In 1861 he resigned and was commissioned captain in the navy of the Confederate States. Assigned to command the Sumter he performed gallant and efficient service. In August, 1862, he took command of the Confederate man-of-war Alabama. He sunk the Hatteras off Galveston, January, 1863, after a brief action, and thereafter his achievements and exploits make a record for brilliancy and efficiency unequaled in the annals of war upon the high seas, in the history of the world. He captured and ransomed or burned eighty-nine merchant vessels bearing the United States flag, and literally obliterated the commerce of the United States from the high seas. He pervaded the Atlantic and the Indian oceans. He carried the Confederate battle-flag in the face of four continents, and surrendered it with a blaze of glory that will glow as long as chivalry shall nerve the hearts of men, or the story of gallant deeds stir the pulses of the human race.

Commodore George Nichols Hollins was born at Baltimore, September 20, 1799. He entered the navy of the United States as midshipman in 1814, served on the Erie in her attempt to break the British blockade of Chesapeake bay, and was subsequently transferred to the President, where he served under Stephen Decatur until captured at Bermuda, where he was held until peace was established. His career thus gallantly begun, continued to be a conspicuous one. In the Algerian war of 1815 he served under Decatur with such merit as to be presented a sword in recognition of his gallantry. Subsequently he was on duty upon the Guerriere, Columbus, Franklin, and Washington, and commanded an East India merchantman for a time. He was promoted lieutenant in 1828, commander in 1841, and captain U. S. N. in 1855. In the latter year he bombarded Graytown in the interests of American residents. In 1861 Captain Hollins resigned his commission, upon which the war department refused to accept the resignation and ordered his arrest. But he eluded the effort made to this end, and in March, 1861, was at Montgomery, then the Confederate capital, where he met Semmes, Tattnall, Brent, and many other naval officers, for consultation with the committees of the Confederate Congress on the means to provide a navy for the new government. Hollins became a commander in the navy of the Confederate States, was assigned to very important duties, and quickly attracted attention by his clever capture, on June 29, 1861, of the steamer St. Nicholas in the Potomac river. On July 10th the naval defenses of the James river were placed under his command, and on July 31st he was put in charge of the naval station at New Orleans, where he defeated the Federal blockading squadron in the following October. Being appointed flag-officer, in December he took a fleet up the Mississippi river to assist in the defense of the works at Columbus, Ky. In April, 1862, he was called back to New Orleans by the appearance of the enemy in force, but before the fall of the city he was appointed to the court of inquiry on the destruction of the Virginia. After the war he resided at Baltimore, and died there January 18, 1878.

Major-General Arnold Elzey was descended from some of the best blood of Maryland, his ancestry being among its earliest and most prominent settlers. His father, Col.

Arnold Elzey Jones, was, in his day, very prominent in the politics of Maryland, having several times represented Somerset county in the State legislature. His mother, Anne Wilson Jackson, of a wealthy Maryland family, was a lady of great culture and refinement. General Elzey was born December 18, 1816, at Elmwood, the residence of his parents, on the Manokin river, in Somerset county. He was graduated at West Point in 1837, and commissioned lieutenant of artillery in the United States army. Finding a number of officers in the army bearing his paternal name, he adopted that of his paternal grandmother, Elzey, by which he was subsequently known. As an artillery officer he served with credit during the Seminole outbreak in Florida, and when war was declared between the United States and Mexico, he was in command of a battery at Brownsville, Tex., where he had the honor of firing the first gun of the war. From this opening gun, until the surrender of the City of Mexico, he was with the armies of Taylor and Scott, participating in nearly every battle, and was twice brevetted for gallant and meritorious conduct on the field. In 1860, with the rank of captain of artillery, he was in command of the United States arsenal at Augusta, Ga., which he surrendered with the honors of war upon the demand of superior forces soon after the fall of Fort Sumter. He then conducted his command to Washington, after which he resigned his commission and made his way to Richmond, where he was commissioned lieutenant-colonel in the Confederate service. At the first battle of Manassas, Elzey, then ranking as senior colonel in Kirby Smith's brigade, had the honor, after General Smith was wounded, of leading the successful charge, on the afternoon of the day's hard fighting, which turned the tide of battle, broke the Federal forces, and ended in a rout of the almost victorious army of McDowell. For this gallant service he was complimented by General Beauregard, who styled him "the Blucher of the field," and was promoted brigadier-general on the field by President Davis, who had witnessed the gallant action. In command of a brigade General Elzey was with Stonewall Jackson all through his celebrated Valley campaign of 1862, and the opening of the Seven Days' fighting before Richmond. At the battle of Port Republic he was slightly wounded in the leg, and his horse shot under him, and in the engagement at Cold Harbor he was desperately wounded, a minie ball entering on the right side of his face just above the mouth and passing transversely entirely through his head and out behind his left ear. This injury prevented his further service in the field, but after his almost miraculous recovery he was promoted major-general and put in command of the department of Richmond, where he continued until the fall of 1864. He then joined General Hood as chief of artillery of the army of Tennessee, and participated in the operations against Sherman's line of communication. After the end of the war, being permitted to return to Maryland, he retired with his wife, and only son then living, to a small farm in Anne Arundel county. Here this intrepid soldier and modest unassuming gentleman passed the remainder of his days, honored for his manly virtues, and beloved for his gentle qualities. He died February 21, 1870, while on a visit to Dr. Frank Donaldson, at Baltimore. His wife, to whom he was married in 1845, then Miss Ellen Irwin, a ruling belle of Baltimore society, still survives him.

Major-General Isaac Ridgeway Trimble was born in Culpeper county, Virginia, May 15, 1802. He was graduated at the national military academy in 1822, and was detailed to survey the military road from Washington to the Ohio river, having won distinction at West Point in engineering. In 1832 he resigned from the army, and becoming chief engineer of the Baltimore and Susquehanna railroad, completed that line to York, Pa., in 1837.

He was subsequently chief engineer of the Philadelphia, Wilmington & Baltimore and the Boston & Providence railroads, and in 1860 was engaged in large railroad operations in the West Indies. During April, 1861, he was in command of the Baltimore organizations for the defense of the city from the Federal troops. He entered the service of Virginia, as colonel of engineers, in May, 1861, and was assigned by General Lee to the duty of constructing the defenses of Norfolk. In August he was commissioned brigadier-general in the Confederate provisional army, and ordered to report to General Johnston, by whom he was put in command of a brigade at Evansport, with the duty of erecting batteries and blockading the river against Federal shipping. Subsequently he was assigned to the command of a brigade of Ewell's division, which he accompanied to the support of Jackson in the Valley campaign of 1862 In this famous series of glorious battles and brilliant maneuvers he bore a conspicuous part, and at Cross Keys was particularly distinguished, where in command of two brigades, he repulsed the attack of Fremont, and being reinforced, in turn advanced and routed the enemy. During the Seven Days' battles before Richmond, his brigade continued to be distinguished, particularly at Cold Harbor, where Trimble led in person a successful charge against the Federal defenses. Moving with Jackson's command against Pope, he fought his men with gallantry at Slaughter's Mountain; and at the time when Jackson lay in the enemy's rear at Bristoe Station, he was roused on the night of August 27th to receive notice that he could if he chose, capture Manassas Junction before morning. With five hundred men, already weary, he marched at once, and by midnight had crushed the Federal resistance at the point of the bayonet, and without the loss of a man killed, captured three hundred prisoners, eight guns and the immense Federal stores. Jackson at once wrote to him, "I congratulate you on the great success which

God has given you. You deserve promotion to major-general," and in his official report he wrote: "I regard the capture of Manassas Junction Station at night, after a march of thirty-four miles without food, as the most brilliant achievement that has come under my notice during the war." In the battle of the 28th before Groveton, he fought on the extreme left, and during the severe battle of the 29th he was seriously wounded. Promoted major-general in January, 1863, he was given the honorable assignment of command of Jackson's old division. In June, 1863, Lee offered him command of the valley of Virginia, to form the left wing of the army, with headquarters at Staunton, and orders to form into brigades "under you all the Maryland troops—a measure I have much at heart." During the grapple of the contending armies at Gettysburg, Pender fell on the first day, and General Trimble was assigned to the command of his division of A. P. Hill's corps. This division he led in co-operation with Pickett in the famous attack against the Federal center on July 3d, and being so severely wounded as to cause the loss of a leg, fell into the hands of the enemy. He was held as a prisoner of war at Johnson's Island and Fort Warren, despite earnest efforts made for his release, until February, 1865, when two Federal major-generals, Crook and Kelly, were finally received in exchange. He hastened to join General Lee, but upon reaching Lynchburg found that the army had been surrendered. As the leader selected by Lee under whom the Confederate soldiers of Maryland were to have been organized, General Trimble holds a position of particular prominence in the military history of his adopted State. His chivalrous character, great personal bravery, and capacity for generalship, were proved on many occasions. It may be said with the hearty approval of all of Maryland's brave soldiers that among them, as Gen. Bradley Johnson says, he performed the most distinguished service, obtained the highest rank and won the greatest fame.'' After the close of hostilities he made his home at Baltimore until his death, which occurred January 2, 1888.

Major-General Mansfield Lovell was born at Washington, D. C., October 20, 1822. He was the son of Dr. Joseph Lovell, surgeon-general of the United States army in 1818, and grandson of a member of the Continental Congress. Receiving an appointment in youth to the United States military academy at West Point, he was graduated there in 1842, with the distinction of being ninth in grade in a class which included some afterward distinguished generals. He received a lieutenancy in the Fourth artillery, which joined General Taylor's army in Texas, in 1845. He was wounded at Monterey in 1846, was appointed aide to General Quitman, went to Vera Cruz and was in the campaign from that place to the City of Mexico, in the assault upon which he was wounded at Belasco gate. He was brevetted captain for bravery at Chapultepec. After the Mexican war he commanded a battery of his regiment for two years, served in garrisons in the South and West, and finally in New York, where he resigned September 18, 1854, having married Emily M., daughter of Colonel Plympton, U. S. A. At New York he was a member of, and drilled the Old City Guard, and was deputy street commissioner from 1858 until 1861, when he went South. Tendering his services to the Confederate government, he was commissioned brigadier-general and in October, 1861, was promoted major-general and assigned to the command of Department No. 1, with headquarters at New Orleans. On account of the inadequacy of his infantry force in the city he was compelled to evacuate when the Federal fleet passed the forts and came up the river. He retired to Vicksburg, was superseded by General Van Dorn, was second in command at Corinth, and commanded the rear guard in the subse-

quent retreat. A court of inquiry relieved him of blame
for the surrender of New Orleans, and Gen. J. E. Johnston in 1864 proposed to give him command of a corps,
but he was not restored to the field by the government.
After the war he resided in New York City, engaged in
civil engineering, until his death in June, 1884.

Lloyd Tilghman, brigadier-general in the Confederate
States army, was born in Talbot county, Maryland, in
1816. He was of a distinguished colonial family, being
the great-grandson of Matthew Tilghman, who was
president of the revolutionary conventions of Maryland,
member of the legislature and Continental Congress,
head of the council of safety, and known in his old age as
the Patriarch of Maryland. A daughter of this ancestor
married Col. Tench Tilghman, aide-de-camp to General
Washington. Lloyd Tilghman was graduated at the
United States military academy in 1836, and was commissioned second-lieutenant in the First Dragoons. September 30, 1836, he resigned and took up the profession
of civil engineering, becoming division engineer of the
Baltimore & Susquehanna railroad in 1836-37; of the
Norfolk & Wilmington canal in 1837-38; of the Eastern
Shore railroad of Maryland in 1838-39; and of the Baltimore & Ohio railroad in 1839-40. He served in the
war with Mexico as volunteer aide to General Twiggs in
the battles of Palo Alto and Resaca de la Palma, and was
captain of the Maryland and District of Columbia battalion of volunteers in 1847-48. He then engaged as prin-
cipal assistant engineer of the Panama division of the
Isthmus railroad, and was engineer on Southern railroads until 1859. He joined the army of the Confederate
States in 1861, and was commissioned brigadier-general.
In February, 1862, he was charged with the inspection
of Fort Henry, one of the most important defenses on
the Tennessee river, and of the neighboring Fort Donelson. He reported defects in the location of Fort Henry,

built before he took charge, which could not be remedied
because of the immediate pressure of the enemy.   On
the 6th of February the fort was attacked by General
Grant with a force of 12,000 men, aided by General Smith
with a smaller body, and seven gun-boats with an arma-
ment of 54 guns.   Tilghman had a grand total of 2,600
men not well armed, and the eleven guns of the fort.
He resolved to retire his infantry, field artillery and cavalry toward Fort Donelson, retaining a small force with
the siege guns to make a stubborn fight.   The retreat
was effected, notwithstanding the enemy was pushing
his infantry to within a half mile of the advance work,
and the gun-boat flotilla had opened fire.   The fort returned the fire with spirit and effect, disabling one of the
gun-boats, but unfortunately losing a 24-pounder rifled gun
by bursting, and a Columbiad by the closing of the vent.
The enemy's entire force became engaged in an advance
which Tilghman saw must become successful, especially
since at one o'clock only four guns remained serviceable,
and the men were broken down with fatigue.   An embarrassing question now presented itself as to his duty,
whether to leave his small band of heroic defenders in
the fort to be surrendered and join his main command
en route to Fort Donelson, or remain and share the fate
of the garrison.   Colonel Heiman, in command of the
escaping force, had returned to the fort for final orders,
and General Tilghman could have left with him.   But
the men at the guns entreated him to stay, and the effect
of his absence would have been the immediate fall of
the fort, which he desired to postpone to the last moment.   His decision was made.   Colonel Heiman was
directed to return to the main body, and General Tilghman took the place of an exhausted gunner and worked
a 32-pounder with good effect.   Soon afterward the
enemy succeeded in breaching the fort, but resistance
was continued for over two hours before the white flag
was hoisted, under which an honorable surrender was

made of 12 officers, 66 effective men and 16 others in hospital. In this gallant fight of a day he lost but five killed and sixteen disabled, and the entire command outside the fort was saved by his prolonged and heroic resistance. General Tilghman was a prisoner of war until his exchange in the fall of 1862, when he rejoined the army of the West, then in north Mississippi, and was put in command of the First brigade of Loring's division. At the battle of Corinth, Miss., he took a prominent part. During the retreat from Holly Springs to Grenada, Tilghman's brigade was assigned the responsible position of rear guard, and repeatedly gave battle to and held in check the enemy. Between four and five o'clock of the evening of May 16, 1863, he was killed on the battle-field of Champion's Hill. He was in command of his brigade, consisting of the Fifteenth and Twenty-second Mississippi regiments, First Louisiana, and Rayburn's and McLendon's batteries, on the extreme right of the line. They received the first fire of that battle, but the fight drifted to the left until after midday, when the enemy advanced in force against Loring's division, and after their first repulse threw forward a line of sharpshooters which, aided by artillery, maintained the action. These sharpshooters occupied a row of plantation cabins near the Confederate line, and were doing destructive work, when General Tilghman directed a gun to be trained upon them. He dismounted to give directions for sighting the piece, when a shell from the enemy exploded about fifty feet to the front, and a fragment tore through his body. He died very soon after receiving this terrible wound, and his body was carried to the rear, and subsequently interred at Vicksburg, escorted by his personal staff and his son, Lloyd Tilghman, Jr.

Brigadier-General Charles S. Winder was born in Maryland in 1829. He was graduated at West Point in 1850, and on advancement from second to first-lieutenant of infantry, U. S. A., was ordered to the Pacific coast. The steamer San Francisco, on which the troops took passage, encountered a hurricane off the Atlantic coast, and for several weeks was reported lost. Lieutenant Winder and his men were, however, rescued and carried to Liverpool. For his coolness and devotion on this occasion he was promoted to captain of the Ninth regiment, March 3, 1855, being, it is believed, the youngest captain in the army. Finally reaching the Pacific coast he went into Washington Territory in 1856, and was engaged in the desperate combat of To-hots-nim-me, with the Columbia river Indians, and other engagements in 1856 and 1858 in the Spokane country, under the command of Steptoe and Wright. Early in 1861 he resigned his commission, and was commissioned, to date from March 16th, major of artillery in the Confederate army. He served at Charleston during the reduction of Fort Sumter, and was in command of the South Carolina arsenal until com missioned colonel of the Sixth regiment, South Carolina infantry, July 8, 1861. He hurried with his command to Manassas, but reached the battle ground at the close of the fight. Promoted brigadier-general in March, 1862, he was assigned to command the Fourth brigade in Hill's division, but on the occurrence of a vacancy was given command of the "Stonewall brigade," in Jackson's division, with which he served in the Valley campaign of 1862. He led the advance and opened the battle of Port Republic and in the campaign on the Chickahominy led his brigade in the desperate and memorable charge which broke the Federal lines at Cold Harbor or Gaines' Mill. In his report of that battle General Jackson describes the forward movement of the brigade, through the swamp, meeting at that point the Hampton Legion, First Maryland, Twelfth Alabama, Fifty-second Virginia and Thirty-eighth Georgia, which were formed on General Winder's line. "Thus formed, they moved forward under the lead of that gallant officer, whose conduct here was marked by the coolness and courage which distinguished him on the battle-fields of the valley." In the subsequent advance against Pope he commanded the division lately under the leadership of Jackson, who was in command of the corps. He was, however, not destined to see the second overwhelming defeat of the Federal army on the historic field of Manassas. While in command of Jackson's division, on August 9, 1862, and directing the movements of his batteries in the terrific artillery duel of the battle of Cedar Mountain, he was given a mortal wound by a shell, and died in a few hours, at the age of thirty-three. Gen. Stonewall Jackson said in his report, "It is difficult within the proper reserve of an official report to do justice to the merits of this accomplished officer. Richly endowed with those qualities of mind and person which fit an officer for command, and which attract the admiration and excite the enthusiasm of troops, he was rapidly rising to the front rank of his profession, and his loss has been severely felt." General Lee also wrote, in his official report: "I can add nothing to the well-deserved tribute paid to the courage, capacity, and conspicuous merit of this lamented officer by General Jackson, in whose brilliant campaigns in the valley and on the Chickahominy he bore a distinguished part."

Brigadier-General George H. Steuart was born at Baltimore, August 24, 1828, and was graduated at the United States military academy in 1848, with a lieutenancy in the Second Dragoons. He served on frontier duty in the United States army; on the march through Texas to Austin in 1848-49, and remained on duty at various garrisons in Texas until 1855, when he was promoted first-lieutenant First cavalry, March 3d, and captain December 20th. Subsequently he was engaged in garrison duty in Kansas, Nebraska and Colorado, in the Cheyenne expedition of 1856, the Utah expedition of

1848, and the Comanche expedition of 1860. Immediately after April 19, 1861, he resigned his commission, and going to Richmond, was commissioned captain of cavalry in the regular army of the Confederate States. Upon the formation of the First regiment, Maryland infantry, he was appointed lieutenant-colonel of that command, and by special good conduct won the commendation of Gen. J. E. Johnston in orders. He was with the regiment under Colonel Elzey during its distinguished service at the first battle of Manassas, and at the promotion of Elzey, Steuart was commissioned colonel. In March, 1862, he was promoted brigadier-general, and given command of a brigade in Ewell's division, consisting of the Forty-fourth, Fifty-second and Fifty-eighth Virginia regiments, to which the First Maryland was added, which he led during Jackson's campaign in the valley, receiving a severe wound at Cross Keys, which disabled him for some time. In the Pennsylvania campaign he commanded a brigade consisting of the Second Maryland, the First and Third North Carolina, and the Tenth, Twenty-third and Thirty-seventh Virginia regiments, in Johnson's division of Ewell's corps, and was distinguished in the assault on Culp's Hill. In the first of the fighting at the Wilderness in 1864, he is found pushing in with his brigade after the repulse of Jones to meet the Federal attack, and continuing in the struggle until the 12th of May, fatal to his division, which held the salient at Spottsylvania, known as the bloody angle, and was overwhelmed on that date by the early morning attack of Hancock. General Steuart was among the prisoners taken by the Federals, and was one of those sent to Hilton Head to be placed under fire of the Confederate batteries. Being exchanged he returned to the army on the Petersburg and Richmond lines and was assigned to command the First brigade of Pickett's division, consisting of the Ninth, Fourteenth, Thirty-eighth, Fifty-third and Fifty-seventh

Brigadier-General James J. Archer was born in Harford county, Maryland, of a distinguished family which has contributed brave soldiers to American battles. He was a graduate of the United States military academy, class of 1826, the class of Albert Sidney Johnston and E. Kirby Smith, and was assigned to the Third infantry. After serving on frontier duty in the West he was promoted first-lieutenant in October, 1833. March 31, 1834, he resigned and was engaged in business as a lumber merchant at Havre-de-Grace, Md., until 1847, and from that date until 1861 as a planter at San Patricio, Tex. He was commissioned a captain in the regular army of the Confederate States March 16, 1861, and soon afterward with the rank of colonel of the Fifth Texas regiment, was in command of the Texas brigade at the Evansport batteries. In May as acting brigadier-general he was on duty at West Point, Va., and after the battle of Seven Pines he was promoted brigadier-general and assigned to the command of a brigade in A. P. Hill's division, consisting mainly of Tennessee and Alabama regiments. Under his gallant leadership Archer's brigade soon rose to prominence in the famous "light division" and won laurels through all the hard fighting which followed. On June 26th in the battle of Mechanicsville, he advanced along the Bethesda road and made a desperate attack upon the Federal position with such valor that the losses of the attack fell principally upon his brigade. Following the retreating enemy he was again engaged with distinction at Gaines' Mill. With Jackson's command in the campaign of Manassas which followed, he was in action at Cedar Mountain, August 9th, Manassas Junction, August 26th, and in the battles of Manassas, August 28, 29 and 30. On the 29th, according to General Lee's report, General Archer "firmly held his ground against every attack." He was subsequently in action at Ox Hill, during the Maryland campaign took part in the capture of Harper's Ferry and the battle of

Sharpsburg, and the encounter of Shepherdstown, and in the following December was in the heat of the fighting at Fredericksburg. He participated in the flank movement and hard fighting of Jackson's corps at Chancellorsville. At Gettysburg, Hill having been promoted to command of corps, General Archer's brigade was in the division commanded by Gen. Henry Heth, which led in the Confederate advance on Gettysburg, Archer's command on the right of division line. The first shot of this memorable struggle was fired by Archer's brigade, and the first Confederate who fell was a private of one of his Tennessee regiments. The brigade occupied McPherson's wood, against which the Federal troops were promptly hurled under the leadership of Major-General Reynolds himself. In the fight which followed Reynolds was killed, and Archer was wounded and with many of his command fell into the hands of the enemy. The service lost at this time, as General Early well expressed it, a "most gallant and meritorious officer." In the summer of 1864, he was one of the six hundred Confederate officers who were sent from Fort Delaware to be placed under fire at Morris Island. Subsequently exchanged, he was assigned on August 19, 1864, to the command of his brigade and Walker's, temporarily united, of Heth's division. But in a few weeks the effects of his wounds and the hardships of imprisonment disabled him for active duty, and caused his death October 24, 1864.

Brigadier-General William W. Mackall, native of Cecil county, Maryland, was distinguished in various capacities in the Confederate service in the Western States. He was graduated at the United States military academy in 1837, a class-mate of General Bragg, and was assigned to the First artillery as second lieutenant. In the Seminole war he gained promotion to first lieutenant, and was severely wounded in an ambush at New Inlet in February, 1839. He served at Plattsburg, N. Y., during the Canada border disturbances in 1840, and on the Maine frontier in 1841-42. In the Mexican war he gained the brevet of captain by gallant service at Monterey, and of major for his record at Contreras and Churubusco. He served as adjutant-general on the staff of Generals Butler and Worth in 1846-48, and subsequently as adjutant-general of the Western division and the Third military department. After two years as treasurer of the Soldiers' Home, he made a tour of inspection of the Florida and Gulf posts, and in 1853 became adjutant-general of the Eastern division, and in 1856 of the department of the Pacific. In May, 1861, he declined promotion to lieutenant-colonel of staff, and then resigned, to offer his services to the Confederate States. He was commissioned lieutenant-colonel, and became adjutant-general on the staff of Gen. Albert Sidney Johnston. He was promoted brigadier-general early in 1862, and was assigned by General Johnston to the command of the Confederate forces at Madrid Bend and Island No. 10, where he was captured, with a large number of men, by the Federal army under Pope, on April 8th. He was exchanged later in the season, and General Beauregard, who had written to Adjutant-General Cooper that he considered " the services of Mackall as a division commander indispensable at this critical juncture," was able to send word to Mackall under date of August 22d, " I am happy to hear of your safe return to the Confederacy, and hope you will soon receive a command commensurate with your merit." Gen. Samuel Jones, commanding the department of Tennessee, asked that General Mackall be assigned to that department to command a brigade, and a special order was issued accordingly. In December following he was given command of the district of the Gulf, and in February, 1863, being succeeded by General Buckner, he took charge of the Western division of that district. In April, 1863, he was appointed chief-of-staff by Gen. Braxton Bragg, with whom he rendered important services during the campaigns of that year until relieved at his own request, after the battle of Chickamauga.   In his general order announcing this event, General Bragg wrote concerning Mackall: " He will proceed with his aides and report to Gen. J. E. Johnston, now commanding the department from which he was transferred.   With a grateful sense of the distinguished services rendered by this accomplished officer in the high position he has filled, the commanding general tenders him his cordial thanks and wishes him all success and happiness in his future career. The general and the army will long feel the sacrifice made in sparing the services of one so distinguished for capacity, professional acquirements and urbanity."   In November, now being on duty in the department of Mississippi and East Louisiana, he was assigned to the command of the brigades lately under General Hébert.   In January, 1864, after serving for a time with Gen. Leonidas Polk, who recommended his promotion to major-general, he returned to Johnston, then in command of the army of Tennessee, and being appointed chief-of-staff, served in that capacity throughout the famous campaign against Sherman from Dalton to Atlanta.   After the removal of Johnston he was relieved from his staff duties at his own request, but he continued to participate in the Confederate operations, and on April 20, 1865, after the surrender of Lee's army, joined with Generals G. W. Smith and Howell Cobb in the surrender of Macon, Ga.   General Mackall died August 12, 1891.

Brigadier-General Bradley T. Johnson, as commander of the Maryland Line, became most prominently the representative Marylander in the South.   Ardent in his devotion to the cause, intelligent in his performance of duty, with a courage that was fearless as was his gallantry conspicuous, he attained a reputation throughout the service, and won repeated commendation and honorable mention at the hands of his superiors. His highest ambition was that his loved State should be properly represented in the great struggle for liberty, honor and home rule. No inducement that would separate him from this great purpose was for a moment considered. As a Marylander he entered the army of the Confederacy associated with Maryland troops. Their fame was his fame; the honor of their record was his honor; and the perpetuation of the story of their privations and the glories of their triumphs was to him the ever-prevailing object of his efforts. To them he gave his loving care, and for them he made the sacrifices of the four years' war. Thus it can be readily understood why, then and since, Bradley T. Johnson has been recognized as the typical Marylander in the Confederate army, and the love and devotion so freely bestowed on the men of the Maryland line have in return followed him to this day, and make glad his declining years.

He was without the great advantages of military education, his early efforts being given to that more prosaic profession, the law. In this he attained a degree of success and was becoming prominently known when the disruption of the Democratic party occurred and the fatal struggle of 1860 was precipitated. When the dire alternative was presented of taking sides against conviction and kindred, or against the Federal government, and the crisis was accentuated by the passage of troops through Baltimore, Johnson, in command of a company of Frederick volunteers, was among the first to unhesitatingly tender his services to defend the city and State. When futility of opposition by the State to the Federal power became apparent he moved his company to Point of Rocks, and declining a commission as lieutenant-colonel in the Virginia service from Governor Letcher, endeavored to organize a distinctively Maryland command. His hopes were realized in the organization of the First regiment, whose record, which cannot be disassociated from the history of his own gallant career, has been eloquently

told in the preceding pages.   Acting first as major, he became lieutenant-colonel after First Manassas, and colonel
in March, 1862.   During the famous Valley campaign
under Stonewall Jackson the ability of Johnson as a commanding officer was abundantly manifested, and in general orders his name received most honorable mention.
On the right flank of McClellan before Richmond he gallantly led his Marylanders to victory at Gaines' Mill, and
during the night of terror and apprehension following the
fight at Malvern Hill he kept vigil among the dead and
dying until dawn revealed that McClellan had withdrawn
to the protection of his fleet.   Subsequently, while recruiting at Charlottesville, it was deemed expedient by the
Confederate war department to disband the gallant regiment, and Colonel Johnson was left without command.
He then readily yielded to the invitation of Generals Jackson and Ewell to accompany them in the operations of
August, 1862.   During Jackson's brilliant movement to
the vicinity of Manassas Junction, Colonel Johnson was
assigned to the command of the Virginia brigade of Gen.
J. R. Jones, temporarily absent by reason of sickness.
After the capture of Manassas Junction, while Hill moved
in the direction of Centerville, and Ewell held the railroad
line at Bristoe station, Johnson took position at Groveton,
a few miles south of the famous stone bridge over Bull
run, to resist the advance of Pope.   This important service he successfully performed until Taliaferro had come
up and Jackson's forces were united.   The sanguinary
battle of the 28th followed, leaving the armies substantially on the old lines of July, 1861, but with positions reversed.   On the 29th, after repeated assaults on the Confederate left under Hill, the attack was made on Johnson's
line, which connected with Hill's right.   Permitting the
enemy to enter the edge of the woods in which he was
stationed he gave command to fire and then to charge,
and hurled the Federals back to their original position,
bringing off two pieces of artillery.   In this crisis he acted

without instruction, the occasion not admitting of delay. The headlong movement was witnessed by General Hood from the hills of Groveton, and the latter impetuous fighter sent an officer over to inquire what command had so magnificently risen to the emergency.   On the 30th Johnson advanced his line to the railroad cut before his position, and there his men repulsed charge after charge. After ammunition gave out they used stones with great effect.   Finally reinforced by Stafford and aided by Pender, the Federals were swept from the field.

During the Maryland campaign General Jones resumed command of his brigade, but Jackson was anxious that the young Maryland officer should be continued in duty adequate to his talent.   He addressed the war department under date of September 4th, as follows: "I respectfully recommend that Col. Bradley T. Johnson, late colonel of the First Maryland regiment, be appointed brigadier-general.   While I was in command at Harper's Ferry, in the early part of the war, Colonel Johnson left his home in Maryland and entered our service, where he continued until his regiment was recently disbanded.   I regarded him as a promising officer when he first entered the army, and so fully did he come up to my expectations that when his regiment was disbanded I put him in command of a brigade, and so ably did he discharge his duties in the recent battles near Bull Run as to make it my duty, as well as my pleasure, to recommend him for a brigadier-generalcy.   The brilliant service of his brigade in the engagement on Saturday last proved that it was under a superior leader, whose spirit was partaken of by his command.   When it is so difficult to procure good general officers, I deem it due the service not to permit an opportunity of securing the services of one of such merit to pass unimproved."   Upon the occupation of Frederick by the army of Northern Virginia, Colonel Johnson was appointed provost-marshal, and his knowledge of the country and its people was of value to General Lee, with whom he was in frequent conference.   When Jackson moved toward Harper's Ferry, he was sent to Richmond with important dispatches from General Lee.   This was the occasion of his appointment as a member of the military court then being organized, with the rank of colonel of cavalry.   The recommendation of General Jackson was for the time not acted upon for the reason, creditable to Maryland, that so many general officers had already been appointed from that State.

On February 4, 1863, General Jackson renewed his recommendation for Colonel Johnson's promotion and urged his assignment to command Taliaferro's brigade of the Stonewall division, concluding an earnest appeal with the words, "I do not know of any colonel who, in my opinion, is so well qualified for the position in question."   A week later Jackson again urged action upon his recommendation. In a few months came Chancellorsville, and the heroic Jackson was no more.   Though his promotion was still delayed, Johnson, upon the call of the Marylanders in the valley, secured his relief from the military court and reached his comrades at Gettysburg on the morning of July 2d, intent upon his cherished plan of organizing the Maryland Line, which he had been selected to command. But the exigencies of the Pennsylvania campaign made this for the time impracticable, and his service until after the return to Virginia was as temporary commander again of the brigade of General Jones.   In November, 1863, he was ordered to Hanover Junction, and there, as has been related, he finally brought together a considerable Maryland command.   Toward the close of February, 1864, operating against Kilpatrick's raid, he had opportunity to render service of great value by the capture at Yellow Tavern of a dispatch from Dahlgren, and promptly acted as the emergency demanded.   Gen. Wade Hampton in a letter to General Lee stated that he was convinced that " the enemy could have taken Richmond, and in all probability would have done so, but for the fact that Colonel Johnson

intercepted a dispatch from Dahlgren to Kilpatrick, asking what hour the latter had fixed for an attack on the
city, so that both attacks might be simultaneous;" and
in his report the gallant South Carolinian complimented
the Marylander for his gallantry in attacking the enemy
at Beaver Dam, with a handful of men, and hanging on
their rear, striking them continually, and never losing
sight of them until they had passed Tunstall's station.
Hampton further expressed his appreciation by presenting
Johnson with a saber.   This promptly won distinction as
a cavalry leader he confirmed by his service against Mer-
ritt's division at Pollard's farm, and under Hampton at
Trevilian's.   June 25, 1864, he received his commission
as brigadier-general and was assigned to the command of
the cavalry brigade lately led by Gen. William E. Jones,
killed at New Hope church.   The service of this command under his gallant leadership is narrated in the preceding pages.   His prime object in the Maryland campaign under Early was the release of the Confederate
prisoners at Point Lookout, which had been discussed by
General Lee and the President.   Regarding the selection
of a leader for this hazardous duty, General Lee had written the President: " It will be well he should be a Marylander, and of those connected with the army, I consider
Col. Bradley T. Johnson the most suitable.   He is bold
and intelligent, ardent and true, and yet I am unable to
say whether he possesses the requisite qualities.   Everything in an expedition of this kind depends upon the leader."   But he was fated not to be permitted to perform
this service, being recalled after he made a detour around
Baltimore to Beltsville by information from Early that
the expedition was about to retire to Virginia.   Later in
July, 1864, he was associated with General McCausland
in command of the expedition to Chambersburg, Pa., and
as he occupied the place with his brigade it fell his lot
to execute the orders of General Early to burn the town.
Justifiable as it was, as a stern and righteous retribution

for the outrages in the valley, the work was no less repugnant to him and to the large majority of his command. He announced that no plundering would be permitted; nothing was to be appropriated but boots, shoes and army stores. Before the work of destruction had ceased many of his men were seen to unite with the residents in efforts to suppress the flames or rescue property. At Hancock his indignant protest prevented a similar visitation upon a community that had representatives in the Confederate service. The disaster at Moorefield followed, where General Johnson narrowly escaped capture and was distinguished by his efforts to retrieve the day. That he was not censurable was evidenced by the refusal of General Early to order the investigation demanded by him soon afterward. During the campaign in the valley against Sheridan he did all that a gallant officer could do in the face of overwhelming opposition. At Winchester, September 19th, he fought from dawn to night, and by a headlong charge of his brigade gave Ramseur at a critical moment an opportunity to reform his lines. When heavy losses made it necessary to reorganize and consolidate commands, Johnson, being junior in rank and not commanding troops from his own State, gave way to others in the field, and in the latter part of November, 1864, was given command of the post at Salisbury, N. C. This had been a Confederate military prison, but on the advance of Sherman through Georgia a large number of Federal prisoners were transferred thither, without adequate preparations for their care. Officers and men were huddled in the overflowing buildings, and boxes and even excavations in the earth were employed for shelter from the rigor of approaching winter. The post was also in danger from the inroads of Federal guerrillas. Under such circumstances General Johnson was called on to take charge, and his active efforts toward restoring order and alleviating distress met with the best of results. He secured the issuing of fuel to the prisoners, and of food identical with

that of his own men; through his representations to the
Confederate government the Federal government was induced to send supplies by their own officers through the
lines; and, through the co-operation of Governor Vance,
all that was possible was done to relieve distress. Finally, in the early days of March, 1865, he was enabled to
start his charge in the direction of Wilmington for deliv-
ery to their friends. Within sixty days the struggle came
to an end, and then as is well remembered those who were
connected with the prison posts were made the subjects of
investigation by military courts. But the archives at
Raleigh and Richmond, and the voluntary testimony of
those he had guarded, were so eloquent of the humanity
of General Johnson that he was promptly relieved of persecution. Finding himself broken in fortune he made his
home at Richmond and resumed the practice of his profession. As soon as the restrictive legislation of the re-
construction period admitted, he entered public life, and
served in the senate of Virginia with distinction. His
heart, however, still yearned for his native State, and in
1878 he removed to Baltimore, where his efforts were at
once enlisted in the organization of the Society of the
Army and Navy of the Confederate States in Maryland,
and in the formation of the Association of the Maryland
Line. The perpetuation of the record of Maryland in the
armies of the Confederacy, and the relief of needy
and disabled Confederates were to him duties paramount to all other obligations. He was at once placed
at the front in all movements which represented the Confederate sentiment of the State. He became and still
continues the president of the Army and Navy society,
and of the Association of the Maryland Line, and he contributed largely in effort and influence to the establishment of the Home for Confederate veterans. Now, in
the fullness of honors and in complete assurance of the
love of his old comrades, he is living in retirement in his
Virginia home. The State holds him in reverence as one

of its heroes, worthy of a place with Howard, Smallwood and Gist, of the Revolution, as their honored successor in the " Maryland Line."   GEORGE W. BOOTH.

Brigadier-General Joseph Lancaster Brent, of Baltimore, distinguished for his service in various arms of the Confederate military forces, was born in Charles county, Maryland, in 1826. He was reared at his native place, and attended college at Georgetown, D. C. When the war broke out, he was in California, but the ties of sympathy were too strong to be overcome by his great distance from home, and he took ship for the seat of war, in company with William M. Gwyn, ex-United States senator, and Calhoun Benham, United States district attorney in California. But on the high seas they were arrested by Gen. E. V. Sumner, and the three were sent to Fort Lafayette, and held two or three weeks, when they were paroled and permitted to go to Washington. They sought to be relieved of this coercion and finally, through the influence of George D. Prentice, a brother-in-law of Mr. Benham, Mr. Brent was discharged from restraint without being required to take the oath of allegiance, which he had refused to do. He proceeded to Richmond in the winter of 1861-62, and at once entered the Confederate service, with rank of captain, on the staff of Gen. J. B. Magruder, in command of the district of Yorktown. After the conclusion of the Yorktown campaign, he was promoted major of artillery and assigned to duty as chief ordnance officer of the right wing of the army of Northern Virginia, under command of General Magruder, as the army was organized by Gen. Joseph E. Johnston. Major Brent held this position until the close of the Peninsular campaign of 1862, contributing to the success of the Confederate arms, and was then assigned to the staff of Gen. Richard Taylor, who was in command of the district of Western Louisiana. He participated in the military operations of this

district as chief of artillery and ordnance, with rank of colonel July, 1862; also commanded First Louisiana brigade
cavalry until, in October, 1864, he was promoted brigadier-
general of cavalry, in which rank he served until the
close of the war.   At the time of the surrender he was in
command of the forces of the front line in the West,
extending from Arkansas to the Gulf, the last line held
by the Confederate army.   One of the most exciting exploits in which General Brent was engaged was the capture of the Federal ironclad Indianola, early in the spring
of 1863.   The Indianola, after running the batteries at
Vicksburg, had proceeded to the mouth of the Red river,
and thence started back up the river.   Unexpectedly to
him, Brent was assigned by General Taylor to take command of two boats and engage the Indianola.   The boats
on the Red river available were the side-wheel steamer,
Webb, which was used as a towboat before the war, and
was without any protection whatever, except tiers of cotton
bales about the boiler, and the Queen of the West, a
gunboat captured a few days before from the Federals
at Fort DeRussy on Red river.   The latter was a modern
boat, with bow strengthened for ramming, but had no
protection for her machinery except tiers of cotton bales.
With this flotilla General Brent started in pursuit of
the ironclad Indianola and overtook her twenty miles
below Vicksburg.   He immediately engaged his formidable antagonist, which carried 11-inch guns, a shot from
which, properly served, would have disposed of either of
the Confederate vessels.   But every time the iron
shutters of the Indianola were raised to allow a gun to be
fired, the men of the Webb or Queen of the West would
open on them with rifles, with the result that the Federal
gunners were demoralized.   Only one ball from the Indianola struck the Queen of the West, and that did no
damage further than scatter a lot of her defensive armor,
cotton bales, like leaves in an autumnal gale.   Meanwhile
the wooden boats rammed the Indianola repeatedly,

until she was surrendered by her commander.   Her crew
were overcome with shame by this capitulation, especially
when they saw the vulnerability of the two boats which
had so daringly given them battle.   Only six or eight
men were lost by Brent in this engagement.   After the
surrender of the armies, General Brent was paroled at
Alexandria, La., in May, 1865, and thence returned to
Baltimore, where he resumed the practice of law, in
which he had been engaged before the war.   In 1870 he
went to Louisiana and engaged in planting until 1888,
when he again took up his residence at Baltimore, which
has since been his home.   While a resident of Louisiana
he twice served in the legislature of the State.   At Baltimore he is held in high regard, and especially by his comrades of the Confederate army.   He is a member of the
society of the Army and Navy.

WEST VIRGINIA

BY

COL. ROBERT WHITE.

ROBERT WHITE

CHAPTER I.

THE PARTITION OF VIRGINIA—THE DILEMMA OF THE
OLD DOMINION IN 1861—PREPARATIONS FOR WAR
—ORGANIZATION OF TROOPS IN WESTERN VIR-
GINIA—THE UNIONIST CONVENTION—ORGANIZA-
TION OF THE STATE OF WEST VIRGINIA.

THE partition of Virginia was called by the Hon.
S. S. Cox, "one of the whimsical excesses of
secession or vicissitudes of war." In a vigorous
expression of his repugnance to the movement he exclaimed, "Forty western counties of Virginia agree to
secede and form a new State without the consent of the
old one! It is anomalous and unconstitutional. It is a
new phase of secession made by the war. It is vigor-
ously opposed, but in vain. The first beginning of recon-
struction thus, and in the very midst of the war, came
out of this despoiling of Virginia. It is one of the scars
made by the war. It remains to commemorate the
policy of force. It inevitably led to the successful attack
which was soon to be made upon State institutions,
including slavery." Thaddeus Stevens, with his charac-
teristic frankness, said that "We know it is not constitutional, but it is necessary." The justification of the
existence—the right to be—of the State of West Virginia
was "military necessity," but its Statehood has been
achieved and is now no longer questioned, though its
birth was Cæsarian and roughly accomplished at that.
The Old Dominion which had voluntarily donated the vast
Northwest to the Union and dedicated it to the use of
white labor, was cloven by the hand it had nurtured into
strength. Yet Virginia and all the South hail West
Virginia and rejoice in its progress as one of the States
of the Union, notwithstanding the nature of its origin.

3

In proper historical review of the creation of this State, we may begin with the fact that Virginia was forced into secession by the military movements which compelled it either to surrender all its resources to the uses of war against its sister States, or to ally itself with secession in order to resist the threatening armed coercion. "The crossing of troops into Virginia with hostile purpose is the act of war," said Robert E. Lee in April, 1861, and that act occurred before the secession ordinance was voted on by the people.

The original ordinance of secession passed April 17, 1861, to take effect on the fourth Thursday in May, 1861, if ratified by the vote of the people, was opposed strenuously in the convention by the delegates from some of the northwestern counties, and notwithstanding its passage, many of those who had resented it returned to their counties to organize open opposition to the action of the convention. The Virginia convention adjourned on May 1st to meet again on June 11th, and immediately upon the adjournment, public meetings were held in various western counties resulting in an informal call for a general convention of disaffected counties, to be held at Wheeling on May 13th.

These proceedings attracted the attention of the administration at Washington. Communication with the national capital was easy, the distance slight and the way entirely open. The call for national assistance in defying the action of the Virginia convention was earnestly made and did not go unheeded. First among the military operations to support the secession of these counties from Virginia were those in the two great neighboring States of Pennsylvania and Ohio. The conference between the vigorous governor of Pennsylvania and President Lincoln, on April 12, 1861, which encouraged the President in making his call for troops, was followed by the rapid military organization of the State and the stationing of large bodies of troops at Chambersburg under

Patterson, and at other points from which invasion could be made into Maryland and across any part of the eastern border of Virginia. The State of Ohio passed an act to enroll the militia of that State on April 12th, providing for immediately mustering and arming its volunteers.

These active preparations were made before Virginia had seceded, and even before the attempt to reinforce Fort Sumter had failed. Then followed the ample answer to President Lincoln's call for troops, after which, it is a strange circumstance that on the 26th of April, Ohio created a debt of $2,000,000 to raise funds to defend the State, the governor deciding the measure constitutional because "Ohio is in danger of invasion." An immense "home army" was organized under orders of May 6th, part of which was to be "the active army of operation;" the enrolled militia of 300,000 men were divided into three corps; the people of the cities promptly raised large sums of money for the support of volunteers, and under all this pressure the State soon had a large force in the field.

Maj.-Gen. George B. McClellan, who had been in the regular United States army, and was, in 1861, the general superintendent of the Ohio & Mississippi railroad, was made major-general of State troops May 1st, and proceeding with great energy in the work, had twenty-two regiments mustered before June 1st to meet President Lincoln's call, besides a large number of other regiments in State camps, at an expenditure, as certified by the governor and auditor, of over $2,000,000.

The preliminary arrangements which rendered such rapid action possible, were made prior to the sailing of the fleet destined to reinforce Fort Sumter, and pending the efforts of Virginia to arrest secession. Through the energetic efforts of the war governors in forwarding troops to Washington in April, the State of Maryland was reduced to Federal control before it could be succored, and by the 1st of May, the entire eastern, north-

ern and western borders of Virginia became the boundary
line across which the first bloody experiment of coercion
by land was to be made.   This long frontier of Virginia
was exposed to the assaults of four armies; one consisting
of regulars and volunteers stationed in and around Washington, one at Fortress Monroe, one under General Patterson along the upper Potomac, and one gathered chiefly
from Ohio, under the command of General McClellan.
To these two last mentioned armies, and particularly to
the able general from Ohio, were intrusted the military
operations which would enforce the movement inaugurated in April in the western counties of Virginia to
resist the ratification of the ordinance of secession, passed
by the State convention, and to overthrow the existing
State government.   For the purposes of this movement,
the situation was exceedingly favorable.   Ohio was on
the western border and Pennsylvania on the northern.
Wheeling, the city chosen as the place where the convention would assemble, was in the narrow strip of Virginia
lying between those two States, and McClellan's forces
were assembling in easy striking distance.   The people
of the nearest counties were generally opposed to the
secession of Virginia, and had been at all times in near
commercial and political sympathy with the people of
the adjacent States.   With these advantages, McClellan
prepared in May to advance into Virginia.

During these movements, so adverse to its wishes and
interests as well as to its sovereignty, the State of Virginia was well advised of the dangers that threatened it,
and began preparations after April 17th to place its
people and their possessions in a state of defense.   Gen.
Robert E. Lee having been appointed by Governor
Letcher to command all Virginia forces until the State
should be formally incorporated in the Confederate
States, directed Maj. A. Loring, commanding volunteers at Wheeling on April 29, 1861, to accept and muster into service such volunteer companies as might offer

themselves in compliance with the call of Governor
Letcher, and to take command of them. His command
was confined to the counties of Wetzel, Marshall, Ohio,
Brooke and Hancock, with special duty to protect the
terminus of the Baltimore & Ohio railroad. At the same
time Maj. F. M. Boykin, Jr., at Weston, was directed by
General Lee to muster volunteer companies into the
service of the State, and posting his command at or near
Grafton, to co-operate with Major Loring in holding both
branches of the railroad for the benefit of Maryland and
Virginia. These officers were directed to give quiet and
security to the inhabitants of the country, and also to
facilitate peaceful travel. Two hundred old pattern flint-
lock muskets were the only arms with which General
Lee was able to supply these important forces.

Lieut.-Col. John McCausland was given similar duties
in the valley of the Kanawha, and Col. C. Q. Tompkins,
of Charleston, was assigned to command. Col. George
Porterfield was directed to repair to Grafton and select
positions for the troops in that section so as to cover the
points liable to attack. The call for troops to assemble
at Grafton was made on the counties of Braxton, Lewis,
Harrison, Monongahela, Taylor, Barbour, Upshaw,
Tucker, Mason, Randolph and Preston. The volunteers
from Wood, Wirt, Roane, Calhoun, Gilmer, Ritchie,
Pleasant and Doddridge were to rendezvous at Parkersburg. Lieuts. J. G. Gittings and W. E. Kemble were
ordered to report to Porterfield for duty. Col. Jubal A.
Early was ordered to Lynchburg to organize and command the forces at that point, and Col. Thomas J. Jackson,
who was at Harper's Ferry, was notified to watch the
threatening movements of the enemy, to occupy and use
the Baltimore & Ohio railroad and the Chesapeake &
Ohio canal. Lieut.-Col. John Echols was placed in command at Staunton, about the same time, with two regiments of infantry.

Thus it appears that so far as Governor Letcher and

General Lee could act in defense of the exposed north-western frontier of Virginia, all dispositions were rapidly and sagaciously made within a few weeks after the proclamation of President Lincoln calling for 75,000 volunteers to act with forces already assembled at Washington, to invade the South through the State of Virginia. These dispositions were made before May 10th, by General Lee under his commission from that State, and on that date the Confederate secretary of war directed him to assume control of the Confederate as well as the Virginia forces in the State, assigning them to duty at his discretion until further orders.

The measures thus energetically taken, were made necessary by the action of the anti-secessionists in the extreme western counties adjacent to Ohio and Pennsylvania, and also by the evident intention of the Federal authorities to seize and occupy these counties at once. The opponents of Virginia's ordinance of secession formed organizations to defeat that measure, and evidences of movements to call in the assistance of the Federal army of invasion alarmed the people. Enlistments in the volunteer army of Virginia were discouraged in many ways so forcibly as to make men afraid to leave their families. Enlistments, especially around Grafton, were therefore slowly secured, and it became necessary about the 1st of May to order at first 400 and later 600 rifles with ammunition, from Staunton, to be sent to Major Goff at Beverly, who was to turn them over to Porterfield. With these arms it was expected that some companies could be supplied for immediate service. General Lee did not think it was prudent at that time to order companies from other parts of the State to Grafton, as it might irritate, rather than conciliate, the population of that region. But Lee was very much concerned at the failure to procure volunteers in the West for the service of the State, and was induced by his anxieties on May 14, 1861, to ask Jackson, at Harper's Ferry, to send some aid to Porter-

field if he could do so without endangering his own position. Porterfield had reached Grafton on the same day
that Lee's letter was written to Jackson, and found no
forces to command. The sparseness of the population
and the general uncertainty prevailing everywhere made
concert of action difficult. Citizens who were true to the
Old Dominion, appeared to be in the minority and needed
protection.

In view of the emergency, Col. M. G. Harman moved
from Staunton, May 15, 1861, with a supply of arms, under
escort of Capt. F. F. Sterrett's company of cavalry, for
the relief of the Northwest. Capt. Felix H. Hull also
proceeded to Highland with the company to recruit and
join Captain Sterrett. Captain Moorman marched to
Monterey and Captains Stover and McNeil were sent to
Huttonsville. Under similar orders, Colonel Goff was
engaged in raising troops in Randolph county, and all
these separate companies were directed to unite as rapidly as possible at a point on the route to Grafton.

These Federal and Confederate military dispositions
around and within the western counties of Virginia had
their special bearings upon the political movements heretofore referred to, the object of Virginia and the Confederate government being to hold the western counties,
while it was the Federal design to facilitate the "dispart-
ing of Virginia." Keeping these military operations
which were occurring in April and May, 1861, before us,
we will consider the action taken at the same time among
the people of that section which led finally to the institution of the State of West Virginia.

The citizens of Virginia inhabiting the western counties
were uncompromisingly divided among themselves in
opinion as to their duty when their State became involved in the Confederate war. They had voted against
the secession of Virginia, and many of their representatives refused to conform to the ordinance of secession.
Hostilities, therefore, were begun first among themselves

by the antagonisms of neighbors and households; and by the recruiting of military companies for both the Confederate and the Federal armies. Allegiance to the commonwealth of Virginia as being the paramount obligation of the citizen held large numbers of Union men to the defense of its action, who formed themselves into military companies and entered the Confederate army. On the other hand many were so resolute in their repugnance to secession as to throw off the restraints of the old Virginia theory of allegiance, and to form companies and regiments for Federal service.

The Unionist sentiment in western Virginia led to a meeting at Clarksburg, April 22d, one week after the adoption of the ordinance of secession by the Virginia convention, at which eleven delegates were appointed to meet delegates from other counties at Wheeling, May 13th, to determine what course should be pursued. Similar meetings followed, and the convention which met at the date fixed, contained representatives of twenty-five counties. The popular vote on the ordinance of secession, polled May (fourth Thursday), was largely for rejection in western Virginia and almost unanimous for adoption beyond the mountains.

The informal convention of May 13th adopted resolutions condemning the ordinance and providing for a general election May 23d, of delegates from all counties favoring a division of the State, for a convention to be held at Wheeling, June 11th. Before that date arrived, on the pretext of defending railroad and other property, General McClellan with his army had entered the State, and Wheeling and the country far beyond were occupied by Ohio soldiers in overwhelming numbers. At the same time also, many companies of Virginia troops, for United States service, were organized, composed of men who afterward rendered gallant service for the cause they espoused.

About forty counties were represented by delegates

at Wheeling, June 11th, and the members before proceeding to business joined in an oath of supreme allegiance to the United States.   On June 13th a bill of
rights was adopted, repudiating all allegiance to the
Confederate States, to which Virginia was now united
by ordinance ratified by popular vote; the offices of governor of Virginia, etc., were declared vacant, a provisional
government was provided for, all officers were required
to take the oath of national allegiance, and on the 19th
a declaration of independence from Virginia was unanimously adopted.   The main argument in justification of
this declaration, was that under the bill of rights the
legislature had no right to call a convention to alter the
constitution and the relations of the commonwealth, without the previously expressed consent of the majority, and
that therefore usurpation had occurred which would
inevitably lead to military despotism.

During the session of this convention, Governor Letcher
issued a proclamation June 14th, to the people of northwestern Virginia, pointing out that the sovereign people
of Virginia by a majority of nearly 100,000 votes, had
exercised the right claimed by the fathers, to institute a
new government, and had united the commonwealth
with the Confederate States.   He declared that the
people had all had an opportunity to vote.   "You, as
well as the rest of the State, have cast your vote fairly,
and the majority is against you.   It is the duty of good
citizens to yield to the will of the State."   He quoted
the bill of rights, "that the people have a right to uniform government; and therefore that no government
separate from and independent of the government of
Virginia ought to be erected or established within the
limits thereof," and therefore, he said, "the majority
have a right to govern."   "But notwithstanding, this
right, thus exercised, has been regarded by the people of
all sections of the United States as undoubted and sacred,
yet the government at Washington now utterly denies

it, and by the exercise of despotic power, is endeavoring
to coerce our people to abject submission to their authority. Virginia has asserted her independence. She will
maintain it at every hazard.'' He also pointed out that
the new constitution had removed the previous inequality
of taxation between the east and west, and he closed an
eloquent appeal for unity in the commonwealth by the
words: ''The troops are posted at Huttonsville. Come
with your own good weapons and meet them as brothers.''

On June 20th, the convention at Wheeling elected a
provisional governor, Francis H. Pierpont, other State
officers and an executive council of five. The convention
purported to represent the whole State of Virginia, and
Pierpont declared that it was not the object of the convention to set up any new government in the State, other
than the one under which they had always lived. A
legislature was elected, which met at Wheeling, July 2d,
and was called the legislature of the restored government of Virginia. This body elected two senators for
Virginia, who took the seats in the United States Senate
vacated by Mason and Hunter. By authority of the
legislature, $27,000 in specie deposited in the Exchange
bank at Weston was seized and taken to Wheeling.
A resolution favoring the division of the State of Virginia was at first voted down in the Senate. The proposition to form a new State, to bear the name of Kanawha, was, however, already very strong, and a convention was called to carry out this plan. Attorney-General
Bates, of Lincoln's cabinet, in a letter to a member of
the convention, strongly opposed it, declaring that ''the
formation of a new State out of western Virginia is an
original, independent act of revolution. Any attempt to
carry it out involves a plain breach of both the constitutions, of Virginia and of the nation.'' He contended that
the plan under which the Unionist Virginians should act,
should be one purporting to preserve the old State government, ''claiming to be the very State which has been

in part overthrown by the successful rebellion. . . . The
Senate admitted your senators, not as representing a new
and nameless State, now for the first time heard of in
our history, but as representing 'the good old commonwealth.' " The constitutional convention met at Wheeling, November 26, 1861, and, influenced more by the success of the United States army than by the grave objec-
tions urged by Bates, framed a new constitution, which
was ratified May 3, 1862, by the "qualified voters" of
forty-eight of the old Virginia counties. Berkeley and
Jefferson counties were subsequently added. The mountain counties of Morgan, Hampshire, Hardy, Pendleton,
Pocahontas, Greenbrier, Monroe, Mercer and McDowell
(including the present counties of Mineral, Grant and
Summers), did not participate in the initial movement,
but were included in the formation of the new State.
At the election of May 3d, Pierpont also was elected "governor of Virginia," to fill the "unexpired" term of Governor Letcher, and he continued to administer the affairs
of the Trans-Alleghany until the new State was established, when he removed his "seat of government" to
Alexandria.

CHAPTER II.

McCLELLAN'S INVASION—THE AFFAIR AT PHILIPPI—
RICH MOUNTAIN AND LAUREL HILL—DEATH OF
GARNETT — OPERATIONS ABOUT ROMNEY — FED-
ERAL OCCUPATION OF THE KANAWHA VALLEY—
FIGHT AT SCARY CREEK—LORING AT CHEAT MOUNT-
AIN.

ON May 24th, Colonel Porterfield, who, with about
100 men, had been holding the town of Fetterman,
fell back to Grafton, and sent Col. J. M. Heck,
who had joined him two days before, to Richmond, to
report the condition of the little force, half armed and
altogether undisciplined, which was attempting to hold
the important post of Grafton, the junction of the roads
connecting Washington with Parkersburg and Wheeling
and thence with the Western States. In response to this
appeal General Lee could only say that he would furnish
some arms at Staunton, Va., and give Heck authority to
recruit a regiment in the valley and mountain counties on
the road to Grafton. Meanwhile, Colonel Porterfield had
received advices of the concentration of Federal troops
on the Ohio river, at Marietta and Bellaire and on Wheeling island, with the intention of invading the State; and
he thereupon caused the destruction of the railroad
bridges at Farmington and Mannington, northwest of
Grafton, and one on the Parkersburg line.

Almost simultaneously Gen. George B. McClellan, in
command of the Federal department of Ohio, issued a
proclamation to the people of western Virginia, declaring that "armed traitors" "are destroying the property
of citizens of your State and ruining your magnificent
railways," that the general government had heretofore
carefully abstained from invading the State, or posting

troops on the border, pending the election, but now "cannot close its ears to the demand you have made for assistance. I have ordered troops to cross the river. They come as your friends and brothers—as enemies only to the armed rebels that are preying upon you." He pledged a religious respect for property rights, and not only non-interference with slaves, but an "iron hand to crush" any servile insurrection. On the same date he ordered Col. B. F. Kelley, commanding the First Virginia infantry (U. S.) at Wheeling, to move toward Fairmount, supported by the Sixteenth Ohio from Bellaire, while the Fourteenth and Eighteenth Ohio, and a battery, were sent toward Grafton from Parkersburg. The troops from the northwest promptly repaired the bridges en route and occupied Grafton May 30th, the force from Parkersburg meeting with greater difficulties which delayed it.

Before this invasion by three or four thousand well-armed men, Colonel Porterfield with his little command moved south on the Tygart river to Philippi, carrying with him the State arms and stores. Before taking this step, which abandoned the Baltimore & Ohio railroad to the invading forces, he had appealed in vain for assistance from General Johnston at Harper's Ferry. Though bodies of volunteer infantry and cavalry formed by patriotic West Virginians joined him, he was compelled to dismiss some of them for want of arms. It was his intention to gather at Philippi a force with which he could advance upon the railroad and destroy its value to the enemy, but he was not able to get together more than 600 effective infantry and 175 cavalry, which, though armed, were but poorly supplied with ammunition and the necessary accouterments. In the meantime the Federals at Grafton had been reinforced by Indiana troops, and General Morris, of Indiana, had assumed command. He sanctioned a movement against Philippi devised by Colonel Kelley, and put under the latter's command. To insure a complete surprise of the Confederates at Philippi, the attacking party was divided.   Twenty-one companies under immediate command of Colonel Kelley started out by rail ostensibly toward Harper's Ferry, and after proceeding 6 miles disembarked and took the wagon road for Philippi, and nineteen companies and a battery were sent forward on the west side of the river from Webster. These forty companies marched through the night in a heavy rain that had quieted Colonel Porterfield's fears of such an attack, and reaching the Confederate camp at very nearly the same time, at daybreak, June 3d, surprised the pickets, opened fire with artillery, and charged with the intention of capturing the entire command.   Such a result should certainly have followed, under the conditions of surprise and great disproportion of numbers. Nevertheless the raw and undisciplined troops, both officers and men, conducted themselves with such courage and coolness that they caused the enemy about as much loss as fell upon themselves, and the whole command, after leaving the town, was restored to the good order which characterized a considerable part of it from the first firing.   About six Virginians were killed and several wounded, but the wounded were not abandoned. On the Federal side the main loss was the severe wounding of Colonel Kelley, as he was leading his men in a charge.   He was reported mortally wounded, but he survived to receive promotion to brigadier-general and to figure prominently in the war history of the State. Porterfield's command then retreated further down the river and through the mountain gap to Beverly, behind the mountain line of Rich mountain and Laurel hill, where more sanguinary contests were soon to occur.

At Beverly Colonel Porterfield reported his misfortune to General Lee, also giving an account of the depredations of the Federal troops and the "state of revolution" which existed in the section in the hands of the enemy. General Lee responded in a kindly letter, giving the welcome information that Gen. Robert S. Garnett had been assigned to command in that region and would soon reach the scene of action with such forces as were available in Virginia to aid the loyal western Virginians in their unequal struggle.

Colonel Heck, whose mission to Richmond has been mentioned, was on the way early in June with a battery of four pieces from Shenandoah county, Captain Moorman's cavalry company, and three companies of Virginia infantry, and Governor Letcher had called out the militia from the counties of Pendleton, Highland, Bath, Pocahontas, Randolph and Barbour. The response to this call seems to have been patriotic and abundant, but Colonel Heck decided to send the major part home to tend the crops, taking but 300 men from Highland, Bath and Pendleton. General Garnett reached Huttonsville, where Porterfield had then collected about twenty-four companies of West Virginians. From these were organized two regiments, the Twenty-fifth Virginia infantry, under Colonel Heck, and the Thirty-first, under Col. William L. Jackson, former lieutenant-governor of the State. With Jackson's regiment, Schumacher's battery, Anderson's half battery, and a company of cavalry, General Garnett occupied the pass on the Philippi road at the south end of Laurel hill, while Colonel Heck, in command of his regiment, a half battery and a company of cavalry, was stationed before the Buckhannon pass over Rich mountain, a few miles west of Beverly. A forced night march was made June 15th to seize these positions in advance of the enemy, who was reported to be advancing. For nearly three weeks these troops were undisturbed, meanwhile being reinforced by the Twentieth Virginia under Col. John Pegram, Col. J. N. Ramsey's First Georgia, and Col. J. V. Fulkerson's Thirty-seventh Virginia. Reconnoissances were made, and in one of these, Lieut. Robert McChesney, of Rockbridge county, was killed by a Federal ambush in Tucker county, June 29th, while fighting gallantly.

While the Virginians were thus preparing to defend the Cheat river line, McClellan, having entered Virginia in person, was promising the Washington authorities, as early as June 23d, an attack which should turn the Confederate position. He had issued proclamations and called for abundant reinforcements; had stationed eleven companies on the railroad at Cheat river bridge, a regiment at Grafton, another at Clarksburg, another at Weston, six companies at Parkersburg, six companies at Wirt Court House, had four companies out against a Confederate reconnoissance, had ordered four regiments into the Kanawha valley, and besides all this, "of his active army fifty-one companies and one battery" were at Philippi, under General Morris, "amusing the enemy," while McClellan had with him at Buckhannon six entire regiments of infantry, six detached companies, two batteries and two companies of cavalry, and more than two regiments expected. He repeated on July 5th his promise to advance, adding that he expected to "repeat the movement of Cerro Gordo," and on July 6th he positively promised that his advance guard would move the next day. Official figures of the numerical strength of his army are lacking, but the statement just made from his reports sufficiently indicates its overwhelming character as compared with the troops waiting on the hills under command of Garnett.

General Garnett, a soldier of twenty years' experience in the United States army, had no false confidence in the strength of his position, and gave the government at Richmond no reason to expect anything but disaster if he should be attacked by the enemy in force. He did not greatly fear such an attack, as he believed McClellan had possession of as much of western Virginia as was desired. In this vein General Garnett wrote, and General Lee, in response, expressed his belief that McClellan would attack and endeavor to penetrate Virginia as far as Staunton, a project that Garnett's object should

be to "prevent, if possible, and to restrict his limits
within the narrowest range, which, though outnumbered,
it is hoped by skill and boldness you will accomplish."
The Forty-fourth Virginia, Col. William C. Scott commanding, was already approaching Beverly from Richmond, followed by the Second Georgia, Col. Edward
Johnson, and a North Carolina regiment under Col.
Stephen Lee. To further relieve Garnett, General Lee
on July 11th ordered Wise to move from Charleston upon
Parkersburg. But reinforcements and diversion were
alike too late. The blow had already fallen.

The entire Confederate force on July 8th consisted of
3,381 men at Laurel hill, 859 at Rich mountain, and 375
at Beverly. The position at Rich mountain, on a spur
near its western base, called Camp Garnett, was fortified
with a breastwork of logs covered with an abatis
of slashed timber along its front, and the position on
the Philippi road at Laurel mountain was similarly
strengthened.

On July 6th the Confederate picket was driven in from
Middle Fork bridge between Buckhannon and Rich
mountain, and that position was occupied by McCook's
brigade, while Morris advanced from Philippi to within
a mile and a half of Garnett's position. On the 9th Mc-
Clellan's three brigades encamped at Roaring Run flats,
in sight of the Confederate camp at Rich mountain, and on
that day and next made reconnoissances in force. There
were now about 1,300 Confederates at Camp Garnett
under command of Col. John Pegram, afterward distinguished as a brigadier-general. He, as well as General
Garnett, underestimated the Federal strength, and he
even contemplated a night attack upon the 10,000 troops
confronting him. But perceiving signs of a flank attack,
he posted pickets on the top of the mountain about two
miles to the rear, and early on the morning of the 11th
he learned that six regiments of infantry, under General
Rosecrans, were already on their way to seize a position

on the summit of the mountain commanding his fortifications.   To meet this he could only send reinforcements
to the mountain picket, making in all about 300 men and
one gun, under Capt. Julius A. DeLagnel, while he asked
Garnett to order Colonel Scott's Forty-fourth regiment
in the valley to hold the road in advance of Beverly.
About 11 o'clock in the forenoon of the 11th, Rosecrans
attacked Captain DeLagnel at Hart's house, on the
mountain, in overwhelming numbers.   The intrepid
300 fought with desperate courage, repulsing two
attacks, and keeping up the fight for three hours, during
which about one-third of their number were killed or
wounded.   Pegram, upon hearing the firing, had hurried
to the scene and ordered up the remainder of his regiment, but becoming convinced that his situation was too
desperate to warrant an attack, he sent this body under
Maj. Nat Tyler to effect a junction with either General
Garnett or Colonel Scott, while he returned to the camp,
where Colonel Heck with a few hundred men and two
guns had been all day confronting McClellan.   The
latter had passed the day, in sound of the musketry on
the mountain, cutting roads and mounting artillery to
assault a force which he outnumbered ten to one.
Heck's command, as soon as Pegram arrived, about
midnight, under his orders, spiked their guns and retreated up the mountain, along which they made their
way slowly next day toward General Garnett's camp at
Laurel hill.   The men under Tyler traversed the pathless
mountain to Beverly, overtook the Forty-fourth at Huttonsville, and retreated to Monterey.

Meanwhile, when Morris advanced toward Laurel hill
there had been brisk skirmishing with Garnett's pickets,
and on the 8th an attempt of the enemy to drive the Confederates from an advanced position at Belington was
repulsed.   But at midnight following the 11th, being
informed of the success of Rosecrans at Hart's farm,
Garnett evacuated Laurel hill.   He was falsely informed

that the Federals had advanced to Beverly, and consequently crossed Tygart valley and over Cheat mountain into the Cheat river valley, down which he was pursued northward by the Federal brigade under General Morris. On the morning of July 13th skirmishing began between his rear guard and the Federal advance, and when Carrick's ford was reached, the rear guard, the Twenty-third regiment, under Colonel Taliaferro, supported by artillery, took position on the high bank as soon as it had crossed, while the enemy brought up infantry and artillery on the opposite bank, and for some time a spirited fire was kept up across the stream, in which Taliaferro lost 28 killed and wounded, the enemy's loss being much greater. The Confederates opened the fight with cheers for President Davis, and twice drove back the enemy from the ford, but finally, having exhausted their ammunition, withdrew in good order to the next ford, about a half mile to the rear. On the further side of this ford the gallant Garnett, having posted the main command 4 miles further back, was waiting for the rear guard, and when it had crossed placed a few sharpshooters as skirmishers behind some drift-wood on the bank, while the regiment was sent on to a position he had selected. The enemy's advance was close upon him, and soon perceiving that he was about to be flanked, he sent orders to Taliaferro to retreat rapidly to the rear. Under the fire of the enemy now, he ordered his skirmishers to fall back, and at that moment was killed by a rifle ball, one of the sharpshooters at the same time falling dead at his side. His riderless horse, dashing to the rear, carried the sad news of the general's death. Thus fell, sharing the post of greatest danger in a disastrous retreat which he could not avoid, the first distinguished martyr of the Confederacy. His command, greatly depleted by the fatigues of the rapid march over the mountain paths, rendered still more difficult by the heavy rain, continued northward under the command of Colonel Ramsey, marching all the following night to a point near West Union, when they crossed the Maryland line to Red House and thence moved southward, the next day, to Greenland, Hardy county, finally reaching Monterey after seven days' arduous marching.

Colonel Pegram's command, which we left in the course of their march of 17 miles along the summit of the mountain to join Garnett, on the night of the 12th made an attempt to cross the valley eastward, but his reconnoissance was fired upon and he was advised that the enemy held Leadsville, in the rear of Garnett's former position. Both commander and troops were exhausted and starving, and it was decided after returning to the foot of the mountain range to surrender. Accordingly at midnight a proposition to that effect was sent to General McClellan, then at Beverly, and on the next day, July 13th, the first formal capitulation of the great war took place, 28 officers and 525 men becoming prisoners of war. They were well treated, and in a few days all were released on parole save Colonel Pegram.

Thus ended in disaster the first completed campaign of the Confederate war. There were many instances of remarkable heroism and valor. In the main the troops fought with coolness and tenacity in the face of fearful odds, and maintained their organizations wonderfully well during exhausting and rapid movements over the most impassable country that can well be imagined. Their marches were made through dense thickets of laurel, over precipitous mountains, across raging streams, and along paths impracticable for ordinary military operations. Yet the conduct of the Confederates under these circumstances, and particularly their stubborn fighting at Hart's house and Carrick's ford would suffice to convince a careful observer that the same sort of soldiers, given chances somewhat even, would yet win a victory glorious enough to lift the cloud of gloom which settled upon the South after this unfortunate campaign. Such a prophet would have found himself speedily justified, for ten days later came Manassas.

Previous to the active operations which we have described, the Federal commanders had sent out various parties to break up meetings of citizens supposed to be in the interests of Virginia, or for the formation of military commands. Col. Lew Wallace, of Indiana, stationed at Cumberland, Md., engaged in such an enterprise June 13th.

The people of Hampshire county were loyal to the Southern cause. This county was on the border line, and suffered untold troubles and horrors during the war then beginning. It would take volumes to contain all that was done and suffered for the Southland by the men and the women and the children of this county during the following four years. When the convention at Richmond passed the ordinance of secession, a meeting of citizens of Romney, the county seat, was held on the 27th of April and patriotic resolutions were passed, calling upon the people to prepare for the worst, and a committee of safety was appointed to look out for the public good. The county prepared for war, meetings were held, men enlisted, money was subscribed to equip volunteers and pay the men, and the county court appropriated $10,000 to be expended under the supervision of a committee appointed for the purpose.

Hearing of this and that some Virginia militia were drilling at Romney, Colonel Wallace made a descent upon that place, June 13th, with 500 Indianians, and reported that he put to rout not only all the military but the inhabitants of the town, including women and children, and captured among others "Maj. Isaac Vandever, a gentleman who, from accounts, has been very active in exciting rebellion, organizing troops, and impressing loyal citizens." No town in the South, except perhaps Winchester, 40 miles away, had a record surpassing that of the town of Romney, in regard to the changing of its occupancy by the armies of each side. It is well established that, beginning with Wallace's raid, at least fifty-six times during the war it passed into the control of the Federal army.

After the evacuation of Harper's Ferry, June 16, 1861, when the army of the Shenandoah retired toward Winchester, Thomas J. Jackson, then ranking as colonel, was stationed near Martinsburg, and after making some demonstrations against the Federal advance, did good work in destroying transportation cars and locomotives on the Baltimore & Ohio railroad.

The Thirteenth Virginia and Third Tennessee regiments, under the command of A. P. Hill, were marched from Harper's Ferry, by way of Winchester, to Romney, a distance of about 75 miles. The Union troops had retired. Upon reaching Romney it was ascertained that a company of Federal infantry, with two field pieces, was guarding the bridge over the north branch of the Potomac on the Baltimore & Ohio railroad, some 18 miles northwest from Romney. Colonel Hill detached Company I, of the Thirteenth, and a company of Tennesseeans and sent them to capture the bridge referred to. About sunrise on June 19th, an attack was made, the Federal soldiers driven from the bridge and the two pieces of artillery captured and carried off. This little fight was quick and sharp, ending in one of the first victories of the war.

Jackson, having advanced to Darkesville, at Falling Waters, encountered the Federals who had crossed the Potomac to attack him, and although fighting in retreat with one regiment of infantry and his cavalry, punished his adversary by the loss of 49 prisoners and several killed, while in his own command there were 12 wounded and 13 killed and captured. Jackson was made brigadier-general a few days previous to this fight.

On June 26, 1861, Richard Ashby, a brother of the celebrated Gen. Turner Ashby, lost his life in a skirmish in Hampshire county. The two Ashbys were in charge of a body of Virginia cavalry, scouting toward Cumberland, Md., when Richard was mortally wounded by a bayonet thrust. His body lies beside that of his brother Turner in the Confederate cemetery at Winchester, Va.

On July 21, 1861, a Federal force under Colonel Kain entered Romney. In the same month Colonel Cummins with some Confederate troops retook it.

The loyal Virginians in other parts of the State were active in expeditions to repress hostile organization. One of these was made by Capt. A. G. Jenkins, afterward famous as a cavalry general, in the latter part of June. He advanced from Charleston to Point Pleasant with a mounted party, and secured the persons of several prominent Union men. Colonel Norton, of the First Ohio, at Gallipolis, crossed the river with 100 men and made a vain attempt to overtake Jenkins, after which he "scoured the country and took 30 prominent secessionists prisoners." These gentlemen, who were carried to Camp Chase, Ohio, were the first to arrive from the South at that noted prison camp. They reached Camp Chase July 5th, but were released a few days later. The names of these loyal Virginians were R. B. Hackney, A. B. Dorst, A. Roseberry, H. J. Fisher, R. Knupp, Jacob C. Kline, Frank Ransom, J. N. McMullen, J. W. Echard, David Long, G. D. Slaughter, A. E. Eastman, J. F. Dintz, Robert Mitchell, S. Hargiss, E. J. Ransom, T. B. Kline, Alexander McCausland, O. H. P. Sebrill, James Johnson, W. O. Roseberry, Benjamin Franklin and James Clark.

On June 6th the Confederate war department, being advised of the contemplated occupation of the Kanawha valley by the United States troops, and fearing for the safety of the Tennessee & Virginia railroad, issued orders designed to protect that region. Ex-Gov. Henry A. Wise, having been commissioned brigadier-general, was ordered to move from Richmond with the force placed at his disposal to the valley of the Kanawha, and Gen.

John B. Floyd, an old United States officer, was specially charged with the protection of the railroad. Wise was instructed to rally the people of western Virginia, and rely upon the people of that section not only for supplies but for arms. In case the enemy should largely outnumber the forces he could gather and equip, with such resources, he was to fall back to the mountain passes. The Confederate government then had more formidable attacks to oppose. Patterson advancing from Maryland was threatening Johnston's army in the Shenandoah valley, McDowell before Washington was advancing upon Manassas, and a large force was needed for the defense of Norfolk and the James river. When Johnston was writing that he must retreat from Harper's Ferry, having but forty rounds of ammunition, the government was forced to rely upon the ability of the West Virginians to defend themselves, and that failing, upon the mountains as a line of defense. Wise left Col. J. L. Davis at Richmond for the organization of Wise's legion from Virginia and North Carolina volunteers, and proceeded to Lewisburg and thence to Charleston.

As early as April 29th Lieut.-Col. John McCausland had been authorized to muster into the State service as many as ten volunteer companies, and direct the military operations of that part of the State. He was told that two companies in Kanawha county, Captain Patton's "Kanawha Rifles," Capt. T. B. Swann's company and two in Putnam, Captain Beckett's and Capt. W. E. Fife's (Buffalo Guards), would doubtless offer their services, and that 500 muskets of the old pattern would be sent and four field pieces. On May 3d a commission as colonel was sent to C. Q. Tompkins, of Charleston, and he was directed to take command of the troops raised in the valley. The latter officer sent Colonel McCausland to Richmond, May 30th, to confer with Governor Letcher on the situation. It was difficult to procure reliable soldiers in large numbers, with perhaps the preponderance of sentiment favoring the Federal cause. By this time McCausland and Tompkins had gathered but 340 men at Kanawha Court House, and when all the companies promised had been formed, the aggregate would hardly exceed 1,000. But with a stout heart Tompkins at once issued from Charleston a proclamation counter to that of McClellan:

Men of Virginia! Men of Kanawha! To Arms!

The enemy has invaded your soil and threatens to overrun your country under the pretext of protection. You cannot serve two masters. You have not the right to repudiate allegiance to your own State. Be not seduced by his sophistry or intimidated by his threats. Rise and strike for your firesides and altars. Repel the aggressors and preserve your honor and your rights. Rally in every neighborhood with or without arms. Organize and unite with the sons of the soil to defend it. Report yourselves without delay to those nearest to you in military position. Come to the aid of your fathers, brothers and comrades in arms at this place, who are here for the protection of your mothers, wives and sisters. Let every man who would uphold his rights turn out with such arms as he may get and drive the invader back.

Out of the troops gathered at Charleston, McCausland subsequently organized the Thirty-sixth Virginia infantry regiment, which he commanded until promoted brigadier-general, and Tompkins formed the Twenty-second, led by Col. George S. Patton, until he fell at Winchester, and afterward by Colonel Barbee. By July 8th, General Wise, who had reached Charleston and assumed command, had a force of 2,600 men, consisting of the First and Second Kanawha regiments, the Kanawha battalion, seven independent companies of infantry, and three companies of mounted rangers. Reinforcements from his legion soon arrived, so that a few days later he had about 4,000 men, with ten small pieces of artillery.

In the meantime Ohio troops had been massed at Gallipolis and Point Pleasant, and Gen. J. D. Cox, an officer afterward distinguished at South Mountain and Franklin, was assigned to the command.   July 11th he began his movement up the Kanawha river, by boat, with advance guards marching along the river roads, while another column moved up the Guyandotte and another advanced overland from Ravenswood.   In anticipation of this advance General Wise arranged to meet the enemy west of Charleston, posting 900 men at Coal and 1,600 at Two Mile and Elk, with outposts at Ripley and Barboursville; while 1,000 men were scattered in the rear from Gauley bridge past Summersville to Birch river, toward Rich mountain.   He could not safely make the Parkersburg diversion suggested by Garnett and Lee.   Instead he asked that Garnett reinforce the Kanawha army, at the very time that the latter general was engaged in his fatal retreat.

On the 16th, Colonel Clarkson, with Brock's and Becket's troops of horse, had a brisk skirmish with the enemy near Ripley, and another fight occurred at Barboursville with the right of Cox's army.

Wise wrote at this juncture that the difficulties of his situation were great, and that "this army here has grown by neglect at Richmond.   It has been literally created by Colonel Tompkins, at first beginning with Patton's company alone, since assisted by my legion, which I have created between this and Richmond."

Cox united his three columns at the mouth of the Pocotaligo, and on the afternoon of the 17th sent Colonel Lowe, with the Twelfth Ohio and two companies of the Twenty-first, to make a landing at Scary creek, where Colonel Patton with about 800 men held a position which commanded the river.   Patton had been ordered by Wise to retreat to Bunker Hill, but he gallantly turned back of his own accord and met the enemy's advance.   The enemy was better armed, and after a half hour's fighting a portion of Patton's command fell back.   He rallied his men, however, and returning instantly to action was fifteen minutes later wounded and disabled.   Capts.

Albert G. Jenkins, Bailey, Swann and Sweeney stood their ground, also Col. F. Anderson, whose two companies on the left had not yet come into action. Now there was a rally by the Confederates and they were gaining the advantage, when a cannon ball from the enemy struck one of Patton's 6-pounder guns, disabling it and killing Lieutenant Welch and fatally wounding a private. The other gun withdrew, and for a time the Virginians were disordered. But A. G. Jenkins came to the rescue and a rally followed in which Colonel Anderson and his men joined, with Bailey, Swann and Sweeney, and reinforcements from Captain Coons on Coal mountain, and the enemy were driven back and forced to recross the river. General Wise, whose report is followed in this account of the fight, reported the capture of Federal Colonels Norton, Woodruff and DeVilliers, Lieutenant-Colonel Neff, Captains Austin and Ward, and some 10 to 20 privates, and about 30 of the enemy killed. His loss was 1 killed and 2 wounded. Colonel McCausland with 800 men followed this up with an attack on Cox's position on the north side of the river, and drove back the enemy to the shelter of their guns on the Pocotaligo.

This fight of July 17th was a very creditable affair for the Virginians and did much to restore confidence that had flagged under the influence of continued "surprises" and retreats. It was the first victory for the Confederate States in an open fight, Big Bethel being rather a repulse by artillery from behind breastworks. McClellan, though he called it "something between a victory and a defeat," took it seriously to heart, and adjured the government, "In Heaven's name give me some general officers who understand their profession." "Unless I command every picket and lead every column I cannot be sure of success," he added, strangely oblivious to the fact that his success thus far had been entirely due to the energy of Rosecrans as a column leader.

General Wise, though jubilant over his victory, realized

the difficulty of his position, and on the 19th sent Maj.
C. B. Duffield to Richmond with official reports and a
letter, in which he complained bitterly of hostile feeling of the inhabitants of the valley, and of the difficulty of defending a position threatened by over
3,000 Federals at the Pocotaligo, 1,500 from Ripley to
Sissonville, and forces from the north by Summersville.
He had an engineer, "Colonel Adler, a Hungarian, a
man of consummate ability, science and bravery," aided
by Prof. Thomas I. L. Snead, of William and Mary, and
Lieut. J. B. Harvie. "We are throwing up breastworks
and defenses at every pass and mean never to be taken,"
he added.

But on the 24th the fears of General Wise regarding
the weakness of his position were justified. Cox, by a
circuitous advance among the hills, came upon the Confederate rear at Elk or Tyler mountain, and as soon as
the outposts were driven in Wise was compelled to retreat up the river. The enemy brought up artillery to
the bluff and nearly succeeded in cutting off 700 of
Colonel Tompkins' command at Coal. They escaped but
were compelled to burn the steamer on which they were
about to start up the river, when the artillery fire was
opened upon them. The retreat was made in creditable
order, and on the 27th Wise and his army passed through
Gauley, destroying the bridges behind them, because
there was a great deficiency of transportation and the
men, worn out with marching and countermarching,
lacking shoes and clothing and without tents, were
obliged to move slowly. He reached Lewisburg August
1st, and reported the enemy following in three columns
from Fayetteville, Gauley and Summersville.

The Confederate forces were now practically expelled
from transmontane Virginia. Wise lay in the Greenbrier valley, and the remnant of the forces that were
with Garnett was at Monterey, beyond the limits of
what is now West Virginia. Among the volunteers who

joined Wise at this time were about 300 from Boone and Logan counties, who mainly entered the Third regiment, Wise legion, later known as the Sixtieth regiment, and commanded by Col. B. H. Jones.

Cox held Gauley, and began fortifications, with an advance guard skirmishing toward Sewell mountain, and a regiment guarding his river communications; while Rosecrans, now the Federal commander of the department, fortified the Cheat mountain pass before Huttonsville, and the mountain pass between Huttonsville and Huntersville. These were advanced posts. His main line was marked by a chain of posts, with a regiment or two at each, at Bulltown, Suttonville and Summersville, between Weston and Gauley.

While the events we have described were taking place, an army was forming at Monterey for the purpose of retrieving the Confederate disasters. Previous to Garnett's defeat there had been assembled near Staunton 5,000 or 6,000 troops for his reinforcement, under the command of Gen. Henry R. Jackson, of Georgia. It will be remembered that the Forty-fourth Virginia was at Monterey during the battle of Rich Mountain. It took a position directed by General Garnett, which happened to be one where no service could be rendered. Col. Edward Johnson's Twelfth Georgia, following, made a forced march to occupy Cheat mountain, but met Colonel Scott returning, was advised of Garnett's retreat and fell back to Jackson's main body. The entire command then retired to Monterey, where, with about 3,500 men, Jackson prepared to combat the expected advance of McClellan by Huntersville and Warm Springs to cut the railroad near Staunton. This, however, was not attempted by the Federals. It was deemed too dangerous an enterprise, and McClellan being transferred to Washington, took with him many of his troops, leaving adequate garrisons at the posts established.

On July 20th Brig.-Gen. William W. Loring, a veteran

of the Mexican war, commander of the department of Oregon during the gold excitement, and experienced in mountain warfare, was assigned to the command of the Northwestern army.   He was advised by General Lee that, in addition ;to the forces he would find at Monterey under Jackson, Brigadier-General Floyd, with the brigade he had organized in southwest Virginia, had been directed to move to Covington, Brigadier-General Wise toward the same point, and Col. Angus McDonald with his cavalry legion from the south branch of the Potomac to Staunton.   On the 21st, the day of victory at Manassas, three Tennessee regiments, reaching Staunton, were put under General Loring's orders.

Loring reached Monterey July 24th, accompanied by an efficient staff, including Col. Carter L. Stevenson, adjutant-general, and Maj. A. L. Long, chief of artillery, and flushed with the assurance of success which pervaded the Confederate States immediately after the splendid triumph at Manassas.   Jackson had found it unadvisable to attempt a direct attack upon the Federal fortifications at Cheat Mountain pass, a narrow gap approachable only by the Parkersburg turnpike, and fitted for effective defense. Col. Edward Johnson, with Anderson's battery, was stationed at Alleghany Mountain pass, supported by Rust's Arkansas and Baldwin's Virginia regiments; Colonel Lee's North Carolina regiment was advanced to Elk Mountain pass, supporting the Bath cavalry at Big Spring. Captain Marye's battery was sent forward to Colonel Lee, and 250 Pocahontas militia being mustered in, 80 of them were put on duty as scouts and guides.   With Johnson at Monterey were Fulkerson's and Scott's Virginia regiments, Ramsey's First Georgia, Major Jackson's cavalry and Shumaker's battery.   General Loring determined to flank the Federal position by way of the Valley mountain.   He ordered Jackson's command over into the Greenbrièr valley and made preparations for an advance from Huntersville.   At the latter point were Maney's,

Hatton's and Savage's Tennessee regiments, Campbell's Virginia regiment (Forty-eighth), Colonel Munford's battalion, Maj. W. H. F. Lee's cavalry squadron, and Marye's and Stanley's batteries. Colonel Gilham was at Valley Mountain pass with his own and another regiment, and Burks' Virginia and a Georgia regiment were en route from Staunton. Loring's force on the Huntersville line was in all about 8,500 effective men. But the prompt advance which was contemplated in the orders of General Lee, was delayed for the establishment of a depot of supplies and the formation of a wagon train.

When General Wise had first been ordered to the Kanawha valley, he had been advised that whenever it became necessary for him to be joined by Gen. John B. Floyd, the latter should have command of the joint forces. The time for this junction had now arrived and trouble immediately resulted. Floyd, also an ex-governor of Virginia, as well as ex-secretary of war of the United States, had been telegraphed to at Abingdon, May 14th, by President Davis, asking him if he could raise a "brigade of your mountain riflemen with their own tried weapons." Floyd immediately responded that he could and would, and he was commissioned brigadier-general soon afterward. At Abingdon and Wytheville and Dublin Depot he took measures to protect the railroad communications of Richmond with Tennessee, until, under the orders of July, he moved to Covington and thence to the vicinity of Wise's troops at White Sulphur Springs. General Wise immediately objected to passing under the command of General Floyd, and an embarrassing situation followed, which in a large measure prevented effective work in the Kanawha valley.

CHAPTER III.

AFTER the danger of invasion from the northeast
had been relieved by the victory at Manassas,
Gen. Robert E. Lee gave his attention personally
to the direction of affairs in the Trans-Alleghany department. He arrived at Huntersville in the latter part of
July, and assumed chief command. The circumstances
were somewhat embarrassing to Lee. Throughout his
entire career as a soldier he manifested confidence in his
subordinates, wisely no doubt, taking upon himself blame
when misfortune came, and treating with indulgence
those manifestations of human nature that do not become
subordinate generals, but often impair their usefulness.

He now had an army of two wings; the right under
Loring, who had outranked Lee in the old army, and
the left nominally under Floyd, but actually divided without prospect of effective co-operation. Establishing himself near the headquarters of General Loring, he maintained constant communication with Floyd and Wise.

To add to the difficulties of the situation, the weather
heightened the disadvantages of the rugged country.
For weeks it rained daily in torrents, and the roads became hardly passable. The army was provisioned with
the greatest difficulty, and the troops, deprived of proper
food and shelter, suffered a terrible scourge of measles
and fever.

In preparation for active operations, Gen. Alfred Beckley and Gen. A. A. Chapman, commanding militia brigades in western Virginia, were ordered to collect as much of their forces as possible.

On the 10th, Colonel Davis, occupying the advanced post at Meadow Bluff, reported the enemy in his front, and Floyd advanced to that place, "peremptorily" ordering Wise to follow on the 14th, to which Wise responded that he would execute the order "as early as possible, and as forces and means of transportation are available." He did not have half enough wagons, his horses were without shoes, and his command was in a very unsatisfactory condition. But he sent forward such men as he believed available, about 2,000, and a few days later occupied Big Sewell mountain. At this juncture, in response to the request of General Wise, General Lee detached from the latter's command Tompkins' and McCausland's Twenty-second and Thirty-sixth regiments, and restricted the immediate command of General Wise to his legion.

General Wise advanced with skirmishing to Dogwood gap, while Floyd occupied Summersville, one of the posts on Rosecrans' line, where he could make a flank attack either on Cox at Gauley or Rosecrans to the north, and he asked for reinforcements from Richmond. General Cox, with about three regiments, had succeeded in impressing his antagonists with an exaggerated idea of his strength, while he was preparing to stand a siege. At Carnifix Ferry was stationed the only reinforcement near him, an Ohio regiment under Colonel Tyler.

On the 20th of August, Lieutenant-Colonel Croghan, in advance of Wise, had two skirmishes on the turnpike, one near Hawk's Nest, in which each side lost a few killed and wounded. The little army was then greatly afflicted with measles, to such an extent that the Forty-sixth Virginia reported but one-third of the command effective. On the 25th, Colonel Jenkins' cavalry was defeated at Hawk's Nest near Piggot's mill by an infantry ambuscade, with a loss of 8 or 10 wounded. Wise,

previous to this, had marched to the Gauley river near
Summersville to aid Floyd, but had been returned to
Dogwood gap. On the 26th Floyd achieved a brilliant
success. Raising a flatboat which Tyler had sunk, he
crossed the Gauley river at Carnifix Ferry and surprised
Tyler's regiment at breakfast near Cross Lanes. Floyd
reported that between 45 and 50 of the enemy were killed
and wounded, and over 100 prisoners and some stores were
taken. The receipt of news of this disaster caused Rosecrans at once to make arrangements to advance toward
Gauley. Floyd was now in a position to attack Gauley
from the rear while Wise advanced, but unfortunately a
strong movement was not made. Floyd being informed
that Cox was abandoning Gauley and marching upon
him, ordered Wise to hasten to his reinforcement, which
he did, only to be informed en route that it had been
ascertained that he would not be needed. Returning to
Dogwood he advanced on September 2d, against the
strong position of the Federals at Hawk's Nest, attacking in front while Colonel Anderson attempted to gain
the rear of the little mountain which the enemy occupied,
covering the turnpike which circled about its base toward
Gauley. Parts of three companies, Summers', Ryan's
and Janes', were sent across Big creek and up the hill,
driving the enemy gallantly, until the Confederates
gained the summit. Meanwhile a howitzer was set to
playing on the hill, which speedily cleared the enemy
from the side next Wise; but the enemy being reinforced,
and commanding the road with a rifled cannon and
Anderson not completing his roundabout march soon
enough, Wise abandoned his project of turning the hill,
and took a position covering Miller's ferry and Liken's
mill. General Beckley's militia had driven the enemy
from Cotton hill on the south side of the river, and was
joined there by General Chapman's militia, whence a few
cannon balls were thrown into the Federal camp at
Gauley. During this period, the troops under Wise and

the militia south of the river kept up a continual skirmishing, and the Federals, annoyed by the hostility of
the volunteers, sent an expedition to Boone Court House,
which, according to General Cox, routed a militia encampment and left 25 dead upon the field.

Floyd remained inactive at Carnifix Ferry, fearing an
attack from Rosecrans, and waiting for reinforcements
for a flank attack upon Gauley.   On the 9th, becoming
alarmed by news of the approach of Rosecrans, he asked
Wise to send troops to his assistance, stating that he had
but 1,600 men to oppose the six regiments of Rosecrans.
Wise returned Tompkins' regiment, but declined to send
more for fear of losing his position.   At the same time
he wrote to General Lee, asking to be separated from
Floyd's command.   In this letter, Wise estimated the
Confederate forces at 1,200 infantry, 250 artillery and 350
cavalry in his legion, Tompkins' regiment 400, Floyd's
immediate command 1,200, McCausland's regiment 400,
Chapman's and Beckley's militia, 2,000.   Repeated orders
from Floyd for reinforcements followed, the last one
written in the midst of battle.

Failing to obtain assistance, General Floyd constructed
intrenchments on the elevations before Carnifix Ferry at
the junction of Meadow river and the Gauley, and was
there attacked at 3 p. m., September 10th, by General
Rosecrans, who had under his command nine regiments,
eight of which participated in the battle.   The odds were
at the least estimate three to one.   The Federal brigade
which made the first attack was commanded by Gen.
H. W. Benham, the same officer who, as a captain, was in
charge of the vigorous pursuit of General Garnett to
Carrick's ford.   His command suffered heavily from an
effective fire of musketry and artillery, which greeted its
first appearance before the works.   Colonel Lytle, commanding the Tenth Ohio in this brigade, was among the
wounded and gained promotion by his gallantry.   Colonel Lowe, of the Twelfth Ohio, was killed at the head of

his regiment.   A series of charges were made upon the works as the various regiments came up, but were gallantly repulsed.   The Federal batteries joined in the attack, replied to with equal spirit from the Confederate guns.   The battle raged without intermission four hours, until night put an end to the fighting.   Both infantry and artillery of Wise's command behaved with great coolness and intrepidity, and General Floyd specially mentioned the excellent performance of Guy's battery, for the first time under fire.   The Federals were repulsed in five separate assaults, and finally withdrew from the front of the works, intending to renew the attack in the morning.   But Floyd, having observed that the Federals had gained during the fight a position from which his line could be enfiladed, determined to abandon his hazardous position during the night, which he accomplished in safety without the loss of a gun.   He had great difficulty in getting his guns down from the cliffs in the darkness over a wretched road, but he made the movement without molestation, and gained a position on the opposite shore where he could command the ferry, a smooth bit of water in the otherwise impassable mountain torrent.   Once over, the bridge and ferryboat were destroyed.   The Confederate loss in this action was but 20 wounded, Floyd himself receiving a slight wound in the arm, while the Federal loss was 17 killed and 141 wounded.   Floyd had abandoned his position, but held one stronger, and still commanded the road by which Rosecrans would march to attack Wise, and with very little loss had inflicted severe punishment upon the enemy.   He should have been captured to give Rosecrans title to claim of a victory.

Floyd considered the battle of Carnifix Ferry decisive so far as the troops with him and Wise were concerned. He reported that he could have beaten the enemy if Wise had come up when ordered, and the North Carolina and Georgia regiments could have arrived before the close of the second day's conflict, but that now the project of opening the Kanawha valley could only be attained by an advance upon the enemy along the south bank of the Kanawha. He estimated the Confederate forces at hand as 4,200 and the enemy at 12,000. The secretary of war responded, conveying the congratulations of the President and himself "on this brilliant affair, in which the good conduct and steady valor of your whole command were so conspicuously displayed," and promising reinforcements. General Floyd soon abandoned the Gauley river, and moved to a junction with Wise near Dogwood gap.

Cox advanced on the 12th and the Confederates retired to Sewell mountain, occupying first the crest of the ridge and later a more defensible position about a mile and a half in the rear, which appears to have been selected by Wise. Here the latter established "Camp Defiance," and in the spirit of that title awaited the advance of Cox and Rosecrans, and disregarded the orders of Floyd to fall back to Meadow Bluff, a point 16 miles west of Lewisburg, in a fertile country, at the union of the only good roads to the Gauley and the New ferries. Meanwhile there was some skirmishing going on with the Federal advance, and Col. Lucius Davis, commanding the First regiment of Wise's legion, operated on the south side of the New river, capturing over 40 prisoners.

Up to this time, General Lee had not visited the forces in the Kanawha valley, and had left the conduct of operations entirely to General Floyd, and we will now turn to that even more rugged and difficult field in which the department commander was endeavoring to dislodge the enemy. The Federal force before Huttonsville was under the immediate command of Brig.-Gen. Joseph J. Reynolds, who with about 5,000 men lay at Elkwater, about 10 miles below Huttonsville in the Tygart valley, on the Huntersville road, while three regiments under Colonel Kimball held the impregnable pass of Cheat mountain,

through which the main road from Huttonsville eastward, the Parkersburg turnpike, led in a narrow defile.
The two posts were about seven miles apart by bridle
path through the hills.

The army of the Northwest, now well organized, and
under the immediate command of General Loring, consisted of the brigades of S. R. Anderson, D. S. Donelson,
William Gilham, H. R. Jackson, and W. B. Taliaferro,
and unassigned commands, amounting nominally to
11,700 men, including about 300 each in the cavalry and
artillery arms.

One portion of the army, the "Monterey division,"
under Gen. H. R. Jackson, was encamped at "Camp
Bartow," near where the Parkersburg pike crosses the
Greenbrier river, and included Jackson's Georgia brigade, Rust's Arkansas regiment, Taliaferro's brigade
(Twenty-third, Thirty-first, Thirty-seventh and Forty-
fourth regiments), Hansbrough and Reger's battalions,
two batteries of artillery, and a few companies of cavalry,
in all about 2,500 effective men.

The other wing of the army, under General Loring, in
camp at Valley mountain, included the brigades of Donelson, Anderson and Gilham (Twenty-first and Forty-
second Virginia and Irish battalion in the latter), Colonel
Burk's command and Major Lee's cavalry. About 3,500
men in this division were effective.

General Lee went to the front early in August, accompanied by his aides, Col. John A. Washington and Capt.
Walter H. Taylor, and Maj. W. H. F. Lee's cavalry battalion. He entered personally upon the work of reconnoissance, a work in which he had contributed brilliantly
to the success of General Scott's army in Mexico, and
hardly a day passed when he was not climbing over rocks
and crags, to get a view of the Federal position. One
day, Captain Preston, adjutant of the Forty-eighth Virginia (the incident is recorded by Gen. A. L. Long), his
regiment being on picket, saw three men on a peak about

a half mile in advance, and believing them to be Yankees, got permission to steal up with two men and capture them. After a tedious climb over the rocks and through the mountain thickets, he suddenly burst upon the unsuspecting trio, and to his amazement found that one of them was General Lee.

About the middle of August, rain set in and continued for several weeks, making the narrow mountain roads impassable, while the troops unaccustomed to exposure fell easy victims to typhoid fever, measles and homesickness. These afflictions rendered nearly one-third the army unavailable if the rain had ceased. During this trying period, General Lee maintained his cheerfulness and busied himself in the exertions to find a practicable route leading to the rear of Cheat Mountain pass, the key to the northwest. Colonel Rust, of the Third Arkansas, finally reported a possible path, and on September 9th, General Lee issued orders for a general advance of the army of the Northwest. There was a skirmish at Marshall's store on the 9th with an infantry reconnoissance of the enemy, in which several were wounded on each side, and on the 11th a Federal outpost at Point Mountain pike, after a brisk skirmish in which they lost 5 killed and wounded, narrowly escaped capture. These were incidents preliminary to the battle which was planned. The attack was to be made early on September 12th. From Camp Bartow, Colonel Rust was to gain the rear of the Federal position at Cheat Mountain pass, with 1,500 men, and attack early in the morning; General Anderson, with two Tennessee regiments, was to get between Elkwater and the gap, and support Rust, while General Jackson was to make a demonstration in front. The pass being carried, the whole Confederate force there under Jackson was to sweep down upon the rear of Reynolds at Elkwater, with the co-operation of General Donelson with two regiments, who was to have gained a flanking position. Meanwhile, Burk and Major Lee

W Va 6

would move to the west flank of Reynolds, and the rest of the forces would advance by the main road up the valley to attack Reynolds in front. The plan was good, but the signal for the general mêlée was to be Rust's attack, and unfortunately that never occurred. Jackson moved up the mountain from the east, and gained the first summit, driving in the picket under Captain Junod, who, with one private, was killed. Anderson promptly in position, drove back a Federal company, and repulsed the attack of another body of Federal reinforcements, with some loss on each side, and cut the telegraph between the two Federal camps, but decided not to make the attack upon Reynolds until the prearranged signal had been given. On the following day, Reynolds sent several regiments against Anderson, reopening his communications, and checked the advance of Loring's reconnoissance from the south. On the 14th, there was a renewal of the Confederate advance, but without result; and on the 15th, an attack upon Cheat mountain was repulsed. But there was no hope entertained of success by General Lee after the fiasco of the 12th. The loss on each side was slight, that of the Federals being reported at 9 killed, 2 missing and 60 prisoners. But among the Confederates great sorrow was felt for the untimely death of Colonel Washington, who fell pierced by three balls while making a reconnoissance with Major Lee, whose horse was killed at the same time.

This movement failed to divert Rosecrans from his advance up the Kanawha valley, and General Lee continued to receive from Wise alarming news of the enemy's advance on Sewell mountain, and from Floyd reports that Wise would not fall back. He repaired promptly to the Kanawha valley, reaching Floyd's camp September 21st, and at once wrote to Wise, using these words: "I beg, therefore, if not too late, that the troops be united, and that we conquer or die together." To this, the indomitable Wise responded that he would join Floyd there or at

Meadow Bluff if Lee would say which, that he laughed the enemy to scorn, and that he was ready to do, suffer and die for the cause, but that any imputation upon his motives would make him "perhaps, no longer a military subordinate of any man who breathes." Lee then "went to the mountain," and on the 23d, learning that Rosecrans had occupied in force the crest of Big Sewell, brought up Floyd to the mountain position which Wise had held with such tenacity. He did this, because it was the most defensible line, and he also caused reinforcements to be sent by Loring, which increased the Confederate strength at Little Sewell mountain to 8,000 or 9,000 men. General Wise was relieved from command, and assigned to another field of equal importance and dignity.

General Rosecrans on Big Sewell mountain had about the same number of men as Lee, but each had exaggerated reports of the strength of the other, and it was difficult for either to make an offensive move. Lee naturally anticipated that Rosecrans would attempt to continue his advance, and waited for an opportunity to thwart it. Thus the two forces observed each other across a deep gorge for eleven days, during which period the Confederates, poorly sheltered from the tempests of wind and rain, suffered severely. "It cost us more men, sick and dead," General Floyd averred, "than the battle of Manassas." Finally, on the morning of October 6th, it was found that Rosecrans had retreated, and on pursuit it appeared that he had fled with considerable precipitation and disorder.

While this was going on, there was renewed activity before Cheat mountain. General Reynolds, on October 3d, set out to make an attack upon Camp Bartow, 12 miles from the summit of Cheat mountain, taking with him 5,000 Ohio and Indiana troops and Howe's battery. Jackson's pickets were driven in early in the morning, but were reinforced by 100 men under Col. Edward Johnson, Twelfth Georgia, who held the enemy in check

nearly an hour, not withdrawing until outflanked and
under fire of six pieces of artillery. This gave time for
a proper disposition of Jackson's little army of less than
2,000 men, for a defense of the works which they had par-
tially completed. An artillery duel now began and continued with energy and with circumstances of romantic
scenery and reverberating thunder from the surrounding
mountains that made the scene one long to be remembered by the soldiers waiting for their part in the fight.
Presently the enemy sent a strong column of infantry
across the shallow river against Jackson's left wing,
which the Arkansans drove back in confusion. On the
other flank a more formidable movement developed,
while a direct attack was made in front. But the enemy
was met with such a well-directed fire of musketry and
artillery, that his whole force finally fell back in disorder,
leaving behind some of their killed and a stand of United
States colors. The combat in which the Confederates
won such brilliant distinction, lasted from 7 in the
morning until 2:30 in the afternoon, when the enemy,
whose well-filled haversacks indicated a purpose to make
a much more protracted campaign, was in full retreat to
his mountain fastness. The official returns on each
side show a loss in killed and wounded: Confederate 39,
Federal 43; Confederates taken prisoner, 13.

Some indication of the sufferings of the soldiers in this
mountain campaign is given in the appeal of Col. John
B. Baldwin to Secretary Benjamin, from his post on the
top of Alleghany mountain. He reported that the country, sparsely settled, producing little surplus at any time,
was now especially barren. Supplies from the Hardy
valley were interrupted by the enemy's incursions, the
roads to Petersburg and Staunton would be impassable
in winter, and even then (October) his horses were on
half rations. Winter rapidly approaching would find
them without huts or houses or tools to build shelters
with. Perhaps some relief was given these gallant men.

At any rate, they were kept there, at Camp Baldwin, or Alleghany, and reinforced by the Twelfth Georgia, Thirty-first Virginia, Anderson's and Miller's batteries, and a detachment of the Pittsylvania cavalry under Lieutenant Dabney, making about 1,200 effectives in all, and put under the command of Col. Edward Johnson.

In December, after an interval of quiet in the Cheat Mountain district, Johnson was attacked by a Federal force of 1,760 men under Gen. R. H. Milroy. At first pushed back by superior numbers, on the right, also assailed on the left, the Confederates fought with such unflinching courage, Virginians and Georgians alike, that the enemy was finally repulsed. This was the bloodiest fight, so far, in western Virginia. The total Confederate loss was 20 killed, 98 wounded and 28 missing; the Federal loss, 20 killed, 107 wounded and 10 missing.

After the retreat of Rosecrans to the Hawk's Nest and Gauley bridge, Lee detached Floyd for a movement up the south side of the New river, and that general crossed about October 16th, with the available portions of Russell's Mississippi regiment, Phillips' legion, the Fourteenth Georgia and the Fifty-first, Forty-fifth, Thirty-sixth and Twenty-second Virginia and 500 cavalry, in all about 4,000 men. In this southern region the enemy was in possession as far as Raleigh, having laid waste the village of Fayette and the country upon his lines of march, penetrated within 70 miles of the Virginia & Tennessee railroad, and produced great alarm among the people of Mercer, Giles and Monroe counties. Floyd occupied Fayette and established his camp on Cotton hill, a rocky mass in the angle of the junction of New and Kanawha rivers, where he startled Rosecrans on November 1st, by opening with cannon on the camp at Gauley. To do this, he had moved his guns by hand over precipitous hills for many miles. With his cannon and sharpshooters, he greatly annoyed the Federals, sinking one of the ferryboats, which served in lieu of the burned bridge. He hoped· that a concerted attack would be made from Meadow Bluff, but the force there was inadequate.

General Lee soon returned to Richmond and in November was transferred to the department of South Carolina, Georgia and Florida, his military reputation for the time under an unwarranted eclipse.

From Rosecrans' army, which was stationed along the river from Kanawha Falls to the Hawk's Nest, Colonel DeVilliers, of the Second Kentucky, was sent across the Kanawha at the mouth of the Gauley by ferry on November 10th, with several hundred men, and a brisk skirmish resulted in the repulse of his attack. On the next day the Federals being reinforced, renewed the advance, and after vigorous skirmishes, Floyd abandoned the front of the mountain and moved his camp to the rear. On the 12th, General Schenck crossed with his brigade and occupied Cotton hill, and General Benham moved from Loop creek to attack Floyd in the rear. But the latter evaded the trap prepared for him, and fell back upon Loop mountain, with little loss, except that Lieut.-Col. St. George Croghan, one of the most gallant officers in the service, fell in a skirmish at McCoy's mill, November 14th, after which Floyd took position on Piney creek.

Previous to this Colonel Clarkson with the cavalry had been sent on a raid toward the Ohio river, and that gallant officer at Guyandotte, November 10th, attacked a body of recruits for a Federal regiment, called the Ninth Virginia, U. S. A., killing a considerable number, and taking 70 prisoners and 30 horses, some stores, and 200 or 300 rifles. Some of the dead were thrown from the bridge into the river. Among the prisoners were K. V. Whaley, member of Congress, and several other Ohio citizens, and Clarkson also brought back with him several citizens of the town. He held Guyandotte until the next day, when a steamboat came up with reinforcements, upon which the Confederates withdrew and the Federals from Ohio set fire to the town, which had already suffered so far as the Union citizens were concerned. Thus the Guyandotte valley was introduced to the horrors of war.

Floyd was ordered to Dublin Depot, in December, and he finally abandoned the Kanawha valley. On December 15th, Col. George Crook, of the Thirty-sixth Ohio, sent out a detachment, which scattered the guards left at Meadow Bluff, burned the encampment, and returned after gleaning the livestock of the neighborhood. Raleigh Court House was occupied by a portion of Schenck's brigade, December 28th. The Huntersville line also was abandoned, General Loring leaving a guard of about 250 men, who were scattered on January 8th by an expedition from Huttonsville, which defeated the Confederates despite their gallant stand in two skirmishes, and entering the town, burned the military stores.

Thus the year closed with no organized Confederate commands in the State except in the northeast, though Gen. Edward Johnson, commanding the Monterey line, still clung to his mountain post on the border, Camp Alleghany, and held two regiments, Goode's and Scott's, near Monterey.

There were some little affairs in the center of the State in December, one in Roane county, in which a noted partisan, Lowerburn, came to his death, and about December 30th a force of Confederate partisans issued from Webster county, drove the Federal garrison from Braxton Court House, and burned the military stores there. But this was followed by swift retaliation, many of the band being killed and their homes burned—26 houses, the Federal commander reported.

At this time 40,000 Federal troops occupied the State, under the general command of Rosecrans, the Kanawha district being in charge of General Cox, the Cheat Mountain district under Milroy, and the Railroad district under Kelley, the West Virginia soldier who was promoted brigadier-general in the United States army after his success at Philippi.

CHAPTER IV.

OPERATIONS IN THE NORTHEAST — KELLEY'S CAM-
PAIGN AGAINST ROMNEY — STONEWALL JACKSON
IN COMMAND IN THE SHENANDOAH VALLEY—HIS
CAMPAIGN TO BATH AND ROMNEY.

ON August 3, 1861, Rosecrans had assigned General
Kelley to the special military district of Grafton,
embracing the Baltimore & Ohio railroad from
Grafton to Cumberland, and the Northwestern Virginia
from Grafton. Under his command nearly 4,000 men
were stationed at Grafton and along the railroad. In
September, Col. Angus W. McDonald, a leader in the
Confederate cause in the lower Shenandoah valley, was
stationed at Romney with his cavalry regiment, the
Seventy-seventh militia regiment under Col. E. H. Mc-
Donald, the One Hundred and Fourteenth militia under
Col. A. Monroe, and one gun under Lieutenant Lion-
berger, in all about 600 men. Upon this command an
attack was made from New Creek Station, or Keyser, by
Kelley's soldiers, September 23d. The advance pickets
being driven in, the enemy attempted to force their passage through the Mechanicsburg and Hanging Rock
passes, of the South Branch mountain, toward Romney,
but were repulsed at the first by Major Funsten, while
Capt. E. H. Myers and Col. E. H. McDonald, with a few
men, defeated the attack at Hanging Rock in true mount-
aineer style, by rolling rocks down upon the road as well
as using their rifles, before which attack the Federal cavalry fell back in confusion, riding down the infantry and
leaving some dead upon the road and in the river. Later
the enemy advanced in force and gained the two passes,
and after some brisk skirmishing the Confederates aban-

doned Romney and fell back toward North River mountain, fearing to be cut off from Winchester. The next morning Funsten's cavalry and the artillery successfully attacked the enemy at Romney, making a daring charge under heavy fire. The Federals began a retreat, and were pursued nearly to New Creek.

On October 22d, General Kelley was assigned to command of the Federal department of Harper's Ferry and Cumberland. On the 25th he massed a still more formidable force at New Creek, and marched against Romney, while Colonel John's Maryland cavalry regiment moved from Patterson's creek to strike the Confederates in the rear. Passing Mechanicsburg Gap without resistance, they found the Confederates on the 26th in position on the cemetery hill at the town, where the little band made a gallant resistance for an hour or more. It was only after an assault by overwhelming numbers that McDonald's command retired, withdrawing their artillery and making another stand east of town, from which they were again compelled to retreat. General Kelley reported the capture of artillery and baggage train and small-arms, but no prisoners. Colonel John's cavalry, mentioned above, was met at South Branch bridge, near Springfield, by Colonel Monroe, and defeated with considerable loss. A Federal force was stationed at Romney, while Colonel Monroe encamped 15 miles east, at the town of Hanging Rock. About two months afterward there was a considerable engagement between some of Kelley's troops and the Confederates, at Blue's Gap, about 15 miles east of Romney, in which the Confederates were victorious. Kelley's men on this march destroyed by fire a group of houses known as the village of Frenchburg, as well as the residences of some of the best people of the county.

On the 4th of November, Thomas J. Jackson, with the immortal battle-name of "Stonewall," earned at Manassas, and the rank of major-general, returned to the valley and assumed command of that district, his only regret at the assignment being that his Stonewall brigade was not ordered at first to accompany him. This separation was so painful as to cause him to say, "Had this communication not come as an order, I should instantly have declined it and continued in command of the brave old brigade."

Jackson was a descendant of a sterling western Virginia family, which first settled in Hardy county and then moving across the Alleghany ridge made their home in Buckhannon. He was born at Clarksburg, and his mother's grave is in the soil of the new State. The spot where reposes the venerated woman who gave this hero birth is thus described:

On the top of a wooded hill near the mining village of Anstead, Fayette county, W. Va., is an old graveyard still used as a burying place by the dwellers in this mountainous region. It is greatly neglected, and many graves are scarcely to be found, though a few are protected by little pens of fence rails. The location is so beautiful and the view it commands is so extensive and exquisite that it is worthy of being well cared for. Among those who lie buried here is the mother of that Christian soldier, Thomas Jonathan Jackson. The grave, or spot, for the grave is scarcely to be recognized, has been kindly cared for by Stephen M. Taylor, formerly of Albemarle county. But no stone was erected until a gentleman of Staunton, Capt. Thomas D. Ransom, one of his old soldiers, seeing the neglected condition of the grave, had prepared a simple but suitable monument: a tall slab of marble with an inscription giving the dates of her birth and death, and adding that it is "a tribute to the mother of Stonewall Jackson by one of his old brigade."

Among the valleys and hills of this romantic part of the Old Dominion, Jackson passed his boyhood and the greater part of his life until appointed to a cadetship at West Point. After his military life in Mexico he was elected to a professorship in the Virginia military institute, situated in the splendid valley which reposes in beauty and grandeur between the Blue ridge and the Alleghany mountains. There a ten years' service, from 1851, allied him again with the western portion of his native State, identified him with its interests, and explains his ardent desire to hold it as a part of the "Old Dominion" forever.

General Jackson was accustomed to speak of western Virginia as "our section of the State," and no one deplored more than he the divisions among its people which exposed them to special severities during the war. After the brilliant victory at First Manassas, his thoughts turned to the reverses which the Confederates were suffering in his home country. Learning that Lee had been sent there, he expressed his wish to "go and give my feeble aid as an humble instrument in the hands of Providence in retrieving the down-trodden loyalty of that part of my native State." In August he wrote to Colonel Bennett, first auditor of the Virginia commonwealth:

Should you ever have occasion to ask for a brigade from this army for the Northwest, I hope mine will be the one selected. This is, of course, confidential, as it is my duty to serve wherever I may be placed, and I desire to be always where most needed. But it is natural for one's affections to turn to the home of his boyhood and family.

When General Jackson arrived at Winchester, he had at his disposal only the militia brigades of Boggs, Carson and Meem, McDonald's cavalry and Henderson's mounted company. Jackson began upon his arrival the important work of organizing, recruiting and drilling these troops, and was soon reinforced by his Stonewall brigade. The disasters which had occurred in the western counties were so dispiriting to the desolate people of that section, and their numerous and urgent appeals for relief and protection were so great that he felt the necessity of a vigorous campaign even in the midst of winter. His spirit was stirred within him as he heard of the rapid advances of the invasion over the land of his boyhood, and thus moved to begin military operations without delay, he petitioned the secretary of war to send the entire command of General Loring to reinforce him at Winchester for the purpose of making an immediate attempt to capture the Federal forces at Romney, commanded by General Kelley. He stated to the secretary of war that it was of great importance to occupy northwestern Virginia at once, and that while the enemy was not expecting attack, during the severity of winter, was the Confederate opportunity of achieving success.

Jackson's plan, as outlined in his letter of 1861, covered a campaign which included a general battle with McClellan, who was to be defeated, and the reoccupation of the northwest counties and the Kanawha valley. The proposed campaign was undoubtedly hazardous, but the ardent spirit of Jackson saw that the chances of a great success were on the Confederate side.

The eagerness of Jackson to be striking a blow against the enemy somewhere would not suffer him to wait for a decision which seems to have been delayed in a too cautious consideration of obstacles. Believing that even his small command could be made effective, before the arrival of the army of the Northwest, and as a good exercise in the chilly December, he moved upon Dam No. 5, on the Chesapeake & Ohio canal, which was being used by the Federals in forwarding troops and supplies. The expedition involved more hardship than danger. Though Banks, with a large force, was near the opposite bank of the Potomac, Jackson deceived that Federal officer easily by making a diversion with Virginia militia toward Williamsport.

Early in December, Taliaferro's brigade of the army of the Northwest—the First Georgia, Third Arkansas, Twenty-third and Thirty-seventh Virginia regiments, arrived, and a few weeks later more of the same army reported, under General Loring, consisting of Col. William Gilham's brigade—the Twenty-first, Forty-second and Forty-eighth Virginia, First battalion, and Marye's battery—and Gen. S. R. Anderson's Tennessee brigade. After Loring's arrival, though Jackson had the general direction of the projected operations against Bath, Hancock and Romney, Loring retained command of his army by the orders of the war department.   The leader of the cavalry was the brave Lieut.-Col. Turner Ashby, whose fame was already foretokened by chivalrous exploits in the campaigns of the summer.

The army under Jackson and Loring, including about 8,000 infantry, besides Ashby's cavalry, moved away from Winchester, January 1st, under a bright, clear sky, with the temperature of the air like that of a crisp, invigorating April morning.   The troops, though ignorant of their destination, marched out of quarters with buoyant spirits and springy step, and all went well for the first day, but with unexpected suddenness the sleet and snow fell upon them with increasing severity, the frozen roads became slippery, the wagons were delayed, and the men forced to bivouac without their tents for a dreary night. The severe storm continued for two days, during which the true and tried soldiery braved adversity and struggled on with the leaders who shared with them the hardships of the march.   Many were compelled by sickness to return, and some whose courage failed them dropped out of line and straggled to shelter, while the larger number pressed on until after the third day they entered Bath, which the Federals had hastily abandoned, leaving a considerable part of their stores.   After only a temporary halt Jackson pushed on after the retreating foe, and driving them into Hancock he sent Ashby under a flag to demand their surrender.   Colonel Ashby, on reaching the Federal front, was received and blindfolded, then led into the town, hearing his name often mentioned by the Northern troops as "The famous Ashby."   Many of them had heard that name called out in the charge of Ashby's men as they rode into Bath, and were now eager to look upon the noted cavalry captain of Virginia. Colonel Ashby was conducted to the Federal officer in command, and on hearing his refusal to surrender returned and reported to General Jackson. In a few minutes McLaughlin's Confederate artillery drove the enemy out of Hancock. Thus far the expedition had attained success nearly equal to Jackson's expectations. The only reverse had been experienced by Monroe's militia, which encountered superior forces of the enemy at Hanging Rock, January 7th. Six days had passed since leaving Winchester, during which time the intrepid soldiers had endured great hardships from long marches in the severe cold over rough roads, but on the 7th they were again on the march against Romney, which was reached on the 10th and occupied. The Federals in a panic had fled from the town, abandoning to the Confederates a quantity of tents and supplies.

Loring's command was now put into winter quarters near Romney, while Jackson returned to Winchester and made his report of the expedition, showing his loss in killed only 4 and wounded 28; and describing the general result of the brief affair, he says: "Shepherdstown protected from shelling, the railroad communication with Hancock broken, all that portion of the country east of the great Cacapon recovered, Romney and a large part of Hampshire county evacuated by the enemy without firing a gun; the enemy had fled from the western part of Hardy and been forced from the offensive to the defensive." It was Jackson's design to advance from Romney on an important expedition, but the enterprise was abandoned temporarily with the view of further aggressive operations in a different direction. He had disposed his forces so as to protect the territory which had been reclaimed. The regiments of Cols. A. Monroe, E. H. McDonald and W. H. Harness were assigned to the region of their homes; Colonel Johnson's regiment was with Harness in Hardy, and three companies of cavalry were left with Loring, one of them "the daring company of Capt. George F. Sheetz, which was familiar with all that section of the country."

But soon after Jackson's return he was directed by the secretary of war to order Loring's army back to Winchester, which he reluctantly obeyed. In consequence of this withdrawal, Kelley reoccupied Romney, and drove the Confederate outpost from Moorefield, February 12th, while General Lander occupied Bloomery Gap two days later, capturing Col. R. F. Baldwin, Thirty-first regiment, and about 50 others. But this last point was reoccupied by Colonel Ashby on the 16th. General Jackson reported that many houses and mills had been burned in Hampshire county by "the reprobate Federal commanders." On March 3d, Colonel Downey's command of Federal forces occupied Romney. Downey evacuated the place later in the spring, when it was again occupied by the militia of the county. In the summer the town was occupied by the Twenty-second Pennsylvania regiment, and afterward by the Hampshire county militia.

CHAPTER V.

AS the season approached for opening military
operations again, after the winter of 1861-62, General Rosecrans was sent to the West, and the general command of the Federals in West Virginia, now called the Mountain department, was given to Gen. John C. Fremont, with headquarters at Wheeling. On the Confederate side there was considerable activity in March on the border. General Johnson had reoccupied Huntersville, and at Camp Alleghany and other posts had a force of about 3,000 men present. Among his soldiers were the Thirty-first, Fifty-second, Twenty-fifth, Fifty-eighth and Forty-fourth Virginia regiments and the Churchville cavalry. Brig.-Gen. Henry Heth, who in a subordinate capacity had gained distinction in the campaigns of the previous year, had his headquarters at Lewisburg, with 1,400 men and four guns, including the Twenty-second and Forty-fifth infantry and the Eighth cavalry, and had called out the militia of Mercer, Greenbrier and Monroe counties.

But the military events in western Virginia were for some time to be subordinate to the great campaigns of the year, the plans of which were speedily developed. As it became evident that McClellan would menace Richmond from the peninsula, Johnston's army withdrew from Manassas about the middle of March, and Jackson fell back from Winchester to Mount Jackson. General

Banks, with 12,600 men in the field, including Shields' division, and 10,500 on post duty, occupied Winchester and Strasburg. Ashby soon reported the evacuation of Strasburg, and Jackson, fearing that Banks would leave the territory, promptly attacked him at Kernstown, where he was repulsed by superior numbers. Retreating to Swift Run gap, he was reinforced by Ewell's division, while Banks pushed up the Shenandoah valley to Harrisonburg. Meanwhile Gen. Edward Johnson's army of the Northwest had withdrawn from Alleghany mountain to Valley Mills, Augusta county, and Milroy advanced to Monterey and thence to McDowell, where he was reinforced by Schenck. The army of the Northwest, backed by Jackson, occupied Bull Pasture mountain and repulsed two assaults by Milroy, who then retreated to Franklin, Pendleton county, while Jackson moved northward to assail Banks.

This battle of McDowell is of special interest to West Virginia soldiers. General Johnson, commander of the army of the Northwest, had command of the troops engaged in the fight, until he fell wounded, when his place was taken by General Taliaferro. Johnson's army had previously been divided into two brigades, under the command of Colonels Porterfield and Baldwin, the First embracing the Twelfth Georgia, Twenty-fifth and Thirty-first Virginia regiments, Hansbrough's battalion and the Star battery; the Second including the Forty-fourth, Fifty-second and Fifty-eighth Virginia regiments and Miller's and Lee's batteries. These seven regiments were the ones which first occupied Setlington's hill, bringing on the Federal attacks, and there they bore with great gallantry the heat of the battle. When it became desirable, the Georgia regiment at the center was reinforced by the Twenty-third and Thirty-seventh regiments, formerly of Loring's command, while the Tenth Virginia went to assist the Fifty-second, which, after repulsing the enemy from its front, was about to make a return blow

W Va 8

on the flank. Almost the entire loss was suffered by the regiments named, mainly by Johnson's army, which lost 388 of the total 498. The gallantry of these regiments was particularly commended by Jackson, and it is but justice to say that here the army of the Northwest, so long condemned to suffer the hardships and none of the distinction of war, won at last a permanent title to fame by gaining for Jackson his first victory in the campaign which established his place as one of the world's greatest generals. At the previous battle of Kernstown, the other division of the old army, Burk's brigade (the Twenty-first, Forty-second and First battalion), and Fulkerson's brigade (the Twenty-third and Thirty-seventh), had also fought with great distinction.

Thus in a blaze of glory the old Army of the Northwest passes from history. During the remainder of the Valley campaign its regiments were incorporated in the divisions of Jackson and Ewell, and the cavalrymen shared the adventures of Ashby. The story of that campaign is elsewhere told, and we return to the consideration of events beyond the Alleghanies.

General Loring had been assigned to the department of Southwest Virginia, and General Heth had gathered near Lewisburg a little force of good fighters called the "Army of New River." His First brigade, under Col. Walter H. Jenifer, included the Forty-fifth Virginia infantry, Lieutenant-Colonel Peters, the Eighth cavalry (Jenifer's) and Otey's battery, while Col. John McCausland, returned from the Fort Donelson campaign, commanded the Second brigade, including his own Thirty-sixth regiment and Col. George S. Patton's Twenty-second.

Early in May, Scammon's brigade of Cox's army was moving toward Princeton, threatening the Virginia & Tennessee railroad. The advance guard of Col. R. B. Hayes' regiment, the Twenty-third Ohio, upon reaching Camp Creek, Mercer county, was attacked and severely handled. All the rolling stock of the railroad had been withdrawn west of Staunton, and General Heth, still at White Sulphur Springs, near Lewisburg, was ordered by General Lee to defend the approaches to Dublin Depot, and Gen. Humphrey Marshall, of Kentucky, commanding the district of Abingdon, moved with about 2,000 Virginians and Kentuckians toward Princeton. The latter point was now occupied by Cox, who also held the Narrows of New river, and the town of Pearisburg or Giles Court House. On the 10th, Jenifer and McCausland drove the Federals out of Pearisburg by a gallant charge, with a stout "rebel yell," and continued to drive them from hill to hill until they made their last stand in the Narrows, from which a well-directed artillery fire dislodged them, leaving the approaches to the railroad in this direction in the hands of General Heth. In this fight Colonel Patton (wounded), Lieutenant-Colonels Peters and Fitzhugh, and Captains Otey, Chapman and Lowry, of the artillery, won especial distinction.

Calling to his aid Colonel Wharton, who was at Rocky Gap with some of the old Floyd brigade, not with Heth, Marshall attacked General Cox at Princeton on the evening of the 16th with such vigor that the Federals retreated in haste, abandoning General Cox's headquarters. From the Federal correspondence Marshall discovered that he was near a superior force of the enemy, and he withdrew from the Federal camp and the ruins of the town, occupying a stronger position, where Wharton soon joined him. Throughout the day there were spiteful skirmishing and artillery combat, and Wharton, attacked in flank, repulsed a Federal regiment with heavy loss. Marshall maintained his position and Cox retreated, frightened by a demonstration toward his rear by Heth, to Flat Top mountain, which bounds on the west the valley of the Blue Stone, in which Princeton lies. Marshall then withdrew. The proposed Federal invasion had been defeated with little loss in his command, 4 dead and 12 wounded. Cox reported a total loss of 113 killed, wounded and missing, while Marshall stated that he left 71 Federals badly wounded at Princeton, and took 29 prisoners.

Heth then marched against Lewisburg, which was held by Col. George Crook with about 1,500 men. With a superior force, including the Forty-fifth and Twenty-second regiments and Cook's battalion, Heth attempted a surprise, and succeeded well at the start, but as he reported, ''one of those causeless panics for which there is no accounting seized upon my command.'' Lieutenant-Colonel Finney, Major Edgar and other officers, while gallantly attempting to restore order, were captured, and 93 prisoners, 66 wounded, 38 dead, four pieces of artillery, and about 300 stand of arms fell into the hands of the enemy. Heth retired beyond Union, to the Narrows.

During June, July and August, 1862, while splendid victories were being won in eastern Virginia, driving the Federals without the State, the enemy remained in unchallenged possession of the West. A few raids and skirmishes alone disturbed the quiet. Some mention of these gleaned from the Federal reports will serve a useful purpose, notwithstanding the tone of enmity which pervades them, in showing the hardships of citizens who maintained allegiance to the Old Dominion, either passively or actively by forming organizations for protecting their property, and watching or annoying the enemy. At Shaver's river in May, a band of Confederate partisans was surprised and several wounded; near Palestine, early in June, a squad of men of the Greenbrier cavalry and White's cavalry was attacked, and Lieutenant Hanover killed, and two others, whose bodies floated down Muddy creek. A scout from Flat Top mountain into Wyoming county reported: ''Took Squire Clendennen, a noted rebel, prisoner, and fired on his son, who escaped to the mountains.'' A surprising affair at Summersville, or Nicholas Court House, July 25th, showed the activity on the other hand of the loyal Virginians. Lieutenant Miller, of the Ninth Virginia (U. S. A.), reported that he was awakened by a shot, and saw the street full of "rebel cavalry, dressed in gray uniforms, yelling at the top of their voices." He went out of the back window and into the woods, and found on his subsequent return that all his comrades had been "gobbled" except those who were as lucky as himself. In Wyoming county, near where Floyd was stationed, in Tazewell, a daring cavalry raid was made by Captains Straton and Witcher, joining the companies of Chambers and Beckley at Horse Pen, and several skirmishes were fought, in which brave men fell, Straton and Witcher both being reported dangerously wounded.

Early in August, General Cox was still at Flat Top mountain and Brook at Meadow Bluff, on opposite sides of the junction of the New and Greenbrier, before which lay Colonel Hayes near Pack's ferry, maintaining the communications of the two commands. Before him, about the Narrows, was General Loring with the Confederate forces. On August 6th, Col. G. C. Wharton with 900 men moved from Peterstown and made a demonstration against the outpost at the ferry, driving the enemy from their camp with considerable loss and destroying two flatboats.

A week or two later General Cox was ordered to retire from the Kanawha with most of his troops, which were sent to Washington and thence to reinforce Pope on the Rappahannock, and Col. J. A. J. Lightburn, of the Fourth Virginia (U. S. A.), was left in command of the Kanawha, with headquarters at Gauley. The Federal force in the vicinity of Franklin and Moorefield had been previously withdrawn, and as soon as Lee was informed of Cox's orders by the capture of Pope's headquarters and letter-book at Catlett's Station, he requested that Loring be ordered "to clear the valley of the Kanawha and then operate northwardly, so as to join me in the valley of Virginia."

During the summer J. D. Imboden, subsequently colonel and brigadier-general in the Confederate service,
had been organizing a cavalry battalion in Highland
county, enlisting refugees from Braxton, Lewis and
Webster counties and other regions, a large majority of
his men having "but recently escaped from Pierpont's
dominion, brimful of fight." In a private letter written
about this time, he gave a graphic picture of the situation
in the mountain region. He said:

No Oriental despot ever exercised such mortal terror
by his iron rule of his subjects as is now felt by three-
fourths of the true men and women of the northwest.
Grown-up men came to me stealthily through the woods
to talk to me in a whisper of their wrongs. They would
freely have given me grain and meat, but dared not
do so. They begged me in some instances to take it
apparently by force, so that they might not be charged
with feeding us voluntarily. Men offered to sell me cattle
or horses secretly, if I would send armed men to seize and
carry off the property. Their pious Union neighbors,
they said, would watch and report their every act as soon
as my back was turned, and the Yankees would strip
them of all they possessed.

In conformity with orders, General Loring on August
22d sent out Brig.-Gen. A. G. Jenkins, with his cavalry,
about 550 in all, to sweep around the northwest by the
Cheat valley, destroy the Baltimore & Ohio railroad, and
fall upon the rear of the enemy in the Kanawha valley,
while the infantry under Loring in person advanced toward Gauley.

In the meantime Imboden, with about 300 men, had
made an expedition, attended by several skirmishes, to
St. George, and thence returned to Cheat mountain.
Jenkins, who expected to surprise Beverly, found it reinforced by General Kelley, and though joined by Imboden
he was not strong enough to attack. Consequently Imboden remained and amused the Beverly garrison, while
Jenkins rode on, crossing Rich mountain by a trail
through the unbroken wilderness. So arduous was this

march that some of his men and horses broke down and
were left behind. Finally emerging from the wilderness he suddenly entered the fertile valley of the Buckhannon, and after the first consternation due to his
appearance had passed, was assailed continually on his
march by the home guards of that region. In one of the
skirmishes Capt. J. M. Ferguson was painfully wounded.
Approaching Buckhannon, by a skillful disposition of his
cavalry and a gallant attack of three parties under Colonel Corns, Captain Spotts and Captain Preston, the enemy was defeated, with a loss of 15 wounded and 20 prisoners, including the commanding officer, Captain Marsh.
Lieut.-Col. A. F. Cook, Eighth Virginia, and three others
of Jenkins' men were wounded.

Jenkins now cast aside his shotguns, armed his men
with handsome new rifles, and otherwise supplied himself, and then destroyed the remainder of the vast stores,
including 5,000 stand of arms, ordnance stores, clothing,
etc. At Weston next morning, August 31st, the Federal
garrison escaped in the fog, leaving but a dozen prisoners,
and Jenkins destroyed all the public property, after
which he drove the garrison out of Glenville, and reaching Spencer, September 2d, surprised and captured Col.
J. C. Rathbone and Maj. George C. Trimble and their
entire command, six companies of the Eleventh West
Virginia infantry. Having paroled the prisoners, Jenkins
went on to Ripley, finding a lone paymaster, whose
funds on hand, $5,525, were applied to the Confederate
cause, and then moved to Ravenswood, where, after resting his men, he forded the Ohio river on the evening of
September 4th, and was the first to carry the Confederate
flag into Ohio. "The excitement of the command as we
approached the Ohio shore was intense," he wrote, "and
in the anxiety to be the first of their respective companies to reach the soil of those who had invaded us, all order
was lost, and it became almost a universal race as we
came into shoal water. In a short time all were over,

and in a few minutes the command was formed on the
crest of a gentle eminence and the banners of the Southern Confederacy floated over the soil of invaders.   As
our flag was unfurled in the splendors of an evening sun,
cheers upon cheers arose from the men, and their enthusiasm was excited to the highest pitch.''

General Jenkins made a considerable march in Ohio,
and surprised the inhabitants, who begged in abject
terror that their homes might be spared from the torch,
by committing no depredations, assuring the people that
though many of his soldiers were homeless and their
families in exile because of such warfare in Virginia, he
did not represent barbarians, but a civilized people
struggling for their liberties.   On more than one occasion, also, he was gratified by the friendly waving of
handkerchiefs, and ''shouts for Jeff Davis and the Southern Confederacy.''   Recrossing the Ohio at Racine, he
made a demonstration against Point Pleasant, proceeded
to Buffalo, crossed the Kanawha, advanced to Barboursville, and thence returned down the Guyandotte valley
to Wyoming.

Lightburn's command in the valley consisted of two
Ohio regiments at Raleigh Court House, two companies
of West Virginia cavalry at Camp Ewing, 10 miles in
advance of Gauley bridge, four West Virginia companies
at Summersville, and the remainder of the Ninth and
Fourth infantry and Second cavalry, West Virginia Federal troops, at different points from Gauley to Charleston.
He soon began concentrating upon hearing of Jenkins'
movements, and the force at Raleigh fell back to Fayette.   Loring advanced with a little army of about 5,000
men, organized as follows:

ARMY OF WESTERN VIRGINIA.

Maj.-Gen. W. W. Loring commanding.   Maj. H. Fitzhugh, chief of staff; Col. C. E. Thorburn, chief of ordnance; Capt. R. L. Poor, chief engineer; Surg. John A.
Hunter, medical director.

First brigade, Brig.-Gen. John Echols: Fiftieth Virginia infantry, Col. Thomas Poage, Colonel Rodgers; Sixty-third, Col. J. J. McMahon; Twenty-third battalion, Lieutenant-Colonel Derrick.

Second brigade, Brig.-Gen. John S. Williams: Forty-fifth Virginia infantry, Col. William H. Browne; Twenty-sixth battalion (Edgar's), Maj. A. M. Davis; Twenty-second regiment, Col. George S. Patton.

Third brigade, Col. George C. Wharton: Fifty-first Virginia infantry, Lieut.-Col. A. Forsberg; Thirtieth battalion sharpshooters, Lieut.-Col. Melvin Clarke.

Fourth brigade, Col. John McCausland: Thirty-sixth Virginia infantry, Sixtieth (?) Virginia infantry.

Artillery, Maj. J. Floyd King, chief of artillery: Otey's, Stamps', Bryan's, Lowry's and Chapman's batteries.

Cavalry, Gen. A. G. Jenkins: Eighth Virginia regiment and other companies. Major Salyers commanding cavalry with Loring's advance.

General Loring approached Fayetteville on the 10th of September, and after driving the enemy in his works, which were of great strength, prepared for an attack. Williams made the assault in front, while Wharton, reinforced by Colonel Patton, made a demonstration against the turnpike to Montgomery Ferry. Williams' brigade drove the enemy from hill to hill by sharp fighting, after which "the artillery dashed in magnificent style over the ridge, down the slope and up to the top of the next hill, where they unlimbered within 300 yards of the enemy's fort, and opened a terrible cannonade upon it." Browne with the Forty-fifth and McCausland with the Thirty-sixth drove the enemy from their front in gallant style. In the meantime, Wharton was making a determined attack, under great difficulty, against another fort which he encountered in his flank movement, and still another fort beyond, in a commanding position, frowned upon the gallant Confederates. Night coming on, they slept upon their arms, within stone's throw of the enemy. Shrouded by darkness the Federals evacuated their works, attempted to fire the town, and made a precipitate retreat toward

Gauley. At Cotton hill, next morning, reinforced from
Gauley, they made a desperate stand against the pursuing Confederates, pouring grape and canister into the
advance, but were finally driven, and the entire brigade, headed by Browne and McCausland, went down the
hill with a shout, giving the enemy time to transfer but
a small part of his force by ferry to the north bank.
Those who got across fired the ferryboat, under the protection of their guns, and the magazines and commissary
stores were seen to be in process of destruction. Dr.
Watkins of the Thirty-sixth, Lieutenant Samuels of
Williams' staff, W. H. Harman and Allen Thompson of
the Forty-fifth, and some others, boldly sprang into the
river, and swam across in a shower of grape and canister,
seized the ferryboat, and brought it back to the south
shore, extinguishing the fire with their hats as water
buckets as they came. Echols' brigade, McCausland and
Patton, crossed the Kanawha, seized the Federal camp
without resistance, and pursued the retreating enemy
across the Gauley toward Charleston on the north bank,
while Williams and Wharton followed them up rapidly
on the south side, with a skirmish at Montgomery's Ferry.
On the following morning the enemy crossed at Camp
Piatt. The artillery was active in the pursuit, keeping
up a fire upon the enemy at their rear, as well as across
the river from Williams' column.

As Charleston was approached, the Federals, who under
the circumstances had displayed much gallantry, the
fighting qualities of West Virginians being proved on both
sides, made a sally across the river to check Williams, but
unsuccessfully, and the enemy soon withdrew, mainly to
a fortified eminence across the Elk river, while a portion
of the command contested the advance of McCausland,
then in command of Echols' brigade, and fired the buildings used for military storehouses. There was a hill on
the south shore, commanding the Federal intrenchments
and artillery beyond the Elk, from which sharpshooters

attempted to keep back the victorious Confederates, but Otey, Bryan and Stamps brought up their guns at a gallop and soon made the Federal infantry abandon their last position.   McCausland, with Derrick's battalion as skirmishers, McMahon, Rodgers and Patton in line, and his own regiment in reserve, Lowry's battery and a section of Otey's, advanced with some brisk skirmishing into Charleston, and on reaching the Elk found the suspension bridge cut down.   The artillery opened a warm fire upon the enemy opposite, while McCausland moved to a ford further up the Elk, where he was able, however, to cross his cavalry only.   By night he was ready to move his infantry over in boats, but on the following morning it was found that the enemy was in full retreat, and it was not thought advisable to pursue further.   Jenkins, meanwhile, had moved down the Coal river and struck the enemy on the flank, compelling him to abandon his proposed march down the Gauley, and take the road for Ravenswood, whence he reached Point Pleasant on the 16th.

In this brilliant campaign, involving a mountain march of 169 miles, the Confederates lost 18 killed and 89 wounded.   Lightburn reported a loss of 25 killed, 95 wounded and 190 missing.   He was compelled to abandon all the immense stores, worth by Loring's estimate about $1,000,000, and did not have time to destroy the important Kanawha salt works.

The Kanawha valley was now in the hands of the Confederate forces, and General Loring at once issued a congratulatory address to his command, and a proclamation to the people of western Virginia, opening with these well-chosen words:

The army of the Confederate States has come among you to expel the enemy, to rescue the people from the despotism of the counterfeit State government imposed on you by Northern bayonets, and to restore the country once more to its natural allegiance to the State.   We fight for peace and the possession of our own territory. We do not intend to punish those who remain at home as quiet citizens in obedience to the laws of the land, and to all such, clemency and amnesty are declared; but those who persist in adhering to the cause of the public enemy and the pretended State government he has erected at Wheeling, will be dealt with as their obstinate treachery deserves.

He appealed to all able-bodied citizens to join the army to "defend the sanctities of religion and virtue, home territory, honor and law," and declared that the oaths imposed by the invaders were void, being "immoral attempts to restrain you from your duty to your State and government."

Loring had considerable success at first in securing recruits and collecting conscripts, but these accessions were checked by rumors of another Federal invasion, and complaints began to go into Richmond of his course in gathering men, also regarding the methods of General Floyd, commanding the State line in Logan and Boone counties. Reconnoissances were made toward Point Pleasant, in one of which General Jenkins had a skirmish near Buffalo, September 27th. Loring at this time had about 4,000 men at Charleston and garrisons at Gauley and Fayette. On September 30th the secretary of war ordered him to proceed soon, leaving a detachment to co-operate with General Floyd in holding the Kanawha valley, toward Winchester, to make a speedy junction with General Lee, destroy the Federal depots at Clarksburg and Grafton, make impressments from the Union men en route, paying in Confederate money, and capture and send to Richmond such prominent Union men as should come within reach. "Assure the people that the government has no animosities to gratify, but that persistent traitors will be punished, and under no conceivable circumstances will a division of the State be acquiesced in."

Loring replied, October 7th, that his most practicable movement was by way of Lewisburg to Monterey, which he had begun that day, and that he had sent out expeditions against the railroad at Parkersburg and Clarksburg, while General Jenkins would be sent against Cheat river bridge. Loring announced to his troops, October 11th, that they would be withdrawn to another field, but soon becoming aware of the increasing strength of the enemy in his department, he advised the government that he could not do more than possibly hold the valley. His infantry, meanwhile, had retired to the verge of western Virginia. He was relieved from command October 15th, and Gen. John Echols, appointed his successor, was ordered to reoccupy the valley, where only Jenkins' cavalry had remained. The army started back toward Charleston on the 17th, though very poorly supplied.

But overwhelming forces were being massed against Echols. Gen. J. D. Cox had been returned to the department of Western Virginia from corps command under McClellan, with his old division, which, with Milroy's brigade, was sent to Clarksburg, while Lightburn was reinforced at Point Pleasant by Morgan's division from Ohio, and a brigade under Colonel Cranor was sent into the Guyandotte country against Floyd. The Confederate artillery checked Lightburn's advance up the Kanawha at Poca on the 23d, and later a stand was made at Tyler mountain and Two-mile creek, but perceiving that the enemy was advancing in force on both sides of the Kanawha, while a division under Crook was threatening his flank by Nicholas Court House, Echols fell back in good order by way of Gauley and Fayetteville toward Raleigh, General Jenkins protecting the rear, obstructing the roads and destroying the river transportation behind him. Crook was in the vicinity of Gauley by November 1st, and the country to the north was in the hands of the Federals as far as Beverly. It was feared that Crook would advance against the Virginia & Tennessee railroad, but according to the reports of Cox and Echols alike, the most effective protection against such a movement was the absolute destitution of the country. Even the inhabitants would find it difficult to survive the winter in this devastated region, and few dwelling-houses were left standing from the Narrows to the Gauley along the main lines of travel. For lack of subsistence, Echols withdrew to the Princeton and Lewisburg line, and Jenkins was ordered into Greenbrier and Pocahontas counties. This was the situation as winter came on in 1862, practically the same as in the previous year at that season.

In the Northeast there had been active operations following the battle of Sharpsburg and Lee's occupation of the lower Shenandoah valley. A few days before Stuart set out on his famous Chambersburg raid around McClellan's army, Col. J. D. Imboden had made an attempt to destroy the Cheat river bridge, but was prevented by the daring of a Union woman, who rode 25 miles through the woods to warn the enemy. He next made a raid to Romney, seized the town and scouted toward the railroad, drawing a party of the enemy into ambush. He reported, "We unhorsed fifteen of the rascals, wounding several; captured two unhurt," and horses and arms. He had now about 900 men, but only 600 armed, and with this little force kept Kelley with 2,500 men running up and down the railroad. Imboden did much to restore order in Hardy county, and reported that the mountains were full of willing recruits for the Confederate cause. He also gathered cattle and other supplies under the orders of General Lee.

In November Imboden made an expedition which, in connection with reports that Stonewall Jackson with 40,000 men had returned to the Shenandoah valley, created consternation in the North and caused the recall of many Federal regiments from the Kanawha valley. Imboden with 310 mounted men set out from his Hardy county camp on the 7th, in a snowstorm, for Cheat river bridge. All the next day he marched along a cattle path over the Alleghanies, his men being compelled by the storm to dismount and lead their horses. At midnight preceding the 8th he learned of the movements of Federal troops threatening him, but nevertheless proceeded to St. George through the snow and sleet, and reaching his destination safely, received the unconditional surrender of Captain Hall, with 31 men, well armed and occupying the courthouse. It was impossible for him to go further, and on his return trip, which he soon began, he had to avoid Kelley's cavalry and the forces of Milroy at Beverly. Fearing Kelley most he advanced toward Milroy with the intention of attacking his baggage train at Camp Bartow. All day the 11th he marched through an unbroken forest, and on the 12th attempted to find Camp Bartow, but the day being rainy and gloomy he was lost in the gloom of the pine wilderness. Finally he learned that the Federal forces were in great commotion, and parties were moving in all directions to cut off his retreat. He managed to gain the rear of 1,300 men moving down South Branch in search of him, and crossing a high mountain safely, reached Augusta Springs on the 14th, evading all the enemy's detachments. It was believed that at this very time Milroy was en route to make a raid on Staunton, which Imboden's raid happened to prevent. Milroy in his advance had captured several cavalrymen, twelve or fifteen citizens, and burned some houses in Highland county. A few days before this there had been a skirmish near Petersburg, in which a herd of cattle seized by the Confederates had been recaptured by Kelley and some prisoners taken, and Milroy had "swept the counties of Highland, Pocahontas, Pendleton and parts of Augusta and Bath," taking in 45 prisoners and some cattle and horses, and immediately after Imboden had left his camp on South Fork with his cavalry, Kelley had swooped down upon the infantry with a large force of cavalry, and captured the camp and supplies and 50 prisoners.

CHAPTER VI.

OPERATIONS OF 1863 — JONES' AND IMBODEN'S RAID AGAINST THE BALTIMORE & OHIO RAILROAD—JENKINS' RAID TO POINT PLEASANT—EXPEDITIONS TO BEVERLY AND WYTHEVILLE—BATTLES OF WHITE SULPHUR SPRINGS AND DROOP MOUNTAIN—AVERELL'S RAID TO SALEM.

URING the early part of 1863, Echols and Jenkins were still in Greenbrier county, but Floyd had withdrawn from Wyoming, which was penetrated by a Federal scouting party in February. In the same month a similar expedition did considerable damage in Pocahontas county. On the 11th a detachment of Col. R. W. Baylor's cavalry had an encounter with the enemy in Jefferson county, and on the 16th, Captain McNeill made his third successful foray against Federal wagon trains near Moorefield.

On December 29th, Gen. W. E. Jones had been assigned to command the Valley district, in the absence of Stonewall Jackson, and Imboden's command, which included McNeill's rangers, came under the direction of Jones. Colonel Imboden's force was then designated as the First Virginia partisan rangers, and his headquarters in Hardy county as Camp Hood. In pursuance of a request from General Cooper he set about making a regular enlistment, and the formation of the "Northwestern Virginia brigade," which in March was composed of the Sixty-second Virginia infantry, the Eighteenth Virginia cavalry, and a battery of artillery. The cavalry brigade under the immediate command of W. E. Jones included the Sixth, Seventh and Twelfth regiments, the Seventeenth battalion, Maj. E. V. White's battalion, and Chew's battery.

During the winter of 1862-63, the citizens of Hardy and Hampshire counties were severely afflicted. The Federal forces were in possession of the region, and had constructed blockhouses along the railroad, and earthworks at various stations, which seemed to insure them against attack. There had also been constructed a number of ironclad cars, carrying pieces of heavy artillery, to aid in the defense of the road. General Milroy levied assessments upon the inhabitants, which caused great suffering, and not content with that issued an order banishing those who in any manner expressed sympathy with their State and the South. Hundreds of families were arrested under this order and forcibly expelled from their homes, without permission to carry with them the necessary means for support. Numbers of helpless women and children were sent through their lines without protection, but found a generous reception among the loyal people of the valley, who, on their own part, had not yet realized the terrible destruction awaiting them. An even greater terror to the citizens were the " Swamp Dragons " and " bushwhackers," deserters and outlaws who harbored in the mountains and made predatory raids, in which the most fiendish outrages were committed.

In the hope of relieving the people from their oppressions, General Jones advanced upon Moorefield, while Imboden's battalion moved toward the same place through Highland and Pendleton counties. Moorefield was attacked January 2d, but Jones was repulsed. He succeeded in compelling the enemy to burn their stores at Petersburg, and then retired to New Market. The services of Colonel Dulaney, Captain McNeill, Lieut. C. H. Vandiver, and Privates J. W. Kuykendall and J. S. Hutton were particularly commended by the general commanding.

As the season for resuming military operations in Virginia approached, it was apparent that the Federals were massing their strength for another advance toward Richmond, and General Lee determined to delay and embarrass such an operation by striking at the railroad over which a great portion of the supplies and reinforcements were sent to the army of the Potomac. Imboden, who had now organized his brigade and had been commissioned brigadier-general, and Gen. W. E. Jones were intrusted with the performance of this work.

Imboden left camp at Shenandoah mountain on April 20th with the Twenty-fifth, Thirty-first and Sixty-second Virginia infantry, the Eighteenth cavalry, and J. H. McClanahan's battery, and was joined by the Twenty-second infantry, Col. A. C. Dunn's Thirty-seventh battalion of cavalry, dismounted, and the Nineteenth cavalry, mostly dismounted, from Samuel Jones' command, making an aggregate force of 3,365 men. He again encountered bad weather, and had to march through snow and sleet, reaching Huttonsville on the 23d. Pressing forward the next day he endeavored to surprise the enemy in camp at Beverly, but warning was given by the "bogus" but heroic sheriff of Randolph county, J. F. Phares, who, though shot though the lungs, managed to reach Beverly and give the alarm. The enemy was strongly posted and made a bold front; but Imboden, by a flank movement, assisted by a gallant cavalry charge, dislodged him, and kept up a running fight for several hours, but failed to capture the garrison. The enemy attempted to burn his stores and destroyed about a third of the town, but many valuable supplies fell into the hands of the Confederates.

Imboden proceeded to a point midway between Philippi and Buckhannon, and soon occupied the latter place, where all the stores had been destroyed and the bridge burned. Col. G. W. Imboden advanced to Weston and found that place abandoned and the enemy concentrating before Clarksburg.

Meanwhile Gen. W. E. Jones had advanced from Rockingham county with his available force to Moorefield, but was compelled to go back to Petersburg to make a crossing of the South Branch, and even then lost some men in crossing the icy stream, swollen by the spring thaw. He was compelled to send back from Moorefield his infantry and artillery. Greenland Pass was found occupied by the enemy, and it was carried by assault, April 25th. The garrison, composed of 52 men of the Twenty-third Illinois, Irish brigade, under Capt. Martin Wallace, and 34 men of Company A, Fourteenth West Virginia, under Captain Smith, displayed heroism equal to their assailants. Throwing themselves into a little church and two other log houses, they met the charge led by Col. Thomas Marshall, Seventh cavalry, supported by Colonel Dulaney, with a destructive fire, wounding Dulaney and a number of the attacking party. A second assault being repulsed, sharpshooters were posted, and Chapman's mounted rifles (Witcher's battalion) secured the stone works close to the building. Under a flag of truce, three times sent in, demands of surrender were made, but the reply was that they were '' Mulligan's men and would fight to the last cartridge.'' Finally, after dark, a general assault was made; Ridgely Brown's and White's battalions stormed the buildings, while Lieutenant Williamson's pioneers applied the torch, and amid the flames the garrison surrendered. In the fight the Confederates lost 7 killed and 22 wounded.

A detachment was then sent to burn the railroad bridge at Oakland, under the command of Col. A. W. Harman, consisting of the Twelfth cavalry, Brown's battalion and McNeill's rangers, while a detachment of the Eleventh cavalry under Capt. E. H. McDonald was sent against Altamont, and the remainder of the force moved on Rowlesburg, where the trestle bridge had been burned some time before by a Confederate party. There they found a garrison of 300, against which the Sixth cavalry was sent in front, supported by Colonel Marshall, with the Seventh, and Col. L. L. Lomax, with the Eleventh cavalry, while Capt. O. T. Weems, with 80 sharp-shooters of the Eleventh cavalry and a part of Witcher's battalion, was ordered to fire the railroad bridge. Both efforts failed, and Jones moved on to Evansville, while Lieutenant Vandiver and 8 men captured Independence and a home guard of 20 men. Jones then crossed the railroad at that point and was joined by Harman and McDonald, who had been successful in their expeditions.

On the 28th the command crossed the Monongahela at Morgantown and marched on Fairmount, which they occupied on the morning of the 29th, capturing the gar-rison of 260 after a brisk fight. Scarcely was this capitu-lation concluded before reinforcements arrived, who began shelling the Confederates, but the enemy was held off, mainly by Harman and Marshall, while under the direction of Lieutenant Williamson and Capt. John Hen-derson the magnificent iron railroad bridge of three spans, each 300 feet, erected at a cost of about half a million dollars, was completely destroyed. The Confed-erate loss at Fairmount was but 3 wounded. At dark the command started out to join Imboden, and finding Clarksburg occupied by the Federals, the Maryland cav-alry under Brown made an attack on Bridgeport, 5 miles west of that place, capturing 47 prisoners, burning the bridge to the east and the trestle work to the west, and running a captured train into the chasm. Next day they reached Philippi, and the captured horses and cattle were sent to Beverly. The junction was completed with Imboden at Weston on the 5th, and on the same day their picket was attacked at Janelew.

Judging his exhausted force not sufficient to meet the enemy in pitched battle, after resting two days General Imboden retired southward, while Jones' cavalry started against the Parkersburg branch of the Baltimore & Ohio railroad. Colonel Harman, with the Twelfth and Eleventh regiments and Witcher's battalion, moved on West Union, where he burned two bridges, meanwhile skirmishing with the enemy, while Jones, with the remainder of the cavalry, destroyed three bridges at Cairo. At Oiltown, May 9th, all the oil and everything connected with the oil works were fired, causing an appalling spectacle. Oil boats burst with a report like artillery, dense volumes of smoke arose, and the inflammable fluid, floating down stream, made a burning river, as Jones reported, "carrying destruction to our merciless enemy, a scene of magnificence that might well carry joy to every patriotic heart." Then turning southward, Jones again united with Imboden at Summersville, whence Col. G. W. Imboden had pursued a force of the enemy to Gauley, capturing 23 prisoners and a wagon train, and the forces returned to their former positions. Imboden reported that he had compelled the enemy to destroy large and valuable stores at Beverly, Buckhannon, Weston, Bulltown, Suttonville and Big Birch, captured $100,000 worth of horses, mules, wagons and arms, burned several bridges, and brought out over 3,000 head of cattle, paid for in Confederate money. But he was disappointed in recruits, only about 400 having been received. He had marched 400 miles and lost 16 men. Jones had destroyed sixteen railroad bridges and one tunnel, two trains of cars and many engines, captured 700 prisoners, and brought off 1,000 horses and a greater number of cattle. His march had covered 700 miles, and he had lost about 75 men. He reported that his men had "shown a skill in gleaning a precarious existence from a country desolated by two years of oppressive tyranny and brutal war that would have won the admiration of the most approved Cossack."

In the spring of 1863, the following was the organization of the army of Western Virginia, Maj.-Gen. Samuel Jones commanding:

First brigade, Brig.-Gen. John Echols: Twenty-second regiment, Col. George S. Patton; Forty-fifth regiment, Col. William H. Browne; Twenty-third battalion, Lieut.-

Col. Clarence Derrick; Twenty-sixth battalion, Lieut.-Col. George M. Edgar; Chapman's battery.

Second brigade, Brig.-Gen. John S. Williams: Sixty-third regiment, Col. J. J. McMahon; Forty-fifth battalion, Lieut.-Col. H. M. Beckley;—— cavalry regiment, Col. James M. French; Twenty-first cavalry, Col. William E. Peters; partisan rangers, Capt. D. B. Baldwin; Lowry's battery.

Third brigade, Col. G. C. Wharton: Fiftieth regiment, Col. A. S. Vandeventer; Fifty-first regiment, Lieut.-Col. A. Forsberg; Thirtieth battalion sharpshooters, Lieut.-Col. J. Lyle Clark; Stamps' battery.

Fourth brigade, Col. John McCausland: Thirty-sixth regiment, Maj. Thomas Smith; Sixtieth regiment, Col. B. H. Jones; Bryan's battery.

Cavalry brigade, Brig.-Gen. A. G. Jenkins: Eighth regiment, Col. James M. Corns; Fourteenth regiment, Col. James Cochran; Sixteenth regiment, Col. Milton J. Ferguson; Seventeenth regiment, Col. William H. French; Nineteenth regiment, Col. William L. Jackson; Thirty-fourth battalion, Lieut.-Col. V. A. Witcher; Thirty-sixth battalion, Maj. James W. Sweeney; Thirty-seventh battalion, Lieut.-Col. A. C. Dunn.

Unattached: Fifty-fourth regiment, Col. R. C. Trigg; partisans, Capt. P. J. Thurmond; partisans, Capt. William D. Thurmond; Otey's battery.

Aggregate present and absent, 9,747.

On March 18th General Jenkins started out from Jeffersonville with a part of his brigade on another brilliant raid across western Virginia, while McCausland made a demonstration against Fayetteville to distract the enemy, and Williams sent the Forty-fifth regiment to Raleigh. The major part of the Federal troops was now withdrawn under Cox to the army of Rosecrans. On March 27th, Jenkins reached Hurricane bridge, Putnam county, and summoned the garrison, mainly consisting of West Virginia Federals, to surrender. The demand being refused, a brisk fight ensued of several hours' duration, ending in Jenkins' withdrawal. On the 29th he reached Hall's landing just as the steamer Victress was passing, with a Federal paymaster on board. The pilot was signaled to touch for passengers, but just before it was too late he realized the situation and the boat escaped, riddled with bullets from the ambushed Confederates. Jenkins reached Point Pleasant on the next day, and surprising the Federal West Virginia company, Capt. John D. Carter commanding, that constituted the garrison, drove it into the courthouse, which was besieged for several hours. The news being carried across the river, preparations were there made to bombard the town, but this calamity was fortunately averted. Jenkins failed to dislodge the garrison, and after several men had been killed and wounded on each side, crossed the Kanawha, and returned on the south side of the river.

An expedition was sent in pursuit from Camp Piatt, by way of Chapmanville, and a sharp skirmish resulted April 5th on Mud river. Minor operations of this period deserving notice were McNeill's brilliant skirmishes with superior forces at Burlington and Purgitsville and Going's Ford, in the vicinity of Moorefield; the handsome repulse of a Federal assault by Col. G. M. Edgar at Lewisburg, May 2d; Colonel McCausland's demonstration against Fayetteville, May 20th, and the rout of a Federal scouting party on Loup creek late in June, by Maj. E. A. Bailey, who captured 29 prisoners and 45 horses. June 28, 1863, Gen. Benjamin F. Kelley became the Federal commander of the West Virginia department.

On June 29th, Col. William L. Jackson, Nineteenth Virginia cavalry, commanding the camp near Huntersville, made an expedition against Beverly, which was held by about 1,000 Federals, hoping to capture the garrison. Advancing beyond Valley mountain, Maj. John B. Lady, with five companies commanded by Capts. D. Evans, W. W. Arnett, Joseph Hayhurst, Duncan and W. W. Boggs, was sent by way of Rich mountain to the rear of the enemy, while Lieut. A. C. Dunn occupied the Philippi road. The pickets, meanwhile, had been quietly captured by Captain Righter, and the main body of Jackson's command was well upon the enemy before his presence was suspected. An advance of the Federals on the Buckhannon road was checked by Captains Marshall and Spriggs, and artillery fire was opened by Lieutenant Thrasher, of Chapman's battery. But no attack was made that day, and on the next morning the Federals being reinforced by Gen. W. W. Averell, now for the first time figuring in this region, Jackson withdrew, and was presently followed by the enemy for a short distance. On July 3d, Maj. D. Boston Stewart's battalion repulsed the enemy's cavalry in a gallant little affair at Daniel's farm. In the various reports the officers specially commended were Majors Claiborne and Lady, Captains Spriggs, Marshall, Righter, Hutton, Evans, Arnett, and Lieutenants Thrasher, Gittings, Wamsley and William Harris, the latter falling mortally wounded in the charge of Stewart's battalion.

Brig.-Gen. E. Parker Scammon was now in command at Charleston, and Col. John T. Toland was in charge of the brigade stationed at Camp Piatt. With seven companies of the Second Virginia, U. S. V., the Thirty-fourth Ohio mounted, and two companies of First Virginia, U. S. V., cavalry, Toland marched against Wytheville, Va., July 13th, through Boone, Wyoming and McDowell counties, with instructions to destroy the railroad. On the 17th the expedition surprised Camp Pendleton in Abb's valley, Tazewell county, capturing J. E. Stollings' company and some stores, but allowing one man to escape, who carried the news to Williams. At the same time McCausland was pressed back from the vicinity of Raleigh by General Scammon, and retreated to Mercer Court House, when, learning that Toland had gone down through Tazewell, he sent his cavalry to follow and moved his infantry to Bland Court House. As Toland approached Wytheville, Major May, from Williams' command, attacked his rear, inflicting severe pun-

ishment and recapturing Stollings' company. Gen. Sam
Jones had had time to throw two companies into Wytheville, under Maj. T. M. Bowyer. A gallant fight was
made against the Federals as they entered the town by
Lieutenant Bozang and his company, but he was wounded
and captured with his men, and the remainder of the Confederate force was driven from the town. During the
street fighting Colonel Toland was killed, and Colonel
Powell, second in command, wounded. The best houses
of the town were burned, Colonel Franklin, who succeeded to command, claiming that soldiers and citizens
alike fired from the houses. The railroad was torn up
slightly, and Franklin then retreated, harassed by the
Confederate cavalry, by way of Abb's valley and Flat
Top mountain.

In May, General Jenkins' brigade had been ordered into
the Shenandoah valley, and in June many West Virginians accompanied him with Ewell's corps into Pennsylvania, fighting at Bunker Hill and Martinsburg in the
defeat of Milroy, and leading the advance to Chambersburg, whence they proceeded almost to Harrisburg before
the concentration was made at Gettysburg. There they
fought gallantly, and on the retreat, under command of
Colonel Ferguson, Jenkins having been wounded, were
one of the two brigades under the immediate command
of Stuart, moving by way of Emmitsburg. Fighting
their way through the Catoctin mountains, they attacked
the enemy at Hagerstown, and after defeating him,
rapidly moved to the relief of the army train at Williamsport. In the fight near that place, according to Stuart's
report, "Jenkins' brigade was ordered to dismount and
deploy over the difficult ground. This was done with
marked effect and boldness, Lieutenant-Colonel Witcher,
as usual, distinguishing himself by his courage and conduct. The enemy, thus dislodged, was closely pressed
by the mounted cavalry, but made one effort at a counter-
charge, which was met and gallantly repulsed by Col.

w va 11

James B. Gordon. This repulse was soon afterward converted into a rout by Colonel Lomax's regiment, the
Eleventh Virginia cavalry, which now took the road with
drawn sabers, and charged down the turnpike under a
fearful fire of artillery. Without this attack it is certain
that our trains would have fallen into the hands of the
enemy." In the fight of the 10th, "Lieutenant-Colonel
Witcher's cavalry, on foot, behind a stone fence on the
Boonsboro road, performed a very gallant part in the
repulse of the enemy, standing their ground with unflinching tenacity."

On July 21st, General Imboden was assigned to command of the Shenandoah Valley district. Gen. Sam
Jones was in chief command of the department of Western Virginia and East Tennessee, with headquarters at
Dublin, with an army of about 10,000 at the various
posts. Echols' brigade, under Col. George S. Patton,
occupied Lewisburg, and Col. William L. Jackson was in
command on the Huntersville line with his regiment, the
Nineteenth cavalry, under Lieut.-Col. W. P. Thompson,
and the Twentieth cavalry, under Col. W. W. Arnett.
On August 21st, Jackson received information from Colonel Arnett that Averell, with a large force, was in Monterey. Averell had crossed to that point from Huttonsville under orders to drive Patton and Jackson from
Pocahontas and Greenbrier counties, destroy the saltpeter
works in Pendleton county, and carry the law library of
the Virginia court of appeals to Beverly. Before reaching Beverly a detachment against Moorefield had been
severely handled by the partisans there. Colonel Jackson, believing Averell's objective was Staunton, called
for aid from Patton, but was soon convinced of the real purpose of Averell. Arnett fell back skirmishing, and Jackson moved to Gatewood. Averell occupied Huntersville
and Camp Northwest, burning the stores, while Jackson,
whom Arnett had joined, skillfully extricated himself
from a dangerous position and retreated beyond Warm

Springs, Bath county, when it appearing that the Federals were withdrawing in turn, he followed toward Camp Northwest.

Averell, meanwhile, had made a rapid movement against Lewisburg, and encountered Patton in line of battle at White Sulphur Springs. The battle was opened on August 26th with an artillery duel, in which Chapman's battery did excellent service, followed by repeated assaults by the enemy, which were repulsed. Col. A. R. Barbee, of the Twenty-second, commanding skirmishers, fell wounded while displaying notable gallantry; the Forty-fifth held its ground with great steadiness; the Twenty-third, under Major Blessing, reinforced the Twenty-second under a galling fire; Major Bailey handsomely repulsed a charge upon the center; Colonel Edgar, Twenty-sixth, whose men had done the first skirmishing, repulsed two cavalry charges, and Colonel Browne and Major Claiborne held the right without wavering. The last attack was made at sunset against Edgar, but was again repulsed. The fight was renewed next day, but the enemy had lost spirit under severe punishment, and retreated, Colonel Corns, with the cavalry, leading in pursuit. A junction was made with Jackson, and Colonel Arnett skirmished with the retreating columns, but his force was inadequate.

In this raid, Averell had about 3,000 men, but claimed that he fought the battle of the 26th with but 1,300. Jackson had 1,000 and Patton 1,900. Jackson's loss was about 20 killed and wounded, Patton's, including missing, 162, Averell's 218. The battle of White Sulphur Springs deserves to be remembered as one of the most gallantly fought in the department of Western Virginia.

The Confederates continued to occupy their positions, and detachments were stationed in the Elk river country and up toward Weston, where several minor skirmishes occurred. In the northeast during September there were several Federal parties sent out from Martinsburg.

On the 4th there was a severe skirmish at Petersburg Gap, and on the 15th one at Smithfield.   On the night of September 6th, 26 men under Captains Burke and Blackford attacked the camp of two companies of Pennsylvania six months' men at Bath, killed Captain Hebble and a number of his men, and brought away 23 prisoners and 50 horses.   On the 11th, Captains Imboden, McNeill and Hobson, with about 150 men, attacked 300 Federals under Major Stephens at Moorefield, at dawn charging into their camp with a yell, effectually surprising the enemy. Thirty Federals were killed or seriously wounded, 8 officers and 138 privates captured, and all the ammunition and supplies taken in charge.   Two attacks were made upon the little band on their retreat, but they escaped with the loss of only 8 or 10 men and some of the captured horses.

Reconnoissances and skirmishes continued all along the line.   On the 24th there was an encounter at Greenbrier bridge with Averell's command.   Bailey, Morrow and Gilmor made a demonstration against Charlestown, October 7th, and encountered a detachment under Captain Summers, who was killed.   The West Virginia, U. S. V., garrison at Bulltown was attacked by Colonel Jackson October 13th, but after a fight which continued through the day, the Federal troops held their fortifications.   Being reinforced the next day they pursued Jackson, but were checked at Salt Lick bridge.

The continual fighting about Charlestown had weakened the Federal force there, but it was thought by the Federal authorities that the Ninth Maryland regiment, under Colonel Simpson, was sufficient.   He made a reconnoissance, and found no force in his front except the Forty-first Virginia battalion under Maj. Robert White, at Berryville, "not the old White (E. V.), but another man," the Federals reported, "whose men say they have been in the valley but two or three weeks." But Imboden joined White, and on Sunday morning,

October 18th, they surprised the Charlestown garrison, surrounding the enemy in the courthouse, jail and other buildings they had fortified in the heart of the town. Simpson was called on to surrender and given five minutes for deliberation, upon which he said, "Take us if you can." An artillery fire was opened at a distance of 200 yards, and the garrison speedily left the buildings and formed for retreat to Harper's Ferry, when they were met by a detachment at the edge of town, and after one volley threw down their arms, the mounted officers escaping. Two hours later the Harper's Ferry forces arrived on the scene and the Confederates fell back slowly toward Berryville, fighting all the day till 10 o'clock at night. They carried safely to Shenandoah county 434 prisoners; their loss was about 6 killed or mortally wounded, 20 wounded and a few stragglers.

Colonel Beckley was about this time organizing cavalry near Logan Court House on the Guyandotte, and a reconnoissance was sent in his direction under Gen. A. N. Duffie, without results.

Early in November, simultaneous with an advance of Federal cavalry in east Tennessee, General Averell set out from Beverly and General Duffié from Charlestown, against Echols and Jackson, General Scammon's infantry brigade to join them at Lewisburg, the united cavalry command then to proceed to Dublin Station and destroy the New River bridge. The first intimation of this formidable movement was received by Jackson, who concentrated at Mill Point and informed Echols, who prepared to move to his relief from Lewisburg. Jackson made a stand at Mill Point, Lurty's battery engaging the enemy, but was soon compelled to fall back to Droop mountain, about half way between Lewisburg and Huntersville, on the west side of the Greenbrier river, where he took a strong position.

Colonel Thompson had gallantly disputed the enemy's advance step by step, and, aided by Lurty's shells, reached the Droop mountain position in safety, giving Jackson about 750 men. Jackson was also reinforced that night and on the morning of the 6th by the Fourteenth Virginia cavalry, the Twenty-second regiment, Derrick's battalion, and Jackson's and Chapman's batteries, which were under the brigade command of Colonel Patton, while General Echols took general command. About 11 a. m. on November 6th the enemy advanced to attack, opening with artillery on the right and threatening the center, but making the serious attack on the left, where Colonel Thompson soon called for help. The Fourteenth cavalry and Derrick's battalion were sent there, then several companies of the Twenty-second, and finally Colonel Patton moved to that point, but was unable to withstand the pressure. Arnett and Cochrane at the center meanwhile gallantly repulsed several charges, but when it became apparent that the left was turned, the whole force fell back under a severe shelling and enfilading fire of musketry. Major McLaughlin, and Captains Chapman, Jackson and Lurty, with their artillery, gallantly held the enemy in check.

The retreat to Lewisburg was rapid, as information was at hand that Duffié was already at Little Sewell mountain in the rear. The Sixteenth cavalry, Col. M. J. Ferguson, from Jenkins' brigade, also participated in the engagement. General Echols reported that he had but 1,700 men in the fight. The total strength of Averell's brigade was about 5,000, and his force in battle must have considerably outnumbered that of Echols. The Confederate loss in killed, wounded and missing was 275. Among the killed was the gallant Maj. R. A. Bailey of the Twenty-second. That regiment went into battle with 550 men and lost 113; the Twenty-third lost 61 out of 350. The total Federal loss was reported at 119.

Echols won the race to Lewisburg, passing through there seven hours before Duffié arrived and much longer before Averell came up. He had successfully avoided the capture of his command that had been planned. General Imboden, at Bridgewater, hearing of Averell's advance, moved toward Huntersville, when he was informed of the battle and retired to Covington, where he checked a detachment which Averell sent out against the furnaces in Rockbridge county. Averell then returned to his post on New creek, the great object of his raid, the destruction of a part of the Virginia & Tennessee railroad, having been defeated by the gallant stand made by Echols, Jackson and Patton at Droop mountain. The battle, though a technical defeat, was a tactical victory.

On November 17th a Federal cavalry expedition left Charlestown with 700 men under Col. W. H. Boyd, encountered Confederate skirmishers at Edenburg, who contested their advance, and at Mount Jackson, in the Shenandoah valley, had a sharp fight with Maj. Robert White commanding his battalion, a portion of Gilmor's battalion, Captain Davis' company, and a section of McClanahan's battery. Major White then took position on Rude's hill and the enemy was handsomely repulsed, after which Davis pursued the Federals and compelled them to break camp near Woodstock. On the same day, the 16th, Captain McNeill, with his own indomitable company and a detachment from the Sixty-second regiment, in all 100 men, attacked a train of eighty wagons near Burlington, en route to Averell, whipped the escort of 100 infantry, and brought away 25 prisoners and 245 horses, though hotly pursued by 600 cavalry. This caused a Federal court-martial.

Early in December another movement against the Virginia & Tennessee railroad was ordered by Halleck, the Federal commander-in-chief, Sullivan (9,500 strong) to advance up the Shenandoah valley to threaten Staunton; Averell's brigade (5,000) to move by Monterey, to destroy the railroad in Botetourt or Roanoke county; while Scammon's division was to make a feint toward

New River bridge. Colonel Moor, also, with two regiments, was to move from Beverly to Droop mountain. General Averell reached Petersburg December 10th.

General Echols, at Lewisburg, suspecting a Federal advance from Charlestown, sent Capt. Philip J. Thurmond on a reconnoissance, and he dispersed some Federal pickets on Big Sewell mountain and forwarded the startling intelligence to Echols of the proximity of a large body of the enemy. Thurmond skirmished with their advance as far as Lewisburg, where Echols made a stand before the town until all public property was removed, when he moved across the river, driving back the enemy's advance with McLaughlin's artillery. Being advised then of Moor's approach from the north, he fell back into Monroe county, where he was joined by McCausland's force, Gen. Sam Jones also arriving and taking command on the 14th. Averell meanwhile, making feints to confuse Jackson and Imboden, made his way safely to Salem on the 16th, and destroyed the stores at that point, destroyed four bridges and injured the track to some extent, but was compelled to make a hasty retreat in the afternoon of the same day. He found his way beset with difficulty, as General Early had reached New Market to direct the movement for his capture, and Gen. Fitzhugh Lee with two brigades had been ordered into the field. Echols was placed near Sweet Springs, and Jackson, ordered in every direction in the confusion, finally brought up at Clifton Forge near Covington.

Averell attempted to re-enter western Virginia by the Sweet Springs road, but meeting Echols, turned off on an obscure road to Covington, reaching there just as a detachment from Jackson was firing the Rich Patch bridge. He succeeded in getting part of his men across when Jackson cut his command in two, Colonel Arnett attacking, while Major Lady, with 50 men, three times during the night repulsed Averell's attempts to get the remainder of his cavalry across the bridge. At daylight

Averell burned the bridge, apparently leaving the rear of his command to their fate; but the latter were stronger than Jackson, and, driving him back, they burned their wagon train, and on the morning of the 20th escaped across a ford which had been declared impassable, losing several men by drowning, and closely pressed by Colonel Arnett. Jackson captured about 150 prisoners and inflicted a considerable loss in killed and wounded. Fitzhugh Lee and Imboden crossed in pursuit the next day, but failed to come up with the raiders.

CHAPTER VII.

OPERATIONS OF 1864-1865—EXPEDITIONS OF FITZHUGH LEE AND ROSSER—EXPLOITS OF GILMOR AND McNEILL—ORGANIZATION OF THE ARMY OF WESTERN VIRGINIA—BATTLE OF CLOYD'S MOUNTAIN—NEWMARKET—LYNCHBURG—RETREAT OF HUNTER THROUGH WEST VIRGINIA—WITCHER'S RAIDS—OTHER BRILLIANT EXPLOITS.

ON the last day of 1863 Maj.-Gen. Fitzhugh Lee started from Mount Jackson, in a snow and rain storm, and marched to Moorefield across North mountain, where he was obliged to abandon his artillery and wagon train. He reconnoitered the Federal garrison at Petersburg and then moved toward New Creek depot, capturing a wagon train, burned the block houses at Burlington, Williamsport, and McLemar's church, and then proceeded toward the Baltimore & Ohio railroad intending to cut it, but was compelled by the sufferings of his men and the impassability of the mountains to turn back on January 5, 1864, bringing into the Shenandoah valley about 600 cattle, 300 horses and mules, and 110 prisoners. Major Gilmor meanwhile drove the enemy out of Springfield, burned their winter quarters and brought off supplies, the main item of which was 3,000 pounds of bacon. All these captures except the prisoners were very welcome in the Confederate army.

Another raid was made January 28th from the Shenandoah valley, under the command of General Early, with Rosser's brigade, Thomas' brigade, Gilmor's and McNeill's rangers, and part of McClanahan's battery. Reaching Moorefield, Rosser was sent to intercept a train of ninety-five wagons en route from New Creek to Petersburg, where the Federals were strongly fortified.   Near Moorefield junction he encountered the Twenty-third Illinois regiment obstructing the road.   This command, driven back, joined the detachments of the Second Maryland and Fourth West Virginia, and the united force attempted to defend the wagons against Rosser, but gave way on the second charge and yielded the rich train to the yearning Confederates.   In the fight Maj. Nathan Goff, U. S. V., was wounded and captured.   The whole command then occupied Petersburg, the garrison fleeing, and gathered some commissary stores and 13,000 cartridges, after which Gilmor and McNeill were sent out after cattle, while Rosser destroyed the railroad and other bridges at the mouth of Patterson's creek.   The enemy then appearing in force, Early withdrew, bringing out 50 wagons and teams, 1,200 cattle, 500 sheep and 78 prisoners, again cheering the hearts of the soldiers in the Shenandoah valley.

In January, 1864, Colonel Ferguson, Sixteenth Virginia cavalry, came into Wayne county, with a large part of his regiment and the Eighth cavalry, and during the remainder of the year the region between the Guyandotte and Big Sandy was practically controlled by the Confederate soldiers.   Under this protection, the Big Sandy river became a channel of trade with Northern merchants.   Judge H. L. Samuels, who had been prevented from holding court in Wayne under the West Virginia State government, reported that "a vast quantity of useful and indispensable articles find their way to Dixie through the medium of these guerrillas.   The stolen horses are laden with this contraband trade.   Sympathizers land large lots of barrels and boxes from steamboats.   I myself have seen seven rebels taken with their arms whose shoes were not worn enough to erase the trademarks of neighboring Ohio merchants."   During this period there were no captures of Northern steamboats on the Big Sandy.

During February occurred two daring exploits at opposite extremities of the State. The first was the capture of the United States steamer B. C. Levi, at Red House shoals, on the Kanawha, on the night of February 2d, by Maj. J. H. Nounnan, with less than 30 men. The Confederates quietly boarded the boat while lashed to the bank, and captured Gen. E. P. Scammon, commander of the Federal division at Charleston, his staff and 13 soldiers. The steamer was run four miles down the river next morning and burned, and the general and his staff were mounted and carried to Richmond.

The other adventure was by Maj. H. W. Gilmor, who threw a Baltimore & Ohio train off the track near Duffield depot, and secured about $900 from the mailbags. The collections made by his soldiers from passengers led General Lee to order an investigation.

On February 25th Maj.-Gen. John C. Breckinridge was assigned to command of the Trans-Alleghany or western department of Virginia. The organization of the army of Western Virginia* in April was as follows:

Echols' infantry brigade, Brig.-Gen. John Echols: Twenty-second, Col. George S. Patton; Twenty-third, Lieut.-Col. Clarence Derrick; Twenty-sixth battalion, Lieut.-Col. George M. Edgar; partisan rangers, Capt. Philip J. Thurmond; partisan rangers, Capt. William D. Thurmond; partisan rangers, Capt. John Amick; battery, Capt. George B. Chapman.

Jenkins' cavalry brigade, Brig.-Gen. Albert G. Jenkins: Fourteenth regiment, Col. Charles Cochrane; Sixteenth regiment, Maj. James H. Nounnan; Seventeenth, Col. William H. French; Twenty-second regiment, Col. Henry S. Bowen.

Saltville garrison, Col. William H. Browne: Forty-fifth infantry regiment, Lieut.-Col. Edwin H. Harman; Ten-

---

* The infantry brigades of the army of Western Virginia constituted G. C. Wharton's division of Early's army of the Valley during the fall and winter of 1864-65, and suffered severely in the disaster of Waynesboro, March 2, 1865, which practically ended the career of the various commands, though a remnant of the division maintained its organization after the surrender at Appomattox.

nessee battery, Capt. William H. Burroughs; Tennessee battery, Capt. H. L. W. McClung.

McCausland's infantry brigade, Col. John McCausland: Thirty-sixth regiment, Lieut.-Col. Thomas Smith; Sixtieth regiment, Col. Beuhring H. Jones; Forty-fifth battalion, Lieut.-Col. Henry M. Beckley; battery, Capt. Thomas. A Bryan.

Jackson's cavalry brigade, Col. William L. Jackson: Nineteenth regiment, Capt. George Downs; Twentieth regiment, Col. William W. Arnett; Forty-sixth battalion, Lieut.-Col. Joseph K. Kesler; Forty-seventh battalion, Maj. William N. Harman; battery, Capt. Warren S. Lurty.

Unattached: Bosang's Company C, Fourth infantry, Lieut. James F. Cecil; Hart's engineer company, Capt. William T. Hart; Botetourt artillery, Capt. Henry C. Douthat; Jackson's horse artillery, Capt. Thomas E. Jackson.

In eastern Tennessee were the Forty-fifth and Fifty-first Virginia infantry, and Thirtieth Virginia sharpshooters, of Wharton's brigade; W. E. Jones' cavalry brigade —Eighth regiment, Lieut.-Col. A. F. Cook; Twenty-first regiment, Capt. W. H. Balthis; Twenty-seventh battalion, Capt. John B. Thompson; Thirty-fourth battalion, Lieut.-Col. V. A. Witcher; Thirty-sixth battalion, Capt. C. T. Smith; Thirty-seventh battalion, Maj. James R. Claiborne—and Floyd King's artillery battalion, the Davidson, Lowry, Otey and Ringgold batteries.

February 10th Maj.-Gen. Franz Sigel was assigned to command of the Union department, and he was succeeded May 21st by Maj.-Gen. David Hunter. The organization of his army in May was as follows:

Brig.-Gen. J. C. Sullivan's division, 6,500 men, headquarters at Harper's Ferry: First brigade, five regiments, Col. Augustus Moore; Second brigade, Col. Joseph Thoburn, five regiments, including Weddle's and Curtis' West Virginian.

Brig.-Gen. George Crook's division, 9,800 men: First brigade, Col. Rutherford B. Hayes, four regiments, including Tomlinson's and Brown's West Virginian; Second brigade, Col. Carr B. White, four regiments, including Duval's and Johnson's West Virginian; Third brigade, Col. H. G. Sickel, four regiments including Frost's and Morris' West Virginian.

First cavalry division, Maj.-Gen. Julius Stahel, 7,600 men: brigades of Tibbits and Wynkoop. Second cavalry division, Brig.-Gen. W. W. Averell, 5,000 men: brigades of Duffié, Schoonmaker and Oley.

These active forces numbered 20,000 present for duty. Besides there was the reserve division, over 16,000 men present, under command of Brig.-Gen. Max Weber from Monocacy to Sleepy creek, and under Brigadier-General Kelley west of Sleepy creek.

The destruction of the saltpeter works of the Confederate army was a constant aim of the Federal troops, and an expedition for this purpose started out from Burlington late in February and destroyed the works at Franklin. The detachment guarding the supply train at Petersburg was severely handled on March 3d by a Confederate detachment from Moorefield. On the 10th a detachment of Mosby's men attacked the pickets at Charlestown, and in the skirmishing which followed Major Sullivan, commanding picket, and several others were killed, and 21 prisoners were taken by the partisans. A considerable number of the Eighth and Sixteenth cavalry regiments were at home on furlough in Wayne and Cabell counties at this time, and previously a body of the Sixteenth had had a brisk fight with Colonel Gallup, of Ohio, in Wayne county. A Federal reconnoissance through the counties in March failed to find any of the Confederates.

Capt. John H. McNeill made an important expedition from Moorefield, May 5th, against the Baltimore & Ohio railroad at Bloomington and Piedmont. Though taking but 60 men he was entirely successful, captured the garrison at Piedmont, destroyed seven large buildings filled with machinery, engines and cars, burned nine railroad engines, seventy-five or eighty freight cars, two trains laden with commissary stores, sent six engines with full head of steam toward New Creek, captured a mail train, releasing prisoners, and burned the railroad bridge. Such exploits retained in this region large bodies of Federal troops sorely needed by Grant in the Wilderness.

Early in May important operations began, which involved the West Virginia soldiers, but which were conducted mainly in the Shenandoah valley and southwest Virginia. Gen. U. S. Grant, ordering a forward movement in all parts of the South simultaneous with his crossing of the Rapidan, directed Sigel to move two divisions of his army down the Shenandoah valley to Cedar creek, while Averell should make a dash into southwest Virginia, destroy New river bridge, work eastward to Lynchburg if possible, and in that case return to Staunton, where Sigel would meet him with supplies. The forces under Breckinridge by two brilliant battles, one won and the other lost, defeated the full carrying out of this plan.

Crook set out with his division in the last of April, marching 6,155 men by way of Fayetteville to Princeton, while Colonel Tomlinson's regiment, with Blazer's scouts, was sent by Lewisburg. At the same time Averell with 2,000 men was sent by way of Logan Court House to Saltville, Va., thence to strike Dublin Depot. On May 6th, Princeton was occupied with skirmishing. On the 7th, having entered Giles county, a Confederate force was found posted at the gap of Walker mountain but forced to withdraw. On the following day in a skirmish on Back creek before Dublin, Captain Harman, the famous partisan, was killed.

General Jenkins, who had only 200 men with him, took a position on Cloyd's farm, at the base of Cloyd's mountain, commanding the road to Dublin, and about 5 miles from that place, where he was joined by McCausland's brigade, fortunately just arrived at Dublin en route to Staunton, and by Browne's Forty-fifth regiment from Saltville, Dickinson's battery and the Botetourt artillery. The battle began early on the 9th with a Federal attack on the right. while a fierce artillery duel was opened at the center. The attack upon Browne, on the right, was repelled at the cost of weakening other parts of the lines, and a gallant charge repelled the Federals from that part of the field; but meanwhile the center was fiercely assailed, General Jenkins falling mortally wounded there, and the left was turned. The whole line then gave way, but was rallied by McCausland, who succeeded Jenkins in command, and the fight was renewed. Still another line was formed, and finally the fourth line repelled the enemy's charge, after which the Confederates moved through Dublin, the rear guard constantly fighting, and across New river bridge. McCausland subsequently fell back to the vicinity of Salem.

Colonel Browne, of the Forty-fifth, reported that his gallant lieutenant-colonel, E. H. Harman, fell mortally wounded while placing in line reinforcements from the Sixtieth. The Forty-fifth battalion, Lieutenant-Colonel Beckley, coming to his aid, made a brilliant charge upon the enemy's position on the ridge from which Browne had been flanked, but were overpowered and driven back. Among the killed of Browne's regiment were Capt. R. R. Crockett and Lieuts. J. R. Brown, C. N. Porter and H. H. Lockett; of the Sixtieth, Lieut.-Col. G. W. Hammond, Maj. J. N. Taylor and Capt. M. McClintic. Morgan's dismounted Kentucky cavalry, under Col. D. H. Smith, reached the field toward the close of the fight, and in a gallant charge Capt. C. S. Cleburne, a brother of Maj.-Gen. P. S. Cleburne, was mortally wounded.

The Federal loss at Cloyd's mountain was 108 killed, 508 wounded and 72 captured or missing; the Confederate loss, 76 killed, 262 wounded and 200 captured or missing. The casualties were mainly in the Forty-fifth, Sixtieth and Thirty-sixth infantry regiments, Morgan's dismounted men, and the Forty-fifth battalion.

Jackson, who had been ordered to the Narrows of New river, and joined by Colonel French, commanding Jenkins' brigade, was called back to meet Crook on his return.

They were pushed back from Newport, and Crook, followed by McCausland, started across Salt Pond mountain toward Union, skirmishing at Gap mountain with Jackson and reaching Meadow Bluff on the 19th.

Averell, with the other Federal column, had captured some of the Eighth Virginia in Tazewell county, but found Saltville strongly held by Gens. John H. Morgan and W. E. Jones, and avoiding that point, his real destination, marched to Wytheville, fought a battle on the 10th with Morgan and Jones, and then by a narrow margin won a race to Dublin, and crossed the river in safety, the Confederates being prevented from following by the swollen waters and the destruction of the railroad and bridges. He then joined General Crook at Union. Thus, with some assistance, the Confederate army of Western Virginia had defeated the main purposes of this formidable raid, saved Lynchburg from attack, and prevented the contemplated junction of Crook and Sigel.

Further down the great valley in the same month of May, the West Virginians in other commands participated in a still more decided check given the other column of invading Federals. Brigadier-General Imboden, in command of the Valley district since July, 1863, broke camp May 2d, at Mount Crawford, and moved to Woodstock to observe Sigel, who was coming up the valley with Sullivan's and Stahel's divisions and five batteries. Imboden's whole force then was a little less than 1,500 men, included in the Sixty-second infantry, mounted, Col. George H. Smith; Twenty-third cavalry, Col. Robert White; Eighteenth cavalry, Col. George W. Imboden; Gilmor's Maryland battalion; Davis' Maryland battalion, McNeill's rangers, and McClanahan's battery. As soon as he had discovered the strength of the approaching enemy he fell back to Mount Jackson. By skillful maneuvers he dealt severe blows to Sigel's reconnoissances and held him back, while reinforcements came up from Breckinridge.

On the 14th, Sigel's advance finally reached Rude's hill, near New Market, pressing back Colonel Imboden. Colonel Smith, in command of Imboden's force during that general's absence to meet Breckinridge, formed his little brigade and held the town until night, artillery firing continuing during the day. In the morning Breckinridge arrived with Echols' brigade, Wharton's brigade (Forty-fifth and Fifty-first regiments and Thirtieth battalion), and the Virginia military institute cadets under Colonel Shipp. The fight was opened by McLaughlin's artillery, and presently the Confederate line advanced, while Imboden's cavalry and McClanahan's battery occupied a hill commanding the enemy's left. The fire from this position scattered Stahel's cavalry, and Sigel fell back half a mile, pressed by the Confederate infantry. Men were falling rapidly now under a destructive artillery and infantry fire, and the Sixty-second regiment and the cadet corps made their famous charge upon a battery at the Federal center, capturing it and the gunners, but suffering terribly in the movement. McLaughlin defeated a cavalry charge and Sigel was soon in retreat. Breckinridge occupied Rude's hill that night. In this battle the Federals lost 831 out of about 6,000, the Confederates 577 out of about 5,000.

Immediately afterward Wharton's and Echols' brigades were called to Lee's army on the Cold Harbor line.

In the latter part of May, a Federal reconnoissance was made through Pocahontas, Webster and Braxton counties, gathering in a considerable number of partisan rangers, and horses and cattle.

Sigel was soon replaced by Gen. David Hunter, who advanced to Mount Jackson simultaneously with another incursion by Crook, who left Meadow Bluff on the last of May to attack Staunton. Thus was begun the Lynchburg campaign, in which many West Virginians served with great credit. Imboden's men stubbornly contested Hunter's advance, and were reinforced by W. E. Jones, who took command.   The little army was badly defeated at Piedmont by Hunter, and Jones killed.   McCausland and Jackson gallantly opposed the advance of Crook and Averell, delaying their junction with Hunter, and meanwhile Lynchburg was reinforced by Early.   On the day that Early's advance arrived, Imboden, McCausland and Jackson went out to meet Hunter's combined army to hold it back long enough to insure the safety of the city, attacking the enemy gallantly at New London, and on Friday, June 17th, 4 miles from Lynchburg, made a brilliant fight, losing 100 killed and wounded, after which they fell back unmolested to the fortifications of the city.

After a battle before Lynchburg, Hunter retreated to Salem.   His rear guard, under Averell, was defeated at Liberty, and near Salem two of his batteries were captured by the Confederate cavalry.   Harassed and headed off by Early, Hunter turned toward Lewisburg, and reached Gauley bridge June 27th, moving thence to Charleston and Parkersburg, whence his army was sent back by rail to the lower Shenandoah valley.   This retreat across the State was the last great military movement in West Virginia.

The campaign of Early's army through Maryland against Washington and the railroad communications of Baltimore was shared by the brigades of Echols, Wharton, McCausland, Imboden and Jackson, and the batteries formerly associated with the army of Western Virginia.   These commands also participated in the campaign against Sheridan in the Shenandoah valley.

When General Early was advancing down the valley of Virginia on his march toward Washington, the Twenty-third Virginia cavalry, under Col. Robert White, with one piece of artillery, was detached from the main command and sent a distance of some 50 miles northwest to capture and destroy the bridge of the Baltimore & Ohio railroad at the junction of the North and South branches of the Potomac.   Upon reaching the hill overlooking the bridge a little after midday, July 4th, it was found that on the western side of the South Branch and near the western end of the bridge there was a blockhouse, occupied by Federal soldiers, as well as an engine with an ironclad magazine attached standing there, also occupied by soldiers. When the location of this blockhouse and magazine was discovered, a shell was fired from the artillery at the magazine. The aim was accurate; the shell entered the magazine and burst inside of it, exploding the ammunition contained, destroying the magazine, and, as was afterward ascertained, injuring some forty of the Federal soldiers. The bridge was then cut, and White retired to rejoin Early's command near Martinsburg.

On June 22d, Gen. John H. Morgan, of Kentucky, was assigned to command the department of Western Virginia and East Tennessee, and soon afterward General Crook was given chief command of the Federal forces. Morgan's operations were all outside the State, and the only Virginia organizations in his army were Col. Robert Smith's battalion, Witcher's battalion and the Sixty-fourth cavalry.

Upon the death of Morgan, Breckinridge resumed command of the department, and under him in November, Colonel Witcher had a brigade consisting of his battalion, W. H. Payne's company and the two Thurmond battalions. The other western Virginia troops were mainly with Early in the Shenandoah valley. Maj.-Gen. John Echols was in command at Dublin, and participated in the defeat of the Federal raid into southwest Virginia in October.

On August 4th, the brigades of Gen. Bradley Johnson (W. E. Jones' old brigade) and McCausland, returning from Chambersburg, Pa., attacked New Creek, and after a severe fight were repulsed with considerable loss. The Confederate command then proceeded to Moorefield, near where they were attacked in camp about daylight, August 7th, by Averell's cavalry, surprised and routed, losing 27 officers and 393 enlisted men as prisoners and 400 horses.

On August 26th the Federals at Huttonsville, 70 strong, were captured by partisans.

In the latter part of September, a brilliant raid was made by Lieut.-Col. V. A. Witcher from Tazewell county through West Virginia. On the 25th he captured and burned the fortified camp at Bulltown, surprised Weston on the evening of the next day, capturing a large amount of stores and seizing over $5,000 from the Exchange bank; destroyed stores at Janelew; at Buckhannon on the 28th captured the garrison, including Maj. T. F. Lang, and burned a very large quantity of quartermaster, commissary and medical stores, and about 1,000 stand of small-arms. Returning to Greenbrier county he brought out 400 horses and 200 cattle. His battalions were under the command of Captains McFarlane, P. J. and W. D. Thurmond.

About the same time Maj. J. H. Nounnan was sent from Tazewell to the mouth of the Coal, but being unable to cross the river, he retired after securing a considerable amount of supplies from a store-boat. Near Winfield his men and a body of Federals collided in full speed, and the Confederates, with Nounnan, were worsted in the mêlée. But his expedition served a good purpose in drawing attention from Witcher.

In the latter part of the same month, Witcher moved into the Mud river region, and rode through Teay's valley against a garrison at Winfield, a company of the Seventh West Virginia. He sent his men into the town in two detachments, Capt. Philip J. Thurmond leading one. In the desperate fight in the streets which followed, Thurmond was mortally wounded at the head of his command.

With continued audacity Witcher turned his attention to the Big Sandy river early in November, on the 5th captured and burned the United States armed steamers Barnum and Fawn at Buffalo shoals, and on the same day captured and destroyed the military stores at Mellonsburg and drove the enemy's cavalry under his guns at Louisa. At Logan Court House, a few days later, this indomitable officer reported that he had collected six companies of recruits, and had four or five other companies forming. He had increased his own battalion to a regiment, and had collected one for Col. Thomas B. Swann.

One of the most notable affairs in other portions of the State in this period was the "greenback raid" under Mosby. Hearing that a train had left Washington with 42 paymasters on board carrying funds for Sheridan's army, he determined to share in the emoluments due to active and faithful soldiers. With about 70 picked men, and Dr. James G. Wiltshire, of Jefferson county, as a guide, he made a night ride and prepared to stop the train at the same place that Gilmor's men had selected in February. One side of the track was raised in such a manner that the locomotive was overthrown, as the train arrived, and Mosby's men went through the cars, capturing Generals Ruggles and Moore, and $168,000 in greenbacks. The train was then burned, and the daring raiders made a successful escape. On reaching Bloomfield, Loudoun county, the money was equally divided, without respect to rank, and the paymasters were forwarded to Richmond. On October 29th an unfortunate attack was made upon a Federal detachment at Beverly, by Maj. Houston Hall. The latter was wounded and captured and his command lost 140 men in the two hours' battle. The opposite result followed an attack upon Green Spring by McNeill's rangers November 1st, the garrison being almost entirely captured, and the horses and arms carried off.

On November 25th General Kelley sent out an expedition to hunt McNeill, which to its great surprise encountered General Rosser with his own and two regiments of Payne's brigade, at Moorefield, Rosser being engaged in a little expedition of his own. The Federals escaped with considerable loss, and Rosser followed close upon their heels to the fortified post of New Creek, which, guided by two trusty scouts, Pierce and Williams, he succeeded in completely surprising, in daylight, capturing Fort Kelley and garrison without a shot, also taking possession of Piedmont. He captured by this brilliant and almost bloodless coup 700 prisoners, about 1,500 horses and as many cattle, and destroyed a vast amount of property, including 200 wagons, a very large amount of stores, government buildings and engines.

On January 11, 1865, General Rosser made another brilliant stroke at Beverly. With 300 mounted men he rode into the Federal fortified camp, where no visitors were expected on account of the inclement weather, and in the fight which ensued 6 of the enemy were killed and 33 wounded. The remainder of the garrison, 580 men, were captured, with all their arms, ammunition and supplies.

On February 5th, Colonel Whittaker, First Connecticut cavalry, succeeded in surprising the famous partisan leader, Major Gilmor, in bed, and hastily carried him to Winchester; and on February 22d Lieut. Jesse C. McNeill, with 25 men, entered the fortified town of Cumberland, Md., and taking Generals Crook and Kelley out of bed, brought them safely into Virginia.

The troops of the department of Western Virginia and East Tennessee, commanded by Brig.-Gen. John Echols, with headquarters at Wytheville, Va., comprised the following organizations on February 28, 1865:

Echols' infantry brigade, Col. Robert T. Preston's brigade of reserves, Gen. George B. Cosby's brigade of Kentucky cavalry, Gen. Basil Duke's brigade of Kentucky cavalry, Col. Henry Giltner's brigade of Kentucky cavalry, Gen. John C. Vaughn's brigade of Tennessee cavalry, Lieut.-Col. Vincent A. Witcher's brigade of Virginia cavalry, Maj. R. C. M. Page's artillery battalion, and Capt. R. C. McCalla's engineer battalion.

Echols' brigade included the Twenty-second regiment, Lieut.-Col. John C. McDonald; Twenty-third battalion, Maj. William Blessing; Twenty-sixth battalion, Lieut.-Col. George M. Edgar. Witcher's brigade was composed of the Thirty-fourth battalion, Maj. John A. McFarlane, and the battalion of Lieut.-Col. Thomas B. Swann. Capt. H. C. Douthat's battery was with the artillery.

The total enrollment of the command was 10,000 men and six pieces of artillery. The largest brigades were those of Vaughn and Echols. But on account of furloughs and for other reasons the aggregate force present was only 4,000. Witcher's brigade was 215 strong and Echols' 662.

On April 2d General Echols began a movement to unite with the army of Northern Virginia, but on reaching Christiansburg, Va., on the 10th, he received a dispatch announcing the surrender of General Lee at Appomattox Court House. General Duke has written, "Strange as the declaration may sound now, there was not one of the 6,000 or 7,000 men then gathered at Christiansburg who had entertained the slightest thought that such an event could happen. . . . That the army of Northern Virginia, with Lee at its head, would ever surrender, had never entered our minds." After a night of excitement and discussion around blazing camp-fires, part of the force proceeded under General Echols to attempt a junction with Johnston's army in North Carolina, while many returned to their homes satisfied that the war was over. Those from West Virginia who went on and those who returned, as well as those who surrendered at Appomattox and with the various commands in the Shenandoah valley, in time mainly accepted citizenship in the new State born in the throes of war, and after enduring the hardships and persecution which followed their home-coming, and the annoyances of adverse legislation, resumed the stations to which their worth entitled them in a free commonwealth and a reunited nation.

CHAPTER VIII.

MISCELLANEOUS DATA — NOTES ON THE CONTRIBU-
TIONS OF VARIOUS COUNTIES TO THE CONFEDER-
ATE SERVICE — RECORDS OF THE TWENTY-FIFTH
AND THIRTY-FIRST REGIMENTS.

IN Hampshire county, before the commencement of the
war, there were two organized and uniformed companies of infantry; one known as the Frontier Riflemen, of which Robert White, afterward colonel of the
Twenty-third Virginia cavalry, was captain, Elias L.
Irvin first lieutenant, Job N. Cookus second lieutenant,
and Daniel T. Kellar third lieutenant; and the other the
Hampshire Guards, John B. Sherrard captain, D. W.
Entler first lieutenant, and Felix D. Heiskell second
lieutenant. The first-named company had about 96 men,
and the last about 80. In May, 1861, both of these companies were ordered by the governor of Virginia to report
to Col. T. J. Jackson, then commanding at Harper's
Ferry. Soon afterward the Thirteenth Virginia regiment
of infantry was organized, with A. P. Hill as colonel,
and these companies were mustered into that regiment
as Companies I and K. The world knows much of the
heroism of the men of that regiment and of its hard service
during the war. In the spring of 1862 the army was reorganized. Captain White was assigned to ordnance duty.
He was afterward authorized, at his own request, to raise
a battalion of cavalry, which he did and became major of
the Forty-first battalion, Virginia cavalry, which was
afterward merged in the Twenty-third regiment, of which
he was colonel. Captain Sherrard, of the Guards, served
during the war and was promoted to the rank of major.

Another company, known as the Potomac Guards, was

raised in that county, and, under the command of Capt. Philip L. Grace, became Company A of the Thirty-first Virginia, one of the regiments of the old Stonewall brigade. Captain Grace was promoted to the rank of major, and afterward resigned.

A company of riflemen was organized in the western end of the county, within what is now the territory of Mineral county. It went into the cavalry service under the command of the gallant Capt. George Sheetz, who lost his life on May 23, 1862, in the valley of Virginia. It became Company F of the Seventh cavalry. Capt. Isaac Kuykendall afterward commanded this company.

Capt. C. S. White commanded Company C of the Twenty-third cavalry, of which company Alexander White became first lieutenant and J. R. Baker, of Hardy county, second lieutenant. The men composing this company came, for the most part, from the county of Hampshire and the adjoining county of Hardy.

Capt. R. Bruce Muse commanded Company F of the Eighteenth cavalry. His command was recruited partly from Hampshire county and partly from the adjoining county of Frederick, in Virginia. Capt. Matthew Ginevan commanded Company C of the Eighteenth cavalry. Company I of this regiment went into the service with D. Ed. Bell, who became lieutenant-colonel, as its captain. In fact, a large number of the rank and file of the Eighteenth were men from Hampshire, such as Maj. Alexander Monroe.

Capt. E. H. McDonald, who commanded Company D of the Eleventh cavalry, and a large number of his men, were natives of Hampshire county. Capt. J. Mortimer Lovett, a Hampshire man, commanded Company E of the Twenty-third cavalry.

Another company, organized first as militia, under Capt. John H. Piles, afterward became Company K of the Eighteenth cavalry. Many of the men from this company of militia enlisted in various other commands.

During the war a great many of the very best people of this county were driven, or fled for refuge from their homes, among them John B. White, the clerk of the courts; Charles Blue, who frequently represented the county in the legislature; and John Kern, Jr., all three of whom died for the cause they loved, while at Richmond, during the war. The county was taken, by force of the bayonet, into the newly-formed State of West Virginia. After the war its people were disfranchised, except a few who called themselves loyal, most of whom were the newly-made colored citizens. The old and respected men were not permitted to enjoy the rights of citizenship. They could not vote, could not hold office, could not sit on juries, could not teach school, could not practice law, and were forbidden even to bring a suit to recover an honest debt. In this and the adjoining counties a great many old Confederate soldiers were harassed by suits for damages and sometimes arrested and imprisoned upon various criminal charges instituted against them in the newly-organized and so-called courts of justice under the new regime. Some were indicted for murder, some for arson, some for larceny, and some for other offenses with which they were charged for acts done as soldiers in civilized warfare. A great many suits were instituted to recover damages, in money, because of acts done by the defendants as soldiers in the army. Judgment after judgment was obtained in the courts below and sustained by the appellate court of the State; but these defendants were generally old Confederates, who had faced trials and oft-times death itself in battle, and bravely did they seek to maintain their rights as belligerents until the Supreme court of the United States at its October term, in the year 1888, decided the case of Freeland vs. Williams, involving the question of the belligerent rights of the Confederate soldiers, in their favor. The case is reported in the 131st United States Reports, at page 405.

There was no organized body of Confederate soldiers from Wetzel, Marshall, or Tyler counties. About fifty men in all entered the service from Wetzel, but in doing so they were compelled to run the blockade, and scattered to the four winds. Some of them were afterward found in Louisiana and Tennessee regiments. Some did not get through at all and were sent to Federal prisons. One party of five included Mordecai Yarnell, who became a member of Company G, Twenty-seventh Virginia, and was promoted to lieutenant; Ephraim Wells, promoted to captain of a cavalry company; Friend C. Cox, who became a staff officer with Gen. W. H. F. Lee; and Robert McEldowney, a member of the Shriver Grays, of Wheeling.

The Shriver Grays, organized at Wheeling, with about 80 men, was organized in May, 1861, with Daniel Shriver, captain; John W. Mitchell, first lieutenant; John B. Leadley, second lieutenant; Pryor Boyd, junior second lieutenant. The company left Wheeling on the 21st or 22d of May, 1861, and went to Harper's Ferry, reporting to Col. T. J. Jackson. It was mustered in as Company G, Twenty-seventh Virginia infantry, of the Stonewall brigade. It served faithfully in that regiment until about May, 1863, when most of the survivors of the original company were transferred to the Thirty-sixth Virginia cavalry battalion, commanded by Maj. James Sweeney, of Wheeling. The battalion participated in the East Tennessee campaign as a part of Longstreet's command, was at the burning of Chambersburg, and in the rear guard after Gettysburg. Captain Shriver was succeeded in command, in the fall of 1862, by Robert McEldowney, previously orderly-sergeant. Captain McEldowney was the last remaining commissioned officer with the Twenty-seventh, on March 25, 1865, when the assault was made on Fort Stedman, and he was there wounded and disabled.

Randolph county contributed the following companies

to the Confederate service: Company A, Eighteenth Virginia cavalry; captains, Haymond Taylor (killed below Winchester) and Job W. Parsons; lieutenants, J. W. Parsons and Elam Taylor. The company participated in every important action in the Shenandoah valley and northwest Virginia. Company I, Nineteenth Virginia cavalry, Capt. Jacob W. Marshall, Lieuts. Jacob S. Wamsley, Jacob G. Ward, George Gay (of Pocahontas, killed at New Mountain), Jacob Simmons and McLaughlin (both of Pocahontas, latter killed at Shepherdstown). This company took part in all the memorable combats in the valley and southwest Virginia after 1863. Company C, Twentieth Virginia cavalry, Capt. Elihu Hutton, Lieut. Eugene Hutton. The service of the company was about the same as that of the last-named. Company F, Thirty-first Virginia infantry, was an exclusively Randolph county organization. Its first officers were Capt. Jacob Currence, Lieuts. Jacob I. Hill, George W. Saulsbury and J. N. Potts. The company was at Laurel Hill and Carrick's Ford, joined Stonewall Jackson at McDowell, and was with him till his death and with Lee to Appomattox, when about a dozen of the company were surrendered. From first to last the company included about 125 men, of whom less than 25 returned to their homes without wounds. At the reorganization in 1862 the officers elected were: Capt. J. F. Harding, and Lieuts. O. H. P. Lewis, W. H. Wilson and Dudley Long (killed at Seven Pines). Harding and Wilson were each five times severely wounded. Lewis, wounded and captured at Cedar Mountain, was one of the prisoners held under fire at Morris island, S. C. Harding was promoted to major of cavalry, and Lieutenant Wilson was the only commissioned officer from early in 1864 until in February, 1865, when he and many of his company were captured beyond Fort Stedman, in the attack upon which they led the charge. Wilson was taking a Federal captain to the rear when captured. Randolph county was also represented in the Twenty-fifth and Sixty-second infantry regiments, and McClanahan's battery. One of the officers of the latter was Lieut. Parkinson Collett, of Randolph.

Hardy county, the seat of which is Moorefield, on the south branch of the Potomac, 38 miles from New Creek (now called Keyser), on the Baltimore & Ohio railroad, was a frequent battle ground, and suffered much from the incursions of both armies. Fremont on the march to McDowell, as well as on his return thence to intercept Jackson in the Shenandoah valley, moved his army through Hardy county. Hardy furnished the following organizations to the Confederate service: The Hardy Blues, 60 men, Capt. J. C. B. Mullen; the Hardy Grays, 60 men, Capt. A. Spangler; the South Branch Riflemen, 60 men, Capt. John H. Everly. These three companies were organized at the beginning of hostilities. The Blues and Riflemen were at Rich Mountain in June, 1861, and surrendered by General Pegram and paroled by General Rosecrans. In time they were exchanged and permitted to return to the service, when the Blues were reorganized with J. J. Chipley as captain, and the Riflemen with A. S. Scott as captain, and both were attached to the Sixty-second Virginia infantry regiment. The Grays were ordered to Harper's Ferry early in 1861, and assigned to the Thirty-third regiment of Jackson's brigade, and shared in that heroic service at First Manassas which won for the brigade and its commander the title of "Stonewall." The company served through the war, and Captain Spangler became colonel of the regiment. Hardy county contributed 55 men to Company B, Eighteenth Virginia regiment, Capt. George W. Stump; 37 men to Capt. George Sheetz' company, of Turner Ashby's old regiment; and 70 men to Company B, Eleventh Virginia cavalry, Capt. William H. Harness. John H. McNeill, the famous ranger, was a native of this county, and organized his company partly of Hardy county men.

In Kanawha county, the company of Kanawha Riflemen, Capt. George S. Patton, was organized at the time of the John Brown raid, and entered the Confederate service in April, 1861. It included some twenty lawyers of the Charleston bar, among them, serving as privates, William A. Quarrier, T. B. Swann, Thomas L. Broun, Isaac N. Smith, S. A. Miller, R. Q. Laidley, J. G. Newman, Nicholas Fitzhugh and Thomas Smith, son of the governor and general. Another Kanawha county company was commanded by Capt. John S. Swann, and an artillery company was raised by Dr. John P. Hale.

Mercer county contributed ten companies to the Confederate army. Monroe furnished the Lowry battery, the Chapman battery, and other organizations. Wayne, Putnam and Greenbrier also made generous contributions. A. J. Jenkins, of Cabell, raised a cavalry company, and afterward a regiment. Thomas L. Broun organized two infantry battalions, of two companies each, in Boone and Logan, and Dr. McChesney raised an infantry company at Peytona, Boone county, called the Boone Rangers.

In Pocahontas county, the scene of many conflicts, some of which are not recorded in history, two infantry companies and one of cavalry were organized in April, 1861. One of the infantry companies, organized at Huntersville, included nearly 100 men, commanded at first by Capt. D. A. Stoner and later by Capt. J. W. Matthews, was ordered to Philippi, where it shared the fate of Colonel Porterfield's forces. The company formed part of Reger's battalion, which was consolidated with Hansbrough's battalion to form the Twenty-fifth regiment, the Huntersville company becoming Company I. The other infantry company was organized at Green Bank in April, 1861, with 106 men, under Capt. James C. Arbogast, and was ordered west on the Parkersburg turnpike, and later stationed at Laurel Hill, as Company G of the Thirty-first regiment. The cavalry company, about 75 men, Capt. Andrew McNeel, went to Laurel Hill, but could not be supplied with arms at that time, and disbanded, about a third of them going into the Bath cavalry, Captain Dangerfield, with which they had distinguished service throughout the war. In the spring of 1862 Capt. William L. McNeel organized a large company of cavalry in Pocahontas, which went into the Nineteenth cavalry regiment, Col. W. P. Thompson. For the same regiment Capt. J. W. Marshall organized a company at Mingo, about half the men being from Pocahontas and half from Randolph. Colonel Imboden raised a company, chiefly in this county, for the Sixty-second Virginia. Captain McNeel and Marshall had many skirmishes in that part of the State, and should have credit for gallant and devoted service. It is estimated that Pocahontas county contributed 60 men to the Sixty-second regiment, 25 to the Eighteenth cavalry, 125 to the Nineteenth cavalry, 10 to the Twentieth cavalry, 20 to the Fourteenth cavalry, 125 to the Thirty-first infantry, 100 to the Twenty-fifth infantry, and 50 to other commands, including Edgar's battalion and Miller's battery. The Twenty-fifth regiment Virginia infantry was organized of West Virginia companies collected on the Laurel Hill line under General Garnett, mainly from Pendleton, Braxter, Webster, Upshur and Pocahontas counties. George A. Porterfield was the first colonel, succeeded by George H. Smith, of Pendleton, and John C. Higginbotham, of Upshur. The latter was killed at Spottsylvania Court House, May 10, 1864, while gallantly leading a brigade in battle.

The Thirty-first infantry was organized at the same time, with the following companies: A, of Marion county, Capt. W. W. Arnett, afterward lieutenant-colonel Twentieth cavalry, succeeded by Capt. W. P. Thompson, promoted to colonel Nineteenth cavalry; B, of Highland county; C, of Harrison county, Capt. U. M. Turner, Lieuts. W. P. Cooper, Norval Lewis; D, of Gilmer county, Capt. J. S. K. McCutcheon, afterward lieutenant-colonel and wounded at Cedar Mountain, and Lieut. John

Campbell; E, of Highland county; F, of Randolph county, Captain Harding; G, of Pocahontas county; H, of Barbour county, Capt. Thomas Bradford, Lieut. I. V. Johnson; I, of Lewis county, Capt. Alfred Jackson, of Weston, afterward lieutenant-colonel and wounded at Cedar Mountain, Lieut. Nathan Clawson. Col. William L. Jackson was the first in command, and early in 1862 was succeeded by John S. Hoffman, of Clarksburg. John G. Gittings, adjutant of the regiment two and a half years, was afterward adjutant-general of Jackson's cavalry brigade.

These two regiments, the Twenty-fifth and Thirty-first, fought together during the war, in West Virginia under Garnett and Edward Johnson, and, after the battle of McDowell, under Stonewall Jackson. In Stonewall Jackson's Shenandoah valley campaign, they, with the Twelfth Georgia and Thirteenth Virginia, formed the Fourth brigade of the army, commanded by Gen. Arnold Elzey, and after he was wounded, by Col. A. J. Walker, of the Thirteenth. The Thirty-first was engaged at Franklin, Strasburg and Winchester, and both regiments at Cross Keys and Port Republic. At the latter combat the Thirty-first lost 116 out of 226 and was saved from destruction by the timely charge of Richard Taylor's Louisiana brigade. The Pocahontas company in fifteen minutes lost half of its men in battle. In the Twenty-fifth Capt. W. T. Gammon and Lieuts. E. D. Camden, J. J. Dunkle and John H. Johnson were wounded, and in the Thirty-first Capt. R. H. Bradshaw and Lieut. A. Whitley were killed, and Lieuts. J. W. Arnett, J. M. Burns and W. C. Kincaid were wounded. The regiments went through the Seven Days battles before Richmond, and in the Second Manassas campaign were brigaded with the Thirteenth, Forty-fourth, Forty-ninth, Fifty-second and Fifty-eighth Virginia, under General Early, Ewell's division, Jackson's corps. Lieutenant-Colonel Jackson, commanding the Thirty-first, and Major Higginbotham, commanding the Twenty-fifth, were both wounded at Cedar Mountain. General Early in his report of that battle specially mentioned the gallantry of Captain Lilley, of the Twenty-fifth, and the color-bearer, leading a portion of his regiment in the face of the enemy, and the color-bearers of the Thirty-first, who advanced waving their flags, and rallying part of that regiment around them. At Second Manassas Early's brigade made a gallant charge, in which Colonel Smith and Major Higginbotham of the Thirty-first were severely wounded. The regiments were at the capture of Harper's Ferry and the battles of Sharpsburg and Fredericksburg. On April 11th they were detached to General Imboden's command in the Shenandoah valley. Under that leader they marched rapidly across the mountains, attacking and routing the enemy at Beverly, and thence by way of Buckhannon, Weston, Bulltown, to Frankfort, Greenbrier county, with several skirmishes. Marching to Buffalo gap, they took cars for Fredericksburg and returned to the army after an absence of just one month. The night following their return they began the march for Winchester, under the brigade command of Gen. William Smith. After marching to York, Pa., they returned to fight at Gettysburg under Ewell, now commanding the corps. Subsequently they participated in all the battles of the Second corps, Mine Run, the Wilderness, Spottsylvania, South Anna, Petersburg, Hatcher's Run, Fort Stedman, and finally stacked arms at Appomattox Court House. The gallant Col. John S. Hoffman led the brigade on the day of the bloody angle fight at Spottsylvania, General Pegram having been wounded at the Wilderness, and his brigade and Gen. C. A. Evans' Georgians were chiefly instrumental in holding the line and saving the army from a terrible defeat. The flag of the Thirty-first, which was presented by the hand of Stonewall Jackson, at the request of the ladies who made it, is yet preserved at the town of Beverly.

Company B, Sixtieth regiment, was organized at Blue Sulphur Springs, by its captain, A. M. Buster, who was succeeded a year later by J. W. Johnson. The company participated in the Seven Days' battles before Richmond, Cedar Mountain, Fayetteville, Cloyd's Mountain, Piedmont, and all the battles under Early in the Shenandoah valley.

"The Twenty-ninth Virginia infantry, recruited in western Virginia, and commanded by Col. James Giles, was detached from Colston's brigade and assigned to Corse's, at Petersburg, in the spring of 1863. A large regiment, composed of sturdy mountaineers, it did good service on the Blackwater, and with Corse was distinguished at Drewry's Bluff and Five Forks." (Harrison's "Pickett and His Men.")

Stephen A. Morgan, a lawyer of Morgantown, and member of the Virginia convention of 1861, was one of six brothers in one of the companies with Porterfield, later Company A, Thirty-first infantry. His widow writes: "The first gun fired against the enemy was by Private T. Night, on picket, killing his antagonist, while Night was wounded in the ear. The first council of war was held at Pruntytown, in the parlor of the house now owned by C. Pierpont Hoffman, by Colonel Porterfield, Col. Edward J. Armstrong, George W. Hansbrough, Mortimer Johnson and Stephen A. Morgan."

For the data embraced in these scattering notes the author is indebted to Capt. J. V. Williams, of Hardy; Capt. E. W. Boggs, of Company E, Twenty-fifth regiment; Henry A. Yeager, commander of camp at Marlinton; John G. Gittings, of Clarksburg, former adjutant of the Thirty-first regiment; Capt. Robert McEldowney, of New Martinsville; George W. Printz, of Beverly; Maj. Thomas L. Broun, of Charleston.

APPENDIX.

McNEILL AND HIS RANGERS.

CAPT. JOHN HANSON McNEILL, whose name was one of the most famous in the Upper Potomac region during the war, was born in the vicinity of Moorefield, Hardy county, in 1815. The family was established in the valley of the South Branch by his grandfather, Daniel McNeill, who immigrated from Pennsylvania about the close of the Indian border war in Virginia. In January, 1837, he married Jemima Harness Cunningham, and a year later removed to the vicinity of Paris, Ky., where he resided six years, occupying himself with stock-raising, and becoming a Knight Templar in the Masonic order. He then, on account of his wife's health, spent four years in his native State, after which he removed to Boone county, Mo., where he was active in the organization of agricultural associations, and was prominent in their meetings. After six years in Boone, he settled in Daviess county, his home at the beginning of trouble in 1861. In this county he was a local minister of the Methodist church. In politics he was an ardent "Union man," opposed to war, but in case there should be war, determined to fight for the South. He raised a company of cavalry under Governor Jackson's call for volunteers to defend the State, and being mustered into service with his men June 14, 1861, joined the command of General Slack, which, after a skirmish with Lyon at Booneville, made a junction with Jackson and fought the battle of Carthage, July 5th. After the defeat of the enemy Captain McNeill harassed their rear, taking several prisoners and making the first capture of a baggage wagon in Missouri. He participated in the fierce battle

116

of Wilson's Creek, and, after the repulse of Sigel, aided in dispersing a column of the retreating enemy, capturing 50 prisoners and one cannon. In September he took part in the famous siege of Lexington, and was severely wounded in the right shoulder just as the capitulation was announced. Here also he suffered the loss of his second son, George McNeill, who had been fighting with him, and in the first attack upon Lexington had earned the plaudits of his comrades by planting the Confederate flag in the city, amid a storm of shot and shell. A few days afterward the boy was shot dead while on picket duty. The period of enlistment of McNeill's company expired in December, and he returned to Boone county to raise another command, and while there he and his son Jesse were captured. After spendng a few days in a jail at St. Louis, Jesse escaped and traveled safely through the Northern States to Hardy county. On June 15th Captain McNeill also escaped, and not long afterward was welcomed by the friends of his boyhood. His home country he found ravaged by the Federal scouting parties, one of which drove him from his resting place a few days after his arrival, and he at once determined to raise a body of men to protect this section of Virginia. Going to Richmond in June, 1862, he obtained permission, after much persuasion, to organize a troop to defend the South Branch valley, and on September 1st he began to collect his men. A fortnight later with 20 men he made a reconnoissance toward New Creek, captured several pickets, and at Ridgeville seized a member of the West Virginia legislature. One of the fruits of the expedition was the famous road mare which McNeill rode thereafter. Evading the Federal cavalry which pursued, the men reached Petersburg and organized, electing McNeill captain. Soon afterward he was ordered to join Colonel Imboden at Bloomery, and en route he attempted to ambuscade a party of Federal cavalry near Romney. It happened that he took position between two bodies of the enemy, and one of his men remarked: "We are cut off," to which McNeill replied, with the instinct of a true soldier: "So are they." His confidence was rewarded by the capture of a considerable number of the enemy. Early in October, when Imboden attempted to destroy the trestle work of the Baltimore & Ohio railroad, McNeill was sent toward Romney with about 30 men, with which he gallantly defeated a Federal detachment of 60, taking prisoner a captain and several others. Imboden's next move was against Paw Paw tunnel, and McNeill's rangers, in advance, surprised and drove the Federal garrison from the fortifications intended to protect this important point on the railroad. Subsequently the command was busied with scouting duty, varied with occasional forays against the "Swamp Dragons," banditti who infested the mountain fastnesses and committed outrages, which they expiated with instant death when captured.

In November they played an important part in Imboden's unsuccessful expedition toward Cheat River bridge, and early in December, hearing that Milroy with 4,500 men was moving past Moorefield toward Winchester, McNeill attacked the wagon train while moving between the two divisions of the enemy, and captured 50 horses and a number of prisoners, losing but one man who was wounded by the discharge of his own gun.

While with W. E. Jones in an expedition toward Romney in January, the Rangers again surprised a wagon train at the site of their previous adventure, and were again successful, burning the wagons and capturing 51 horses and 23 prisoners. In January, Imboden's force was mustered into the regular service, and half of McNeill's men were transferred to Captain Scott's company, Imboden's battalion. The remainder, only 17 in number, gladly followed their captain back to the South Branch valley. Their number was increased to 27, and soon afterward they gave notice of their presence by suddenly descending upon a wagon train, which a Federal party had loaded with hay at the expense of the inhabitants and were leisurely hauling into Moorefield. The daring troopers dispersed the guard of 150 men, capturing 71 prisoners and 106 horses, and burned the train, and then safely conveyed their prizes to the Shenandoah valley. This exploit was announced in general orders to the army by General Lee as one of "the series of successes of the cavalry of Northern Virginia during the winter months." Near Harrisonburg the company was recruited to 60 men, and John H. McNeill was elected captain, Jesse McNeill first lieutenant, J. S. Welton second, and B. J. Dolan junior second lieutenant. Early in March, with the commendation of General Imboden, Captain McNeill applied to the secretary of war for authority to take 600 men and destroy the trestle work and Cheat River bridge. This was readily granted, Secretary Seddon in his letter to Gen. Sam Jones referring to McNeill as "a very brave and enterprising partisan officer." Gen. W. E. Jones, however, did not approve the plan. But he granted McNeill a few companies for another expedition to the northwestern grade. With these companies, Harness', Heiss', and Kuykendall's, of the Eleventh cavalry, and Captain Stump's of the Eighteenth cavalry, McNeill started out and captured another wagon train. Kuykendall's company and a detachment under Lieutenant McNeill were ambuscaded, but escaped with slight losses.

McNeill and his men rendered valuable services during Jones' successful expedition against the Baltimore & Ohio railroad in April, 1863, and continued in their adventurous duties, capturing in June one of Milroy's trains between Berryville and Winchester, until General Ewell entered the valley, en route to Pennsylvania, when the command reported to Ewell. They participated in the defeat of Milroy, and pursuing his command captured many prisoners and wrought great destruction on the Bal-

timore & Ohio railroad.   In Pennsylvania they collected
supplies for the army, and assisted in scouting duty.   On
the retreat the Rangers were with Imboden guarding the
trains, and were distinguished for gallantry in battle on
the occasion when Imboden's brigade of 1,600 repulsed
the assault of a division of Federal cavalry.   On other
occasions previous to the withdrawal of Lee across the
Potomac, McNeill and his men abundantly demonstrated
their soldierly qualities in frequent cavalry encounters.

Returning to the South Branch in August, the Rangers
performed one of their most famous feats in making a
night attack upon a column of Averell's cavalry, which
was carrying away a number of citizens, utterly routing
the enemy, and restoring the prisoners to liberty.   They
were with Imboden during Averell's raid, and subsequently the Rangers, with 40 men under Capts. Frank
Imboden and Hobson, successfully surprised the Federal
camp of 500 men at Moorefield, on the morning of September 10th, driving the enemy from the town and capturing 150 prisoners, 11 wagons, 40 horses, 250 guns, and
the supplies and equippage of the camp.   To secure their
safe retreat Lieutenant Dolan drove away a Federal battery which had opened from a ridge across the river.
Then joining Imboden in the valley, the Rangers participated in the attack upon Charlestown, October 18th,
and Captain McNeill, under a flag of truce, entered the
town and presented the demand for surrender, which was
complied with.

Returning to the South Branch valley in November,
the Rangers, now 80 men, were reinforced by 90 from
Imboden's brigade.   On the 16th they ambushed a
train at the mountain pass near Burlington, and captured
30 prisoners and 245 horses, escaping afterward by unfre-
quented mountain paths.   They skirmished with the
rear of a Federal expedition down the valley; then
assisted Gen. Fitzhugh Lee in his foraging expedition;
and in January, in addition to other exploits, defeated the

Ringgold battalion sent out to effect their capture. In April they made a raid against the Swamp Dragons and succeeded in destroying much of their stores of plunder, but on the return were ambuscaded by the desperadoes in a deep and narrow gap of Fork mountain. A fierce fight followed, in which the Rangers were so fortunate as to escape without loss and inflict severe punishment upon their enemy. In May, 1864, when Crook and Averell were raiding in southwestern Virginia, McNeill advanced against Piedmont, on the Baltimore & Ohio railroad. While he with 40 men demanded and received the surrender of the garrison at that place, two detachments of ten each were sent to the east and west to cut off communications. One of these squads, under John T. Peerce, stopped a train at Bloomington, and found it full of Federal soldiers. With supreme assurance Peerce demanded their surrender, and fortunately the colonel agreed to capitulate, as he did not have a round of ammunition with him. By firing the machine shops, engine-houses and buildings, and turning loose the locomotives, McNeill caused a damage estimated at $1,000,000 to the United States government. Having accomplished so much with almost incredible daring, he left the town under fire of artillery hastily brought up, and escaped with a cunning equally wonderful the forces sent out to intercept him, reaching Moorefield in safety, after an absence of only five days. Not long after this the Rangers suffered from the enemy adopting their own tactics, being surprised in camp, and two men, John B. Fay and Samuel Daugherty, captured. But McNeill's men would not rest under such a misfortune, and ten, with the fleetest mounts, under Lieutenant Dolan, hurried in pursuit. Coming up with the rear guard, they dashed into the Federals, and not only rescued their own comrades but made prisoners of the men who were guarding them. After the battle of New Market, McNeill went to the Shenandoah valley, scouted before Hunter previous to the latter's advance,

then annoyed his rear guard, and when the flank movement was being made against Jones, cut his way through
a Federal regiment and apprised the Confederate commander of his danger.   While the captain was absent on
this duty, a detachment under Lieutenants McNeill and
Dolan remained near Moorefield, severely punished a
raiding party sent against them in June, and about the
18th attacked their mortal enemies, the Swamp Dragons,
who were escorting a train of provisions furnished them
by the Federals.   The fight that resulted was a hot one,
and Lieutenant Dolan was mortally wounded.   This
officer was a native of Ireland and a citizen of Wheeling,
and a man of remarkable bravery.   The "old captain"
now rejoined his men, and a few weeks later they rode
into a camp of 300 Federals at Springfield, and captured
80 prisoners and 145 horses.   He had with him 70 men.
He learned from his prisoners that they were a part of a
picked body sent out by General Kelley against McNeill,
with orders to kill, capture or drive him from the valley.
The horses taken enabled him to remount not only his
own men but a company of Missourians under Captain
Woodson, who had been permitted to join him.   The 4th
of July, 1864, he celebrated by driving the Federal garrison from Patterson Creek station and burning the railroad bridge.   Immediately after this the Rangers joined
General Early's expedition through Maryland to Washington, and were under the orders of the general as
scouts.   In the cavalry fight at Frederick they resisted
the onset of the enemy until McCausland came up, and
at Urbana they again checked the pursuit. Subsequently
they were active in scouting and collecting supplies in
their region, until after the battle of Winchester between
Early and Sheridan, when the band went into the valley
to assist the defeated Confederates.   In this service Captain McNeill came to his death.   One foggy morning in
October, 1864, while leading a charge on a cavalry camp
on Meems bottom, at a bridge over the Shenandoah,

near Mount Jackson, far in advance of his troop, he was mortally wounded by a shot from the rear. This is believed to have been accidental, though it has been charged that the shot was from a recent recruit, and in revenge for some incident of company life. The famous captain died at Harrisonburg a few weeks later. His son, Lieut. Jesse C. McNeill, succeeded to the command, but on account of his youth General Early hesitated to give him full control. Chafing under this lack of confidence, young McNeill was anxious for some opportunity to display his daring, and finally it was presented. The adventure which he proposed in February, 1865, was no less than to enter the town of Cumberland, on the Potomac, and Baltimore & Ohio railroad, pass unchallenged through the garrison of 6,000 or 8,000 soldiers, and make prisoners Gens. George Crook and B. F. Kelley. Comrade J. B. Fay, of Maryland, had proposed such a scheme to the elder McNeill, and he took part in the planning of the expedition.

Fay was a native of Cumberland, and several times during the war had entered it, even remaining at one time in safety an entire week. On account of his well-known courage and discretion, it was agreed that he should reconnoiter, ascertain the location of pickets, the sleeping apartments of the generals, and gain all other information necessary to success. A lad from Missouri, C. R. Hallar, a member of the Rangers, whose coolness and courage had been often tested, accompanied Fay, and without loss of time the north side of the Potomac was reached, friends were found and interviewed, the situation around Cumberland ascertained, and when the night of this adventure ended the two bold Confederates were safely away near Romney, enjoying breakfast with their friend, Vanse Herriot.

Lieutenant McNeill had been engaged during this time in selecting and preparing 25 men, well mounted and armed, whom he moved slowly toward the Potomac in the direction of Cumberland. The rendezvous was reached, where McNeill's men were joined by about 12 others from Company F, Seventh Virginia, and Company D, Eleventh Virginia, Rosser's brigade. When Fay and Hallar had reported, a night ride was at once made over mountain and valley, on icy roads and through snow drifts of such uncertain depth on the mountain top, that the men were compelled to dismount and lead their horses. The Potomac was crossed before daylight; but notwithstanding their fatiguing haste, it was too late to reach Cumberland over the unpicketed national road, as had been planned. Dauntless, however, the men refused to abandon the enterprise, and resolved to advance on a shorter route, guarded by two lines of pickets. McNeill, Fay, Vandiver and Kuykendall riding in advance, encountered a Federal cavalry picket within two miles of Cumberland, whose challenge was first answered by "Friends from New Creek," and next by a quick charge, a pistol shot and the capture of the party. From these captured pickets the countersign "Bull's Gap" was extorted, and the prisoners themselves, mounted on their own horses, were forced to accompany the Rangers until the adventure was ended.

The second picket post, a mile nearer the city, was taken by a ruse. It consisted of five men of the First West Virginia infantry cozily enjoying the early hours before day in a shed behind a log fire. At the approach of McNeill's party one of the pickets picked up his musket and advancing a few steps made the usual formal challenge, which Kuykendall answered according to army regulations. But the Rangers continued to crowd up and with a dash closed in around the fire, capturing the pickets without firing a gun.

This success secured for McNeill the entry into the slumbering city without alarm being given. With the promptitude which the nearness of daylight demanded McNeill detailed two squads of ten men each to make the captures. Sergt. Joseph W. Kuykendall, Company F, Seventh Virginia cavalry, a special scout for General Early, who knew Kelley personally, as he had once been a prisoner in his hands, was charged with the pleasure of reversing the old conditions by the capture of this general. Sergt. Joseph L. Vandiver, who had the style of a field marshal, and could easily pass for a full general, was appointed to take General Crook. Fay, Hallar and others were detailed to cut all telegraph lines, while specific instructions to guard various points were given to the remainder of the troop.

These dispositions being made, the command moved on the pike into Green street, around the Court House hill, crossing Chain bridge, and marched up Baltimore street, the main thoroughfare, in the dim light of approaching morning. Some people were astir, but the intrepid Rangers rode on carelessly, whistling well-known Federal army tunes and now and then guying a sentinel. The first halt was made in front of the Barnum house, since then named the Windsor, where Kuykendall's squad proceeded to their work, while the others rode on to the Revere house, where General Crook was sleeping. Kuykendall's band dismounted without exciting the suspicion of the sentry, who was easily disarmed by Sprigg Lynn, the first man in advance. Entering the hotel and going to the second floor, Major Melvin, Kelley's adjutant-general, was caught in his bed, and the information gained that the General was in the adjacent room. He was at once awakened and told that he was a prisoner. "Prisoner!" said the nervous officer; "to whom am I surrendering?" Kuykendall satisfied his anxiety on that point by saying: "To Captain McNeill, by order of General Rosser." That was so sufficient under the circumstances that the general and his adjutant were soon dressed and mounted on the horses of two troopers, who, yielding their saddle seats to their captives, rode behind out of the city.

The Revere house party penetrated that hotel without further trouble than disarming the careless sentry and having the door opened by an agitated little negro, who exclaimed: "What kind of men is you, anyhow?" General Crook's room was entered after a courteous knock at the door, and the curt reply, "Come in," from the general. Vandiver, Gassman, Daily, Tucker and others promptly accepted the invitation. With the air of a general in authority Vandiver addressed the surprised Federal officer by saying: "General Crook, you are my prisoner!" "By what authority, sir?" said Crook, who had not yet risen from his bed. "General Rosser, sir; Fitzhugh Lee's division of cavalry," was Vandiver's emphatic reply. General Crook rose out of his bed in astonishment, saying: "Is General Rosser here?" "Yes, sir," said Vandiver without a moment's hesitation; "I am General Rosser. We have surprised and captured the town." General Crook could not gainsay the bold declaration and submitted at once. He said, in referring to the event at a later day, that Vandiver "looked to him like such a man as Rosser might be," and doubtless he did.

The Rangers now secured headquarter flags, and riding quietly down Baltimore street entered the government stables, and chose several fine horses, among them General Kelley's favorite charger, Philippi. All being now well mounted, the Rangers rode away more rapidly, disarming guards as they went and announcing to sentries that they were General Crook's body-guard going out to fight some rebels. Excited and jubilant, they hastened away over the snow-clad roads, pursued unavailingly by parties of Federal cavalry, and after fighting back their pursuers, or eluding them, reached a point of safety from which their distinguished prisoners were sent to General Early's headquarters. In the twenty-four hours they had ridden ninety miles, much of the time at night, while the route traversed included mountains, hill and streams, upon which lay the snow and ice of winter.

This famous exploit, which received special mention in a report of Gen. R. E. Lee to Secretary Breckinridge, was the last notable service of the Rangers. Lieutenant McNeill now received his captain's commission, but the war presently ended, and the command was paroled. Subsequently he married and removed to Illinois. The men returned to civil occupations and became honored citizens, in various professions and callings, not only in the Virginias and Maryland, but in other States of the North and South.

BIOGRAPHICAL.

Brigadier-General William Lowther Jackson was born at Clarksburg, Va., February 3, 1825. He was educated for the legal profession and was admitted to the bar in 1847, soon afterward being elected to the office of commonwealth attorney for his native county. His career as a jurist and public official during the ante-war period was prominent and distinguished. He was twice elected to the Virginia house of delegates, served twice as second auditor of the State, and superintendent of the State library fund; held the office of lieutenant-governor one term, and in 1860 was elected judge of the Nineteenth judicial circuit of the State. He left the bench early in 1861 to enlist in the Virginia forces as a private, and was rapidly promoted. In May, 1861, Major Boykin, writing from Grafton, recommended that General Lee appoint Judge Jackson to military command at Parkersburg, as "a gentleman of great personal popularity, not only with his own party, but with those opposed to him politically, and devoted to the interests of Virginia, to the last extremity." With the rank of lieutenant-colonel, Virginia volunteers, he reported for duty to Colonel Porterfield, in Randolph county, in June. Out of the companies collected at Huttonsville, two regiments were organized, and one, the Thirty-first, was put under his command, with which, after General Garnett's arrival June 14th, he took possession of the pass at Laurel mountain. After the disastrous close of the West Virginia operations, Colonel Jackson became the volunteer aide of his cousin, Gen. Stonewall Jackson, in the Valley campaign, and his services were gratefully mentioned in the official report of the battle of Port Republic. He continued in this capacity with Jackson through the campaign before Richmond, the Second Manassas campaign, and the Maryland campaign, including the battles of Harper's Ferry and Sharpsburg.   On February 17, 1863, he was authorized by the war department to raise a regiment for the provisional army within the lines of the enemy in West Virginia.   Early in April he had his regiment, the Nineteenth Virginia cavalry, organized, and was elected colonel.   His command was brigaded under Gen. A. G. Jenkins, in the army of Western Virginia, under Gen. Sam Jones.   He joined in the expedition against the Baltimore & Ohio railroad, in April, under General Imboden, and secured 300 or 400 recruits. In July he commanded a second expedition to Beverly, where and at Huttonsville he was engaged with Averell's Federal force.   He continued in the department of Western Virginia, frequently opposing Federal incursions, his command increasing to the dimensions of a small brigade of cavalry, during the remainder of 1863. In the spring of 1864 he was stationed at Warm Springs, and in the organization under Breckinridge he was given command of a brigade of several cavalry regiments.   In May he was engaged against Crook's expedition; in June he took part in the defense of Lynchburg, and in July he participated in command of his brigade in the expedition through Maryland to the defenses of Washington.   On the retreat, defending the rear, he repulsed a Federal attack at Rockville, Md.   He was promoted brigadier-general, and in the Valley, after this, he was engaged in almost continuous movements and engagements, and participated in the battles of Winchester, Cedar Creek, Fisher's Hill, Port Republic and other affairs, in command of a brigade of Lomax's division.   The spring of 1865 found him still in the field, but on April 15th he disbanded his brigade.   Soon afterward he removed to Louisville, Ky., where he resumed the practice of law.   A few years later he was appointed circuit judge, and by subsequent elections was continued in that office until his death, March 24, 1890. His judicial career was distinguished by high moral courage, as well as professional ability, and he was regarded as one of the leading jurists of the State. He was a descendant of John Jackson, an Irishman who settled in Maryland about 1748, and twenty years later removed to the Buckhannon river region, western Virginia. His son Edward was the grandfather of Judge William L. Jackson, also of Gen. Stonewall Jackson. His elder son, George, member of Congress, was the ancestor of John G. Jackson, M. C., Gen. John J. Jackson, U. S. A., a famous Whig leader, and Jacob J. Jackson, governor of West Virginia. The younger son of the original settler was Edward, whose son, Col. William L. Jackson, married Harriet Wilson, and became the father of Judge William L. Jackson. Jonathan, another son of Edward, was the father of the immortal Stonewall Jackson.

Brigadier-General Albert Gallatin Jenkins was born in Cabell county, Va., November 10, 1830, and was educated at the Virginia military institute and Jefferson college, Pa., being graduated at the latter institution in 1848. He then entered upon the study of law at Harvard college, and in 1850 was admitted to the bar, but never practiced the profession, returning instead to his extensive plantation. But he did not entirely devote himself to agriculture, taking an active and influential part in public affairs. He was a delegate to the National Democratic convention of 1856, and was then elected to the United States Congress, serving in the Thirty-fifth and Thirty-sixth Congresses, from 1857 to 1861. Upon the secession of Virginia he heartily supported his State, and while a soldier was elected as one of the representatives of Virginia in the first congress of the Confederate States, which met at Richmond, February, 1862. Here he creditably performed his duties, but it was mainly as a daring and chivalrous cavalry officer that he is remembered. He organized a company of mounted men at the beginning of hostilities, and soon gained the general attention by raiding Point Pleasant, in the latter part of June, and making prisoners of a number of prominent gentlemen who were conspicuous in the movement for the separation of the State. In the battle of Scary Creek, July 18th, he saved the day at a critical moment; soon had the command of a colonel, became lieutenant-colonel of the Eighth cavalry regiment, and was recognized as one of the leaders in the military occupation of the Kanawha valley by the Virginia forces. After Wise and Floyd had retired to Greenbrier county he remained in the Guyandotte valley, fighting for his home and the Old Dominion. He was promoted brigadier-general August 5, 1862, and in the latter part of August and the first of September made a daring raid through western Virginia, and was the first to unfurl the flag of the Confederate States in Ohio. In his report of this achievement General Loring wrote: "That brilliant and enterprising general executed the plan with such success that in his march of 500 miles he captured 300 prisoners, destroyed many garrisons of home guards and the records of the Wheeling and Federal governments in many counties, and after arming his command completely with captured arms, destroyed at least 5,000 stand of small-arms and immense stores. Prosecuting at least 20 miles of his march in the State of Ohio, he exhibited, as he did elsewhere in his march, a policy of such clemency as won us many friends, and tended greatly to mitigate the ferocity which had characterized the war in this section. The conduct of his officers and men has received my unqualified approbation, and deserves the notice and thanks of the government." In March, 1863, Jenkins made another brilliant raid to the Ohio river, and three months later he was on the Susquehanna, before the capital of Pennsylvania. In May he was ordered into the Shenandoah valley, in command of the cavalry, with

headquarters at Staunton, and in June was ordered northward to report to General Ewell, with whom he co-oper-
ated in the defeat of Milroy at Winchester. He fought
at Bunker Hill, and at Martinsburg led the advance
guard of the army to Chambersburg and made a reconnoissance to Harrisburg. He was wounded on the second
day of the Gettysburg battle, but his men, under the
command of Colonel Ferguson, won approval in the.cav-
alry fight of July 3d, and during the retreat to Virginia,
especially at Williamsport, under the eye of Stuart. In
the fall General Jenkins returned to the department of
Western Virginia, and in the spring of 1864 was stationed
at the narrows of New river. Falling back before Gen.
George Crook he collected a force at Cloyd's mountain,
where a gallant fight was made, on May 9th. In the heat
of the conflict General Jenkins fell, seriously wounded,
and was captured and paroled by the enemy. A Federal
surgeon amputated his arm at the shoulder, but he was
unable to withstand the shock and died soon afterward.

Brigadier-General John McCausland, one of the most
conspicuous figures in the warfare in the valley of the
Shenandoah and on the borders of Virginia, held important
Confederate commands, and gained a national reputation
as a brilliant leader and persistent fighter. He is the
son of John McCausland, a native of county Tyrone,
Ireland, who came to America when about twenty-one
years of age, and first made his home at Lynchburg, with
David Kyle, whose daughter Harriet he subsequently
married. He became a prominent merchant and finally
resided at St. Louis, where he rendered valuable service
as commissioner of taxation. His son, John McCausland,
was born at St. Louis, September 13, 1837, and in 1849
went with his brother to Point Pleasant, Mason county,
where he received a preparatory education. He was
graduated with first honors in the class of 1857 at the
Virginia military institute, and subsequently acted as

assistant professor in that institution until 1861. Upon
the secession of Virginia he organized the famous Rockbridge artillery, of which he was elected commander; but
leaving Dr. Pendleton in charge of that company, he
made his headquarters at Charleston, in the Kanawha
valley, under commission from Governor Letcher, with
the rank of lieutenant-colonel, for the organization of
troops in the military department of Western Virginia.
He gathered about 6,000 men for the commands of Generals Wise and Floyd, who subsequently operated in that
region, and formed the Thirty-sixth regiment, Virginia
infantry, of which he took command, with a commission
as colonel. This regiment, made up of the best blood of
the western Virginia counties, was distinguished under
his leadership in the campaign of Floyd's brigade in
West Virginia, and in the latter part of 1861 moved to
Bowling Green, Ky., to unite with the army of Gen.
Albert Sidney Johnston. At Fort Donelson, Colonel
McCausland commanded a brigade of Floyd's division,
and after bearing a conspicuous part in the gallant and
really successful battle before the fort, brought away his
Virginians before the surrender. After reorganizing at
Nashville, he remained at Chattanooga with his command until after the battle of Shiloh, when he moved to
Wytheville, Va. During 1862 and 1863 he was engaged
in the campaigns in southwestern and western Virginia
and the Shenandoah valley, under Generals Loring,
Echols and Sam Jones, taking a conspicuous part in the
battle at Charleston, September, 1862. Early in May,
1864, he was ordered by Gen. A. G. Jenkins to move his
brigade from Dublin to meet the Federal force advancing under General Crook from the Kanawha valley. He
took position on Cloyd's farm, where he was reinforced
by General Jenkins, and attacked by the enemy May
9th. After several hours' fighting, Jenkins was mortally
wounded and the Confederate line was broken by the
superior strength of the enemy. Colonel McCausland

assumed command and made a gallant fight, forming two
new lines successively, and finally retired in good order,
repulsing the attacks of the Federal cavalry, and carrying with him 200 prisoners.   In this battle the Federals
outnumbered the Confederates three to one. By his subsequent active movements, General McCausland delayed
the contemplated juncture of Crook and Hunter and rendered the Federal movement upon Dublin a practical
failure.   He was immediately promoted brigadier-general and assigned to the command of Jenkins' cavalry brigade.   After the battle at Port Republic, June 5th, he
stubbornly contested the advance of the Federals under
Hunter and Crook, all the way to Lynchburg, his command of about 1,800 men being the only organized force
in the front of the enemy.   His tenacious contest saved
the city, and in recognition of his services the citizens
presented him an address of congratulation, accompanied
by a handsome cavalry officer's outfit, horse, sword and
spurs. Early arrived from Cold Harbor in time to relieve
McCausland from the pressure of the Federal troops,
and McCausland and his troopers were soon upon their
heels, intercepting Hunter at Falling Rock, and capturing his artillery and wagon train.   Sweeping on down
the valley, he was a conspicuous figure in the July raid
through Maryland, levying $25,000 tribute from Hagers-
town, winning a handsome cavalry fight at Frederick City,
and made the first attack at the ford of the Monocacy
across which Gordon moved to strike the Federal flank
at the defeat of Wallace.   Joining in the demonstration
against Washington, D. C., the daring commander
actually penetrated into the town of Georgetown, but
was compelled to retire before the Federal reinforcements.   He returned with Early's army to the Shenandoah valley, and soon afterward was ordered to make a
raid upon Chambersburg, Pa., and destroy it in retaliation for the destruction which attended the operations
of the Federals in the valley. This duty he faithfully

W Va 18

performed. In command of a brigade of Lomax's cavalry division he participated in the Valley campaign against Sheridan, and subsequently, attached to Rosser's division, fought before Petersburg, made a gallant struggle at the decisive battle of Five Forks, during the retreat was engaged in continuous fighting, and finally cutting his way through the Federal lines at Appomattox, brought a number of his men to Lynchburg, where he once more saved the city from rapine by repressing the efforts of the stragglers that infested the suburbs. After the close of hostilities he spent a year or two in Europe and Mexico, and then returned to Mason county, where he has ever since resided in quiet upon his farm at Grimm's landing.